438 Days

AN EXTRAORDINARY TRUE
STORY OF SURVIVAL AT SEA

JONATHAN FRANKLIN

D1340383

PAN BOOKS

First published 2015 by Atria Books

First published in the UK 2015 by Macmillan

This paperback edition published 2016 by Pan Books
an imprint of Pan Macmillan
20 New Wharf Road, London N1 9RR
Associated companies throughout the world
www.panmacmillan.com

ISBN 978-1-5098-0019-3

Pan Macmillan does not have any control over, or any responsibility for,
any author or third-party websites referred to in or on this book.

1 3 5 7 9 8 6 4 2

A CIP catalogue record for this book is available from the British Library.

Printed and bound by CPI Group (UK) Ltd, Croydon, CR0 4YY

Visit **www.panmacmillan.com** to read more about all our books
and to buy them. You will also find features, author interviews and
news of any author events, and you can sign up for e-newsletters
so that you're always first to hear about our new releases.

To my father, Tom Franklin, who from an early age taught me the value of a well-placed comma, a properly tended Japanese garden and a devilish sense of humor, and who has always exemplified the power of positive thinking

Contents

José Salvador Alvarenga's 6,000-Mile Drift from Mexico to the Marshall Islands

Day 335
10/18/2013

Hawaiian Islands

Day 365
11/17/2013

Marshall Islands

Palmyra Atoll

Ebon Atoll

Day 425
1/16/2014

Day 395
12/17/2013

Days 218, 247, 277, 306
6/23/2013
7/22/2013
8/21/2013
9/19/2013

Day 189
5/25/2013

Day 159
4/25/2013

Pacific

Brisbane

AUSTRALIA

Sydney

Auckland

NEW ZEALAND

N
W E
S

UNITED STATES

San Francisco

Los Angeles

Gulf of Mexico

Miami

Havana

Mexico City

Costa Azul

EL SALVADOR

Day 71
1/27/2013

Day 130
3/27/2013

Clipperton Island

Panama Canal

EQUATOR

Day 41
12/28/2012

Day 11
11/28/2012

Day 100
2/25/2013

Lima

O c e a n

Scale at Equator

0   1000 miles

0   1000 kilometers

———— Major Shipping Routes

———— Salvador Alvarenga's Drift

⬤ Nights of the Full Moon

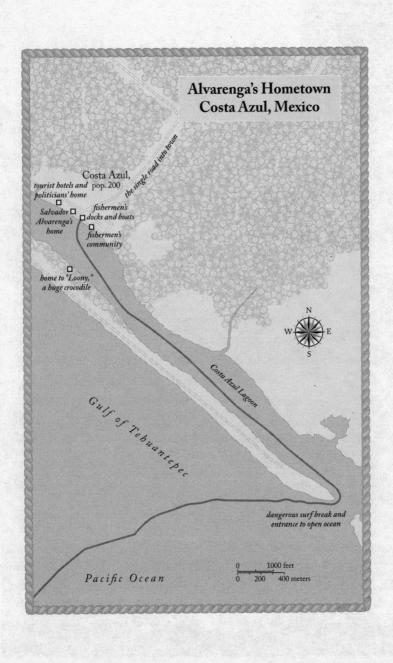

**Alvarenga's Hometown
Costa Azul, Mexico**

the single road into town

Costa Azul, pop. 200

*tourist hotels and
politicians' home*

*Salvador
Alvarenga's
home*

*fishermen's
docks and boats*

*fishermen's
community*

*home to "Loony,"
a huge crocodile*

N
W   E
S

Costa Azul Lagoon

Gulf of Tehuantepec

*dangerous surf break and
entrance to open ocean*

Pacific Ocean

0   1000 feet
0   200   400 meters

CHAPTER 1

The Sharkers

H is name was Salvador and he arrived with bloody feet, said he was looking for work—anything to start—but to those who saw the newcomer arrive, he looked like a man on the run.

———

Salvador Alvarenga had walked on rocks for six full days along the Mexican coastline to reach the beach village of Costa Azul. He carried only a small backpack and his clothes were worn. From the moment he entered Costa Azul in the fall of 2008, he felt a deep sense of relief. The mangrove swamps, nearby cornfields, crashing ocean and protected lagoon reminded him of his home in El Salvador, but here no one wanted to kill him. Only a few hundred people lived in the beachside community, though it was densely populated by flocks of migrating birds, many making the 2,000-mile annual journey south from California. Thousands of sea turtles embarked from coastal hatcheries to breed and migrate—some making the 12,000-mile swim across the Pacific Ocean to China. The town was half ecotourism paradise, half lawless Wild West—ideal cover for a man trying to escape his past and embark on a new life.

Quick with a smile and a helping hand, the round-faced, light-skinned Alvarenga arrived without a visa or working papers, so he pretended to be Mexican. He vigorously defended the lie if anyone questioned his story. Once, when Mexican policemen stopped him and suggested he was a foreigner, Alvarenga broke out with a stanza from the Mexican national anthem.

War, war without truce against who would attempt
To blemish the honor of the fatherland!
War, war! The patriotic banners
Saturated in waves of blood.

Alvarenga had a terrible singing voice made worse by an over-dose of confidence. His rendition was off-key and overflowing with nationalistic pride. Convinced by the enthusiasm of his off-the-cuff performance, the police released him.

Costa Azul is a lost corner of Chiapas, Mexico's poorest state and a region where emigrants tend not to stop as they continue on the long trek north to the United States. Few arrivals see much of an economic salvation in the tattered local economy. But the thirty-year-old Alvarenga wasn't looking at land—his eyes were focused on the Pacific Ocean and had been since he was eleven years old and had run away from school to live at the beach with friends. Costa Azul would serve not as home but as home base. He would launch seaward for multiday ocean journeys to the richest remaining fishing grounds along Mexico's plundered coastal ecosystems.

Insulated from the fury of the Pacific Ocean by a miles-long island that creates a natural lagoon, and surrounded by tangled mangrove forests untouched by loggers, thousands of fish inhabit this postcard-perfect lagoon, discovering only too late their fatal error when speared alive on the knife-sharp bill of a blue heron or crushed in the jaws of a crocodile. Like the migrating birds, Alvarenga was attracted to the protected lagoon and its unending supply of easy-to-catch fish. From afar, it gleamed like a refuge. While vicious storms roared offshore, sometimes lasting for weeks, the mangrove jungles absorbed and sheltered this small community. Like the eye of a hurricane, Costa Azul's beauty had an eerie ability to disguise imminent danger.

"Going out to sea might seem simple but it is a monster you must face," explains a colleague of Alvarenga known as El Hombre Lobo ("The Wolfman"). "If you are going to face the sea you have to be ready for all it can toss at you, including the wind, a storm or a big animal that might eat you—all those dangers. People go out for these little seaside trips, that is not the ocean. The ocean is out there past 120 kilometers [70 miles]. The folks on the beach here live comfortable, they go to sleep in a bed, but out there, you feel terror. Even in your chest you feel it. Your heart beats different."

Though Alvarenga arrived in Costa Azul by walking across sharp rocks and through thick coastal swamps, nearly everyone else reaches the town by way of a narrow paved road from Mexican coastal Highway 200. The seven-mile spur off the main highway ends at the Costa Azul waterfront and offers two options that cleave the town. Turn right and there are chic ecoresorts with flavorless Mexican food, twelve-dollar margaritas and private birding tours that capitalize on the fondness of English tourists of pecking incessantly at a personalized list of bird sightings. Palm-studded white sand beaches lure these tourists with the promise of privacy, virgin scenery, hummingbirds, rosy spoonbills, osprey and dozens more species that flitter and fly with abandon. The waiters may question the wisdom of allowing tourist children to frolic by the lagoon's edge, where a crocodile the size of a station wagon visits frequently, but since they are never encouraged to express opinions to the guests or highlight local dangers, they keep their concerns to themselves. Most of the homes between the hotels have been purchased by local businessmen and politicians who envision a gold mine of tourism as soon as Mexico sheds its reputation as a bloodstained narco-state where bars occasionally get firebombed and waitresses decapitated. That is the nice side of the tracks.

On the left side of town sits a row of low-budget fishing shacks and an oceanfront dock packed with a dozen canoe-shaped boats twenty-five feet long and capable of hitting 50 mph, especially when powered by a pair of 75-horsepower Yamaha outboard motors. This is the part of town where Alvarenga arrived. He had a decade's experience as a fisherman and hoped to find a boss or *patrón* willing to give him a shot at fulfilling his lifelong dream of being his own captain on a small fishing boat. But he needed to go slow. Visitors to this tough-guy neighborhood are immediately confronted with stares and a few basic questions. *Who are you? What do you want?* Like an IRA bar in Ireland or certain Italian restaurants in Boston's North End, Costa Azul maintains an insular tribal loyalty that binds the men together. There is no such thing as a casual visit to these quarters. A local fisherman suggests why the scene is so edgy: "You want to see what's really going on in the Chiapas region? Go out to the island at two a.m. and watch all the narco-boats running north; they are moving two million dollars a night in cocaine up this coast. The entire police force for the state of Oaxaca [just north of Chiapas] has been paid off."

Alvarenga was not a narco or willing to run even the occasional cocaine bale up the coast, despite the promise of riches. At sea off the coast of Mexico, he had seen the savage fate of fishermen who gambled in the business of "Los Kilos" and run afoul of drug lords. Once he had motored up to a fisherman's half-sunken boat and found the hull riddled with bullets. He tried to haul it home but it sank. There was no sign of the crew. Being eaten alive by sharks was probably the least violent way they could have died. At least sharks didn't torture.

When he arrived in Costa Azul, Alvarenga said little. His actions spoke volumes as he quietly found a broom and began sweeping the streets, picking trash up from the docks and making himself a home under a tree. As he opened up to the locals, Alvarenga's enthusiasm, his generosity in lending a helping hand to local fishermen and his diligent sweeping up of the touristy part of town quietly impressed them. "Without anyone telling him what to do, he would pitch in, he was always helping. That is how you win people over," recalls Jarocho, a veteran fisherman who works in Costa Azul. Alvarenga appeared too clean and organized to be a vagabond yet he shared few personal details regarding his past. When he chose, he was a dazzling storyteller, eager and able to entertain the audience as he unveiled stories of his adventures at sea.

A local chef initially paid the stout and muscled young man for his labor in food. Then he gave him a few fifty-peso notes [worth four dollars], and before the first month was over Alvarenga gained work as a fisherman's assistant. "These jobs fixing the lines are boring but he liked to bring them in perfect," remembers Jarocho. "He would say, 'Boss, Boss, this one lacks twenty hooks.' And if the nets weren't stored just right he would unroll them and he would fold it perfectly; he would say, 'This is what brings in the money, a missing hook here and there and you catch less.' He would always pay attention to the details."

Alvarenga's goal in Costa Azul was to join up with its clan of some one hundred fishermen. The protected lagoon allowed them to escape the wrath of seasonal winds that form in the Atlantic Ocean and Caribbean Sea but through a quirk of geography hit hardest on this, the Pacific side of Mexico. These storms begin in the Gulf of Mexico then swirl southwest, where the winds are channeled through a narrow gap in the Sierra Madre mountains. The bottleneck doubles or triples the wind speed—meaning that a fresh 20 mph wind in the Caribbean Sea comes out as a 60 mph blast that scientists describe as "a wind jet."

This screaming wind tunnel blasts into the Gulf of Tehuantepec, an area just off the coast of Costa Azul. For years Alvarenga had been fishing farther south—near the Guatemalan border—but he knew the deadly legacy of these storms was measured in missing boats and lost fishermen. He had heard late-night stories of being trapped by winds that locals simply called a Norteño. These northern winds were so frequent that local newscasts did not even bother to give them a proper name like Katrina or Sandy, but simply referred to them as Cold Front #6 or Cold Front #26 and warned fishermen to stay at port.

This wind tunnel is so notorious and well marked on nautical charts that sailboats often chart a detour hundreds of miles out to sea to avoid the dreaded Gulf winds. "During the winter months . . . you can expect gales almost every day . . . winds of fifty to sixty knots [70–80 mph] are not uncommon," reads a description in *Roads Less Traveled*, a respected online travel guide. "Every year, hapless vessels both large and small get caught out in the 200-mile-wide gulf when it shows its malicious side. Even large ships are unable to resist the storm force winds and fast building and breaking seas. Vessels have no option but to turn downwind and brace themselves for a long and frightening ride south and out to sea for 200 to 300 miles, at which point the effects of the Tehuantepec winds begin to fade."

If ever there was a place not to head to sea in a small, easy-to-roll boat, this was it. But jobs are scarce in Chiapas. Overfishing has decimated the fish population along entire stretches of the Mexican and Central American coast. The high-value fish—what's left of them—are driven farther out to sea. So the fishermen follow. To fill the icebox, these fishermen now commute 50 miles, 75 miles and even 100 miles off the Chiapas coast. Only after a dangerous five-hour trip crashing through the waves can they cut the motor, drop their 2-mile-long line studded with up to seven hundred hooks and hope the tuna, mahimahi, marlin and sharks are biting. Sharks are their preferred catch. Unlike some nations where only the fins are sold, in Mexico shark steak is a traditional offering on restaurant menus. Despite attempts at conservation and evidence of a population collapse, thousands of tons of sharks are hauled every year from the dangerous waters of the Gulf of Tehuantepec.

In recompense for the risks, fishermen are paid minimal wages. They live on the long tail of a global economy that prices a single half-pound serving of tuna at $25 in the Costa Azul resort restaurants but for which they earn only 40 cents. But when the fish are running and a sixty-hour shift can earn a man $250 cash, straight into his pocket, there are no limits on the fervor and party madness that erupts on Costa Azul's left bank. A band of outcasts and soci-

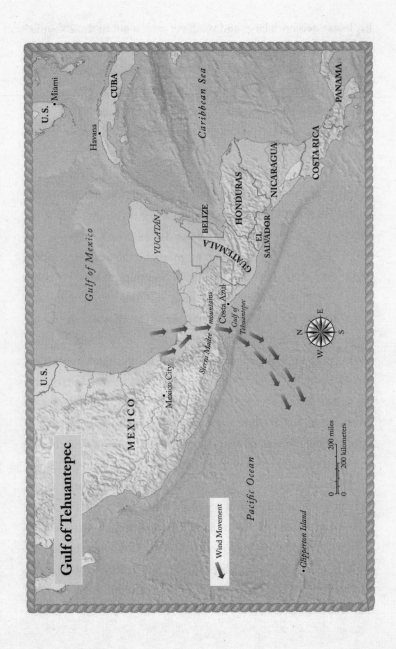

Gulf of Tehuantepec

ety's castaways, they are bound together in tribal unity and by the codes and deadly instincts of professional hunters. The Wolfman explains the philosophy in simple, deadly terms. "Poverty makes you do strange things. Poor people have to do whatever is necessary to get food. If you don't have a job other than fishing in the ocean, what option do you have?"

Like fishermen in villages worldwide, the local crews that launch from Costa Azul face a bleak future: give up fishing or every few years adjust to the realities of overfishing and travel farther out to sea. Alvarenga chose the latter. He didn't even see it as a risk. He preferred to live on the water. In his first thirty years, life on land had provided as many problems as pleasures—some nearly fatal, as a pair of deep scars on his head and arms so clearly attested.

The bar fight was partly his fault—Alvarenga was drunk and rowdy that night at the bar in El Salvador—but four men versus one? Or was it six versus two? Alvarenga stood no chance of winning the fight, and not content with punching him to the floor of the bar, the hooligans took Alvarenga outside, stabbed him repeatedly and left him for dead in the street. When his mother showed up to recover her son she said a prayer and called a priest—clearly her son was about to die. But Alvarenga fought back. He never lost consciousness and he comforted his mom, told her to hold on, that he wasn't leaving yet.

Alvarenga received eleven stab wounds, three broken ribs and a concussion. His memories of that signature event are scattered, as he only remembered waking up inside a hospital room covered in bandages. Doctors were impressed that he lived. Three weeks later when he returned to his home in the small village of Garita Palmera, he received a new shock. In his absence, someone had slit the throat of one of his assailants. A war of revenge commenced and Alvarenga was allegedly next on the hit list. El Salvador has a murder rate that regularly out-bleeds Baghdad and Kabul. Alvarenga knew all too well the Spanish saying *Pueblo Chico, Infierno Grande* ["Little Town, Big Hell"] and was fearful that he would be killed before the year was out. Friends begged him to flee, called him stupid for staying a day more. Alvarenga tried to make a go of it in town, but the shadow of violence was never far. He went on the run—not just out of town but out of the country. He stopped running in Guatemala, where he lived under a false name, and then migrated to Mexico. He'd left behind his entire life, including his girlfriend, his parents and Fatima, his one-year-old daughter.

He went on the run and found his refuge aboard boats. Alvarenga never felt steady on land, as if solid ground was an illusion for a spinning planet. Home was a rocking boat, far from shore and its false advertising of stability. At sea he felt free.

———

Rising through the ranks during his four years in Costa Azul, Alvarenga ruffled few feathers as he bounced from boss to boss, searching for his ideal balance of independence, cash and decent treatment. "I will tell you something, I am very protective of my family, and I invited him to eat at my house. Why? He looked and acted like a good person. I would tell him to sleep at my house, and we gave him a hammock," says Jarocho. Eventually, in a privilege rare among his tribe, Alvarenga was awarded private living quarters.

In time, various fishing *patrones* competed to lure Alvarenga away from his current boss. They were constantly tempting him with offers of a new boat, new lines and gear in exchange for switching teams and home port. Alvarenga, however, was content in his position—he earned enough to live out his modest fantasies and, unlike in his native El Salvador, the violence in Mexico tended to focus around the drug trade and its easily identifiable tentacles. If he avoided that world, he could revel in the simple anonymity of life in Costa Azul.

Alvarenga was free to work as hard, as long and as sporadically as his party lifestyle permitted. During his four years in Costa Azul, he was rarely involved in fights or ugly incidents. His longtime fishing partner Ray explains, "I never saw him get into a fight except when some guys were breaking up the furniture at Doña Mina's [a local restaurant]. There was an ugly fight with chains and you could tell this guy knew how to rumble. But he was always looking for a laugh, he was the life of the party."

Alvarenga's own scarred history plus a decade of watching colleagues drink themselves into jail had convinced him that he was safer drinking and partying with a few trusted friends than mixing it up at the tequila-infused cantinas that his fellow fishermen routinely trashed. For Alvarenga it was the ideal lifestyle. Four-day drinking binges might be followed by ten days of nonstop fishing. Or vice versa. Hangovers were inconsequential at this stage in Alvarenga's life—he either drank them off or went on a two-day fast where his body simply purged the alcohol out of his pores. Despite brutal thirty- or sixty-hour shifts far from shore in the open ocean, he never complained. Optimism was his trademark. "Even if he didn't catch more than one or two fish, which for many guys would have made them sad, he always came in happy," says Bellarmino Rodríguez Beyz, who was his direct supervisor onshore, a former colleague and a close friend. "Even if he had nothing when he came to shore he would be yelling as he docked his boat, 'I nailed it, absolutely nailed it.'" Oblivious or immune to the woes of the world, Alvarenga lived in peace, the type of guy who could snore on a public bus, allow his head to slump onto a random shoulder in the movies or dream under a tree in a park.

Decidedly low tech and dangerous, the fishing operations out of Costa Azul allowed a man to gamble with his life and his luck. No *patrón* would ever order a man out to sea if a sudden Norteño storm was forecast, and unlike larger, more commercial ports along the Mexican coastline, in Costa Azul there was no pesky harbormaster with the ability to prevent boats from heading to sea during raucous weather. Each man was free to calculate (or miscalculate) the cost/benefits for himself, to stay ashore or head out to sea. Alvarenga, a simple but generous man who could barely read and could write little more than his name, reveled in this ancient mariner's world. He saw beauty in the simplicity. One long line with seven hundred hooks. A small fishing boat. One mate. Scattered on the deck of his boat were the ingredients of his life: the assorted flotsam of knives, buckets and bloodstained utensils. Man versus the elements. It fit his style. "If you are a real fisherman, you fall in love with the ocean," said Alvarenga. "Some fishermen like to go out one day and then stay ashore the next, not me. As soon and as often as I could, I went out to sea until the bosses told me not to. It is love because the ocean gives you food, she provides money and it is a habit. When you love the ocean you love the adrenaline, the energy. You battle the ocean. It is your enemy. You share combat and you fight. She might kill you but you are defying death."

Alvarenga risked his life every time he ignored the warnings to stay in port and instead braved the sea seeking an extra day's catch. He was confident he could outmaneuver the waves and routinely arrived home with his icebox packed to the brim, a thousand pounds of fresh fish testament to his skill and courage. When fellow fishermen were flipped, sunk or lost, Alvarenga was among the first to volunteer to search for missing colleagues, regularly risking his life to do so. All this bravery made him very attractive to many local women. Alvarenga laughed as he described the chaos when girlfriends crossed paths outside his humble beach home. "My boss Mino used to radio me from shore and say 'Warning! Warning! Multiple women outside your *palapa*!' When that happened it was better to stay at sea."

The evening of Thursday, November 15, 2012, was a moment to celebrate. Packed on ice in two trucks lay four thousand pounds of fresh fish from the deep sea: tuna, marlin, mahimahi, hammerhead and thresher shark. A hundred miles offshore—where only the bravest fishermen dared travel—everything was biting. At the market price of 20 Mexican pesos a kilo—roughly 70 cents a pound and subtracting the 50 percent share for the boss and huge gasoline expenses, the men had, on average, US$150 in pocket. In a local economy where a meal for two cost $4 and a beachside hotel room ran $7 a night, each man packed a substantial bankroll.

The *compañeros* were together and a beach party commenced. Instead of a three-day bender, the men were raging half speed. With the fish biting, most planned to drink only until two a.m., catch a few hours' sleep, then head out to sea after breakfast. A northern storm was forecast, which meant dry, gusty winds, sometimes reaching hurricane strength, but no rain. This was likely the last shift for days—there would be plenty of time for heavy-duty partying while they waited out the cold front.

Alvarenga and friends lazed in hammocks inside their beachside hut. Corona beer cans, tequila bottles and pint-sized plastic bottles of Quetzal, a cheap grain alcohol, littered the yard. Reggaeton music bleated from a stray cell phone and the men lamented the perpetual shortage of single women. They had purchased enough Sierra Madre marijuana to stone the entire Sixty-first Battalion of the Mexican Army, which, due to a raging cocaine war, was posted just up the road. Fat joints—like props from a Jimmy Cliff reggae film—circled the room. Two naked lightbulbs swung in the night breeze. Iguanas thumped noisily as they walked across the roof. Nighthawks and owls hunted for prey as fruit bats looped through the palms. Loony, a massive crocodile, was set to make his nightly midnight crossing of the lagoon, his eyes reflecting a bright red from the lights on the docks.

The men's banter was nonstop slang, profanities and inside jokes. Alvarenga was known as Chancha—an affectionate version of Piggy—thanks to his voracious appetite. Mino, his supervisor, describes Alvarenga as a man who ate practically anything that landed near the grill. "We had just roasted a tuna fish and he already had a mahimahi sliced open and ready to cook. . . . He could eat and eat and never get fat. I told him, 'Chancha, you must have parasites.'" Another colleague suggests Alvarenga's nickname was a reference to his skin color. Unlike the coffee brown of most local fishermen, Alvarenga's skin was closer to pink, like a piglet.

Although they had polished off platefuls of food in a massive multicourse meal, marijuana provoked a mad hunger. Greedily but with a collective humor, the fishermen harassed their *patrón*, Willy, to buy more food. Willy, a quiet mustachioed man, watched over his flock of fishermen like a veteran teacher stuck with a class of juvenile delinquents. But he agreed and sent a teenager running with orders to restock the table.

As they awaited the grilled chicken and more cold Coronas, Alvarenga opened a fiberglass cooler that held bait for the next day's fishing trip. The fishermen were planning to lay 2,800 hooks, so they had stocked the coolers with hundreds of pounds of sardines to use as bait. But Chancha was hungry now. "It will be yeeeeeearss before the food arrives," he said impatiently as he grabbed a sardine as long as his hand. Its eyes were stuck in a glazed stare and its flesh was cold after being flash frozen with a blast of nitrogen. Alvarenga lifted a tortilla off the foot-high stack in the middle of the communal dining table where the fishermen always ate. He plopped the sardine on the tortilla, rolled it like a jellyroll and, knowing he had an audience, bit off the entire tail. With a broad smile on his round face he began chewing through the raw, half-frozen sardine.

"You are going to get food poisoning," Willy groaned.

"It gets cooked by the juices in my stomach," laughed Alvarenga as he prepared a second sardine.

When the chicken arrived, the men ate with gusto, chugged beers and tossed the cans in the lagoon. There was little risk of driving drunk—few of them owned a car. Nor would wheels much serve them. Their world was the sea—their commute was into the Pacific Ocean off the coast of Mexico. While lesser men fished the lagoon for snapper and flounder and the shrimpers went out twelve miles to work the farms, the deep-sea guys, this crowd, would motor straight out to sea, long past the point where they could see shore. Only when they reached fifty miles, sometimes a hundred miles, would they prepare their lines. They called themselves Los Tiburoneros—"The Sharkers." It didn't matter that they often caught more tuna or mahimahi than shark; they still cultivated the association with the ocean's most notorious predator. Among the hierarchy of coastal fishermen, Sharkers were elite and viewed as a bit mad. Sharkers had their own slang, private jokes and deep scars or missing fingers that chronicled the day-to-day brutalities of fishing in the deep sea from tiny boats. Sharkers earned more. And died younger.

CHAPTER 2

A Stormy Tribe

Salvador Alvarenga awoke at sunrise, rolled out of his hammock clad only in surfer shorts and walked four steps to where the jungle turned into lagoon. The loudest noises were street dogs barking in the distance and birds singing atop palm trees shredded by stormy winds. Barefoot, his shoulder decorated by a death's head tattoo, Alvarenga carved fresh imprints in the sand as he strolled to inspect his twenty-five-foot fishing boat in the predawn glow.

Alvarenga was planning to leave early so he needed to run an inventory on his boat. Thieves had been pilfering gear; unclipping one boat's propeller, stealing spark plugs from another and on occasion filching an entire motor. Heisting a motor took two men, and at night, in the sand, it was an unwieldy operation, so usually the robberies were quick hit-and-run operations. Alvarenga's boss had bought a watchdog that they tied to a stake and was supposed to keep an eye on mischief. Within a month, the dog was dead. "One night I heard a commotion outside, by the edge of the lagoon, and I came out and saw this animal tossing the dog. Then there was a whole lot of screaming. The dog went flying," said Alvarenga. A crocodile had the dog in its mouth and was dragging it across the lagoon. There was no way to save the dog—it would be crazy to jump in the water to fight a nine-foot croc. After the incident, Willy didn't buy any more watchdogs and Alvarenga stopped taking long swims across the lagoon.

As he inspected his boat, Alvarenga noticed the anchor and chain were missing—but it was a colleague, not a thief, who had snatched the gear to use in a shallow-sea coastal-fishing gig. Alvarenga didn't mind the lack of an anchor. The extra deck space allowed him to better pack spare fuel, drinking water and a sedan-sized pile of buoys that would float his line across the ocean's surface when he began to fish later that day. Besides, he was headed on a deep-sea mission where the ocean was hundreds of feet deep; an anchor was useless.

Alvarenga loved the simple lines of the fiberglass craft. No cabin or roof. Just a long narrow canoe-shaped boat that many people in Mexico called a "banana boat." It was designed to carve up the waves like a huge surfboard, making it agile, fast and easy to roll. Atop the deck, a fiberglass crate the size of a refrigerator lay mouth skyward, the lid in the sand. Though empty, the box reeked of rotten fish. This crate was the measure of Alvarenga's finances. If he could fill the icebox with fresh fish (1,500 pounds) he had enough money to survive for a full week. But Alvarenga was never a man interested in just surviving; he enjoyed life to its fullest—inviting friends to seafood buffets, drinking Corona beer until sunrise, dating three women at a time and picking up the tab for his colleagues after all-night parties in local restaurants.

If the fish weren't biting or the storm was too wild, he went hiking and hunting. With either a borrowed rifle or his trusty sling-shot, Alvarenga disappeared for days as he stalked animals in the wooded mountains just inland from the mangrove jungles that guarded the coast. In the mountains, hunting and camping with a friend or two, Alvarenga found his cherished respite and distance from society as well as an abundant supply of meat: raccoon, opossum, coati, iguana and migrating birds were all fair game in his battle to satiate a raging capacity to ingest food. Alvarenga owned no refrigerator or pantry. It was literally slingshot to mouth as he shot his prey then ate it. Alvarenga had few living expenses. The fishing cooperative—The Shrimpers of the Coast—paid his housing and utilities. Instead of health insurance, he knew that if he was injured, his colleagues would patch him up, and if his wounds were life threatening, they would rush him to the nearest hospital. Local doctors were experienced in the art of reattaching a severed finger or patching chunks of flesh ripped away by fishhooks. Accidents at sea were common, but as long as the crew was able to stay near the boat, they could usually survive. However, if the boat sank, it was often the sharks that ended the story.

Alvarenga's boat, at twenty-five feet, was as long as one and a half pickup trucks and as wide as one. With no raised structure, no glass and no running lights, it was virtually invisible at sea. With a draft of less than two feet and the engine mounted on the back, when the motor was full out, the bow and the front third of the boat tilted out of the water and could shoot through the waves or maneuver the tight waterways of the mangrove forest. Police often stopped these boats on the open ocean under suspicion that they were running north with drugs or immigrants, traditions as old and storied as fishing along this outlaw coast. The police would tell the crew to lift up their shirts, then feel up the fishermen's bellies, checking that the men had not swallowed plastic-wrapped balls of cocaine. Usually the fishermen submitted to the surprise police or navy inspections, even slicing open their fresh fish to prove that they were not stuffed with cocaine. But if they were smugglers, they rocketed through the shallows where they nearly always escaped—in the worst case, running the boat directly into the thick mangrove branches, abandoning ship and seeking refuge in the dense jungle. Cargo—be it cocaine, pot or immigrants—was left behind. In the mangrove forest, lethal and aggressive fer-de-lance and jumping viper snakes awaited. These snakes are well camouflaged, their skin mimicking the speckled brown of splotchy leaves on the forest floor. The vipers are aggressive and quick to strike if a predator approaches. Bites can be fatal, yet it is a risk the *contrabandistas* willingly assumed, knowing that the police rarely followed anyone into the mangroves. The authorities often remained on the water, resigned to seizing the suspect boat and towing it back to the naval base, where it was held for ransom, like a car towed for illegal parking.

Alvarenga partied hard and loved the challenging day-and-a-half or three-day fishing shifts. He was an accomplished fisherman who routinely brought home five hundred pounds more "product" than the other boats. On days like this, when the fish were biting, Alvarenga was sure he could repeat the bonanza of the previous day's haul. He was determined to set out early. He had spent hardly any money the night before and still had nearly US$150. But there was never enough cash. On a good night of partying, he could spend all that and more on beer for his friends, food for his date and tequila for all.

Alvarenga planned to leave at ten a.m. and work straight through until four p.m. the next day. In preparation for a thirty-hour shift including a night at sea, Alvarenga packed into a gray five-gallon bucket a carefully wrapped small mirror, a razor, his toothbrush and two changes of clothes. Even at sea as he chopped the heads off the tuna or was slathered in thick shark blood, Alvarenga shaved daily. He brushed his teeth at all hours of the day and checked the mirror to make sure he maintained a modicum of civilized existence. His job allowed him the kind of lifestyle where he could simply dump his dirty work clothes into the corner and wear them again and again, never washing the clothes. When they were fouled or bloodstained he tossed them in the trash, purchased another cheap pair of shorts and a T-shirt and restarted the month-long cycle. But when it was time to hit the town, Alvarenga spiked his hair, splashed on cologne, shined his shoes and shaved.

Alvarenga and his mate packed their boat with the cadence and confidence of men on autopilot. Among the coastal fishermen, the respective roles of captain and mate are marked with a military-style discipline and respect for rank. Captain Alvarenga, anchored at the stern, would run the motor and steer while Ray Perez, his skinny twentysomething mate, dashed about the boat fixing gear, setting lines and organizing equipment. On land, Ray was a wild outlaw who raised havoc with colleagues and the law. But at sea he was a loyal companion and a tireless worker, and the two men filled the shifts with raucous laughter.

Loading the boat was a two-hour process and involved over a thousand pounds of equipment, including 70 gallons of gasoline, 16 gallons of water, 100 pounds of sardines for bait, 700 hooks, miles of line, a harpoon, 3 knives, 3 bailing buckets, a cell phone (in a plastic bag to avoid seawater), a GPS tracking device (not waterproof), a two-way radio (battery half charged), several wrenches for the motor and 200 pounds of ice. Draped over the entire pile of gear was a mountain of empty bleach and detergent bottles—the blue, white and pink containers adding a carnivalesque touch of colors to the scene. The heaviest items were the gasoline containers, which sank the boat to just 20 inches above the waterline. The forward bench was smeared a lighter shade of white, evidence of recent epoxy and reinforcement work to seal a cracked strut.

The largest item on the boat was a five-foot-long and four-foot-high icebox with a removable lid. When filled with ice and fish, the box was so heavy it had the potential to flip the craft if it shifted at sea. Securing the icebox to keep its bulk centered was a basic safety requirement. Alvarenga used the biggest icebox available; its size was both a macho bragging right and a testament to his unceasing ability to fill it with fish.

Along the shore, a convoy of ten boats prepared to embark at roughly the same time. Like trucks at a loading dock, the boats were lined up side by side in a flurry of last-minute activity. As they pushed off, Alvarenga shifted the motor into reverse and pulled away from shore. He turned the boat around and began motoring toward a rough surf break where the estuary waters met the open Pacific. Exiting the lagoon was a tricky navigation among sand bars and crashing waves. Several fishermen had been killed at the break and six months earlier Alvarenga had been in a boat—but not at the helm—when it rolled down the face of a wave, turned over and nearly crushed him in a tumult of rolling boat, flying equipment and thundering water.

The flotilla of fishing boats continued five minutes into the open ocean, then the engines were cut to idle. The boats gathered and aligned side by side. Like covered wagons crossing a desert, these travelers had a ritual of joining for one last powwow before each faced destiny on his own. For the fishermen, this was a combina tion of a town hall community update and gossip around the office watercooler. Given their love of marijuana and absence of any official oversight, the men smoked one cigar-sized joint after another. No one could remember how the "last toke" tradition started but it was now a fixture, most likely a legacy of the fifty-year tradition of Mexican fishermen smuggling loads of marijuana north up the coast to the lucrative US market. The men shouted out jokes and insults rained down. Laughter bounced from boat to boat.

After the smoke, Alvarenga headed west and, navigating in the open ocean, followed his handheld GPS to the spot where he and Ray had caught so many fish the previous day. It took them six hours to get there. They were now in the middle of the Gulf of Tehuantepec, and they spent another two hours baiting the hooks, laying out the line and settling in. By seven p.m. they had the entire two-mile line stretched out behind them. The stars were bright, a strong but pleasant breeze whipped out of the northeast and Alvarenga smoked several more joints with Ray. They laughed and shared stories of conquest, failure and recent engine troubles. Four days earlier their motor had died and they had been hauled to shore by a nearby colleague who was fortuitously close when he heard Alvarenga's SOS calls on Channel 2—the bandwidth used by fishermen in the Gulf of Tehuantepec. Neither man was afraid of the scenario—colleagues were always nearby. "We survived lots of storms together," says Ray. "When the waves would slam us from one side to another he would say, 'Go to sleep. Get a blanket.' I would ask, 'What about the waves?' and he would say, 'Take a nap.'"

Anxious to check if they had any catch, at ten p.m. the duo motored down the line. They quickly confirmed another huge haul. A hammerhead shark was thrashing just below the surface, trying to rip out a hook set deep in the mouth. They waited until two a.m. and Ray began to bring in the line. He hauled the hammerhead to the side of the boat, where Alvarenga used a gaffing hook to prevent it from escaping. Ray then bashed it on the top of the head with a handcrafted wooden club. Whether it was shark or tuna, the men always tried to kill the fish while it was still in the water. Other fishermen used a homemade Taser—a crude system rigged from a car battery and two long wires with clips that could be inserted into the flesh of the fish to deliver an instant and deadly electric shock. Like a slaughterhouse for cows or chickens, this killing of the fish was the brutal back-office that consumers never saw or even imagined when they filled a shopping cart with canned tuna or ordered a fresh mahimahi steak at a restaurant. For Alvarenga and Ray it was crucial to kill all the fish before hauling them aboard. A snapping shark might sever a pair of toes or remove a chunk from the lower leg. Sailfish and marlin, with their spear of a bill, were particularly feared.

For two hours Ray pulled in the line. It was an exhausting chore that required extremely strong shoulder and forearm muscles. Again it was another sumptuous payday: mahimahi, hammerhead shark, thresher shark and a sailfish filled the icebox—1,200 pounds they guessed. In a single cast of their line the icebox was nearly topped off, so there was no point tossing it out again; they would zip to shore in five hours, shower, change clothes, eat, restock the boat and head out for a second and final round. Their thirty-hour shift would now be sixty hours of nearly nonstop work. If all went well they would nail a third consecutive big catch, an uncommon streak of luck.

As they motored back, the men were half awake, having managed only sporadic bouts of sleep over the past several days. They wanted to smoke marijuana but there was none left. Onshore, that too could quickly be restocked. Enthused and giddy, they decided to tell their boss not to pay them—like poker players they wanted to build a stash, gamble they could win the next round and then collect all their winnings. Three hundred dollars apiece was a guarantee they could finance a two-day party with piles of marijuana, bottles of tequila and cases of beer. Neither man had any doubts that he could instantly spend all the money. Of all the pleasures, Alvarenga most loved gourmet meals, especially shrimp dishes on plates the size of a hubcap. He could eat the entire banquet alone or with friends. He often treated colleagues to a free meal and always maintained a substantial positive balance in the local favor bank.

As they arrived at shore Ray made a surprise announcement. He needed to sign probation papers at the local prison. He was out on bail for armed robbery and had itchy fingers—Ray stole so often that trouble was never far away. He kept a pistol stashed in the small of his back and—as he made sure everyone knew—kept a .22 caliber bullet in the chamber.

Ray tried to spin the delay in a positive way by reminding Alvarenga (who had never been imprisoned) that every visit to prison meant he received back a percentage of his bail money. "We will have more money to party," Ray told Alvarenga as they hurriedly packed the boat in preparation for the next trip.

"I told him to wait for me," says Ray. "I packed the boat, the ice, the bait, everything and rushed to court. . . . We knew exactly where the fish were biting, it was a perfect moment." With Ray temporarily out of action, Alvarenga became impatient. He wondered if his regular mate would even make it back by midday, so he started searching for a temporary worker. Alvarenga made the rounds of day laborers—a roaming band of men who walked the lagoon waterfront with a bag of food, a sack of clothes, perhaps a favorite knife and a keen desire to grab a day's work in exchange for a fifty-dollar cash payday upon return to shore.

Alvarenga found a young man eager to work: his friend Wolfman was always training apprentice fishermen and could be counted on to raise an extra crewmember on a moment's notice. Wolfman arranged for Alvarenga to head out with Ezequiel Córdoba, a twenty-two-year-old with the nickname Piñata who lived at the far end of the lagoon, where he was best known as a star on the village soccer team. Alvarenga and Córdoba had seen each other occasionally on the soccer field but had never spoken, much less worked together. Alvarenga suspected that as a crewmate he was far from ideal. Córdoba was accustomed to the calm waters of the lagoon and had less than two years' experience deep at sea. Alvarenga knew the risks of heading out with a rookie—many a landlubber friend had pleaded to go fishing, and then spent the bulk of the trip vomiting and begging for solid ground. But time was tight so Alvarenga, after first dismissing the young man, finally relented in the face of Córdoba's pleas and told him to wait at the docks while he went to eat.

Under a tin-roofed structure with no walls or windows, a long blue wooden table served as breakfast table and de facto community pub and gossip hall for the fishermen. Breakfast was no tea and crackers snack but heaps of eggs, refried beans, potatoes and onions all slathered with cheese and green jalapeño sauce. Alvarenga drank his morning coffee and listened to the talk of a brewing storm. The warnings of a dangerous northern storm system descending on the Gulf of Tehuantepec did little to thin the ranks. Like Alvarenga, most of the fishermen were listening to even stronger countervailing arguments: schools of tuna, sharks in hunting packs and the always thriving Mexico City fish market, where every day, beginning at 2:30 a.m., millions of dollars' worth of sea creatures were bought, sold and shipped.

"I am going with this new guy, but I will be back in time for the party," Alvarenga told his supervisor Mino at the beachside breakfast. Alvarenga was reminded that he was in charge of bringing food to a party the following evening. He must not forget: it was his job to purchase fifteen chickens for a birthday party in honor of Doña Mina—a local chef who served as den mother to many of the fishermen.

"There's a storm coming," Willy, the owner of the boats, warned his employees, though experience taught him that, short of a hurricane or crushing hangover, there was little that would keep Alvarenga and many of the others from embarking.

Alvarenga was more worried he might head to sea without his customary stash of lemons and salt to make ceviche. "I always brought extra supplies in case we had to stay out an extra day, got a bit lost or blown off course by a storm. You have to go to sea prepared. I was accustomed to staying out longer than the others. When they didn't get a good catch, they would come back in. Not me. I would stay out and try again, set the line at another location. I was a good fisherman."

Shark fishermen at sea have few cooking options—there is no oven, no stove and lighting a fire aboard carries obvious risks. Alvarenga prepared for the overnight trip by arranging for a local cook to prepare cow livers. He brought enough of the roasted meat to stuff a couple pounds of tortillas. Aboard the boat and out at sea, he used a bench as a cutting board to chop cilantro, onions and tomatoes. (Tomatoes were cherished at sea though they tended to get mashed long before mealtime.) For a feast he needed only fresh tuna, a sharp knife and a splash of salt water. As he left for sea, he figured the storm might slow down the fishing and cause him to stay for two days instead of one so he grabbed a handful of extra lemons. He also paid two hundred pesos (seventeen dollars) for two fist-sized wads of marijuana buds wrapped in newspaper. It was a ritual for every trip. At sea, especially at night as he waited for the sharks, tuna and mahimahi to attack his lines, he smoked one thick joint after another as he enjoyed the stars.

United in their defiance of weather reports, the ten fishing boats motored straight into the tangle of waves where the Costa Azul estuary is slammed by incoming breakers from the Pacific Ocean. Under full power, the fishermen hunkered down as they timed the wave sets. White foam blew off the waves and floated like snow. The key was to accelerate swiftly in the brief calm between breakers. Soaked from the splashing waves and half blind from salt in his eyes, Salvador Alvarenga steered with his left hand and held tight to a thick pole with his right to keep from bouncing out of the boat. In a day, perhaps two, he would be heading back to shore, another stash of fish in the cooler. Then he planned to collect his wages for the last several days. "I liked money," said Alvarenga. "But no one could say I was a crook, and if they saw me drunk with a woman they at least knew what it had cost me to get that money. I held my head high wherever I was."

Alvarenga wore a black balaklava-style mask with holes cut out for his eyes and nose. "La Terrorista," the other fishermen joked, but the scorching sun grilled his white skin. Alvarenga didn't have their copper-colored skin or genetic protection against the harsh sun. The Alvarengas had originally come from the mountains of Spain. They held up well in snow and cold but not in this tropical heat, which in less than three hours could turn a man's skin to swollen bubbles of burned flesh.

Alvarenga scanned the waves and set his course at 280 degrees west-northwest. The radio in his bucket was beeping but Alvarenga never noticed because it was buried with his clothes. Many fishermen used the radio nonstop, like truck drivers chatting on the CB, but for Alvarenga life at sea meant going off the grid. He often spent two days at sea without a single call to shore. Alvarenga sought a total escape from the static and confusion of day-to-day life onshore.

As he blasted through the waves and the mountains of the coast began to hunch toward the horizon, Alvarenga was relaxed. He did not realize he was traveling west at roughly the same pace at which a huge Norteño was stealthily forming and advancing from the northeast. The storm was still behind the coastal mountains; it had yet to show its face. Had he stopped for lunch, he would have noticed that while the sky above was blue, from the northeast skid marks of thin gray clouds pushed forward, unassuming advance scouts for a storm not yet rattling the warning system by which veteran fishermen track changes in weather hours before those on land notice even a whiff of danger. The storm, which shadowed Alvarenga, was now showing up on meteorologists' maps as "Cold Front #11." It was gaining strength on land but had yet to reach the men far offshore.

Alvarenga knew the danger of storms better than most, but he was on a streak—he had just caught half a ton of fish and there were plenty more to be taken. He expected storms this time of year— November was always rowdy. The key, he explained to Córdoba, was to read the wind, waves and clouds. A glimpse at the waves and sky was information enough for him to calculate the punch of any storm. Today's gusts had teeth—he could feel the power as the cloud bank built over the mountaintops to the east. But Alvarenga accepted the challenge and refused to change his plans. Had he traveled with access to either the Internet or meteorological reports, they would have changed drastically. Lacking any clear warnings, the two men took positions: Alvarenga at the helm and Córdoba prone, like a figurehead stretched out on the bow, scanning for debris that could destroy or flip their boat. Floating coconuts—practically invisible during choppy seas—made a horrific *clack!* when they smacked the hull. Tree trunks were capable of catching the propeller and catapulting the boat end over end. Abandoned fishing nets could foul the motor. A submerged sea turtle could destroy the propeller.

Their journey out to the fishing grounds in the Gulf of Tehuantepec required five hours of constant vigilance and barely an hour into the trip Córdoba felt seasick and homesick—he had signed on for a day job, not a torture session. His stomach was in his throat, his tongue frantic as it searched for stability. Córdoba's eyes rolled with the waves. Vomiting only lasted as long as his stomach had something to offer, then Córdoba began dry heaves, a convulsion that—lacking any lubricant—made his throat feel like it was afire.

"The new guys always vomit and grab the rail. They get dizzy and are not sure what to do. There's nothing they can do," said La Vaca, a fellow fisherman. "I told Ezequiel not to go so far out that day, the storm was tough. I didn't go out."

Two decades aboard small boats had taught Alvarenga to internalize the sequence and predictability of wave patterns. "To be a good fisherman you have to get your mind in order, to know how to attack the sea, how to catch the fish. I could look for a certain color of green and know that we would find fish. The movements of the birds also help, you can see them eating fish."

A novice would not last five minutes without flipping the boat in the choppy eight-foot waves. Alvarenga hardly noticed. Like a practiced surfer, he simultaneously spotted and translated the subtle messages embedded in each wave. With constant adjustments to the throttle and steering, he threaded a path. When a wave ambushed them, Córdoba was knocked off his feet and smashed hard to the floor. He scurried back into position but Alvarenga noted that his novice deckhand would need constant scrutiny. Sitting in the stern, Alvarenga had more stability. They were running a course nearly parallel to the waves, making them susceptible to being sideswiped from the right and rolled. When a wave forced the boat sideways Alvarenga would gun the engine hard, cut the boat into a tight 360-degree spin and again set up his attack angle.

There were no other boats on the horizon—not that Alvarenga could see more than half a mile. There was no rain but the chop and spray glazed his eyes. "The ocean was bouncing around, I told Córdoba to hang on," said Alvarenga. "We were going over the waves, they were not so big but still we were bouncing out of the water, slamming down." Alvarenga knew a feared Norteño was building.

"It was obvious, you could smell it. I could feel it in my body, but I had experienced this many times before." These coastal storms were characterized by violent gusts of wind but little rain and could last for days, said Alvarenga, who recalled a ripping wind but no rain and scattered high clouds. "The day was nice and sunny," he said. "It was hot."

As the men roiled farther out to sea, the wind increased from 20 mph to a sustained 30 mph, still well under the 72 mph mark for a Category I hurricane, but enough to fill the young Córdoba with fear. "It's a wind that whistles," explained Alvarenga. "The waves come this way, that way. And the waves are breaking in all directions. Each one is two meters [six to seven feet] high and smashing into each other." As the wind ratcheted up, the conversation ceased. Córdoba clung to the bow, gripping the rail.

At five p.m. the two men arrived at the designated fishing grounds and extended their two-mile line while baiting seven hundred hooks evenly spaced along the length of the contraption. To keep the line afloat, every twenty yards an empty plastic bleach bottle was tied to the line. Snaking behind the boat on the ocean's surface, it looked like a line of trash. "After we threw out our lines we talked more," said Alvarenga.

By eight p.m. the line was fully extended and floating out behind them, creating a powerful drag that provided stability from waves seeking to push and pull them in all directions. The men had nothing to do but wait for fish to attack the bait. Córdoba fell asleep. Alvarenga smoked marijuana and kept an eye on the line. Container ships from the nearby port of Salina Cruz were known to slice through and cut the lines. Even waving strobe lights in their path was no guarantee that the dronelike ships would change course. Many were on autopilot and the tiny fishing boat captains did their best to scurry away at the first sign of an approaching container ship.

Around one a.m. Alvarenga felt a deep warning. The voice of the storm picked up and Alvarenga took note. The swells gathered strength and the boat began to tilt sideways like a ride at an amusement park. Córdoba was terrified and losing control. "Get us out of here. Let's go back," he screamed at Alvarenga. "We are going to die."

"Shut up," Alvarenga ordered. But as the winds and waves jacked up, the boat began to fill with water. Alvarenga told Córdoba to start bailing. Using a bleach bottle with the top sliced off, he began furiously dumping seawater back into the ocean. Despite Córdoba's frantic bailing, the crashing waves filled their boat with water faster than they could empty it—Alvarenga now joined the bailing effort.

"We've got to bring the lines in now, this Norteño, it's a complicated one," Alvarenga yelled to the young mate. Córdoba didn't react. "Dumbass! Move it!" Alvarenga shouted. "Let's crank up the motor. Start pulling in the line."

Under normal conditions, the captain would watch as the deckhand labored for hours to haul in the line, but the storm winds were whistling, so Alvarenga donned thick gloves and, wary of the hooks, began to assist Córdoba as they hauled in the line, yard by yard. Waves were dumping two inches of water into the boat at a time, so while Córdoba pulled, Alvarenga bailed. Working together, Alvarenga and Córdoba managed to recover half the line. They were exhausted but jubilant, as they had landed a fantastic catch: ten fish including tuna, mahimahi and sharks. Blood from the recently killed fish splattered the boat, then washed to the floor in a sloshing crimson pool. The dangers of getting hooked, bit or gaffed were constant. Even the shark's skin was dangerous; like a file it could flay an uncovered thigh or arm. "It shaves off your skin, peels it right off in slices. With all that salt water it hurts. Basically it shreds you," said Alvarenga. "It is like a road rash from a motorcycle crash."

Alvarenga guided the motorboat and continued to haul in the fishing line as saltwater spray skewed his vision. His twenty-five-foot boat kept getting yanked and dragged so violently it was impossible to stand up without holding tight to the rail. With jugs of extra gasoline and the wooden box to store the net taking up most of the floor space, there was little room for Alvarenga to move. Then Alvarenga made a radical decision. They didn't have enough time to haul in the entire line—instead he would cut it off. He knew it was thousands of dollars' worth of line and hooks that would float away, with hundreds of dollars' worth of catch still hooked, but the storm was turning ugly. Alvarenga took out his fishing knife and sliced the blue cord. They were free. But without the stabilizing drag provided by the long fishing line, they began to bounce as if being shaken by a giant. Córdoba was crying as Alvarenga shined a light on his compass, set a course of 70 degrees east into the gale and in the dark of night aimed for home. If all went well, Alvarenga figured, he would be eating chicken and drinking beer before sunset and then enjoy a weeklong fiesta while he waited out the storm.

CHAPTER 3

Ambushed at Sea

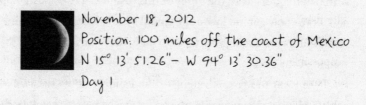

November 18, 2012
Position: 100 miles off the coast of Mexico
N 15° 13' 51.26" – W 94° 13' 30.36"
Day 1

Alvarenga sat huddled in the stern, his face covered by the ski mask and sheltered by the hood of his jacket as he gunned the outboard motor. He aimed toward a shore he couldn't see. Next to him Córdoba—on his knees—bailed nonstop in a losing battle to clear seawater from the deck of the boat. Visibility was sporadic. Alvarenga could use moonlight and see for a few hundred yards, and then clouds of spray and surging waves would make him feel like he was being spun around in a whirlpool with no sight of the horizon and only glimpses of the swirling stars. "We were taking a bath the whole time," he said. "But I didn't think we would sink. The waves were not breaking inside the boat, they were lifting and dropping us."

With the wind now roaring at 50 mph, the sea was white with foam and waves smacked the boat, knocking Alvarenga off course. Like a professional athlete readying for a match, Alvarenga took stock of his opponent. It would be a five-hour competition, and though he had spent years navigating these waters, Alvarenga knew better than to get cocky. Every storm had its quirks and his first task was to understand this storm's rhythm and flow. Alternately accelerating the engine, then suddenly letting up on the throttle, Alvarenga deftly slid the boat among eight- to ten-foot swells. Amid the chaos of cross currents and gale-force winds, Alvarenga searched for clues as to the order of this madness. He couldn't stop and let the bow get too low, or he would be flooded. Alvarenga motored cautiously, angling the bow up high, like a surfboard with the weight at the back.

If he went too fast, Alvarenga risked sliding down the face of a wave, planting the bow underwater, where he would then be vulnerable to a second wave that could instantly fill the boat. If more than half the boat flooded, the men were doomed as the sunken boat would ride flush with the ocean and no amount of hand bailing could refloat it. They would die—in which of the many possible ways hardly mattered. It would be either gruesome and quick or a slow torture over the course of days. Sharks were never far. No one would find their bodies; the cause of death would be "lost at sea" and the only clue a patch of scattered gear floating off the coast.

Getting sideswiped by a wave was equally dangerous, as not only would the boat be flooded but the men were likely to be swept overboard. Being washed off the boat even with a life jacket—and only Alvarenga had one—was a harrowing experience that many Mexican fishermen never lived to recount. The boat might be carried west by the wind and the fishermen east by a current. Alvarenga was an exceptionally strong swimmer, but in stormy waters? Could he swim back to the boat? That would be his only option as Córdoba was unlikely to instantly discover his sea legs and take the helm. And if Córdoba were to flip overboard? Alvarenga would try to swing the boat around in a circle and maneuver close enough for Córdoba to grab the rail. But that would take at least two minutes and Córdoba's body on the surface plus the presence of bloody water would be a shark magnet. Córdoba might be dead by the time Alvarenga returned—or in the process of being shredded. "People think that a shark bite is a clean cut, but that is the Hollywood version," said Alvarenga. "You have to realize that these sharks have seven rows of teeth, and when they grab, they rip back and what is left looks like long, thin pieces of string cheese."

Alvarenga ignored the growing pond of seawater sloshing at his feet. An inexperienced navigator might have panicked, started bailing and been distracted from the primary task—aligning the boat with the waves. Alvarenga needed to regain the initiative. The storm had ambushed him. As he threaded a precarious path through the waves, he realized he was advancing too fast. He slowed the engine. Speed was secondary to precision.

To further stabilize his craft, Alvarenga directed Córdoba to deploy a sea anchor. Made from a string of floating buoys, this long tail aligned the bow with the waves, providing drag and more stability. In this case, empty bleach bottles were affixed to a long piece of extra fishing line taken from the wooden crate. "If I hadn't put those buoys out, we would have sunk after the first few waves. Even with the buoys, every wave was rough as the bow of the boat slammed through it," said Alvarenga, who had often resorted to this homemade system to navigate fierce storms. Despite the sea anchor and Alvarenga's navigational skills, the spray and crashing waves dumped hundreds of gallons of seawater into the boat. While Alvarenga steered, Córdoba was now frantically tossing the water back into the ocean, pausing momentarily only to allow his shoulder muscles to recover.

While Alvarenga tensely negotiated their slow advance toward the coast, Córdoba continued to unravel. As the weather worsened, his resolve disintegrated. At times he refused to bail and instead held the rail with both hands, vomiting and crying. Córdoba had signed up to make fifty dollars, an honest two-days' wage. He could kill, gut and store fish all day if necessary. He was capable of working twelve hours straight without complaining and was athletic and strong. But this crashing, soaking-wet journey to the coast? He was sure their tiny craft would shatter and sharks would devour them. He began to scream his fears aloud, especially the part about being eaten by sharks. Triangular fins had been slicing the water as they killed and hauled in the fish, and both men feared that if the boat flipped they would live only long enough to realize who was eaten alive first.

An occasional burst of lightning provided a glimpse of their predicament. But Alvarenga could harvest little information from this millisecond of light as his eyes were bombarded with pelting salt water but not a drop of rain. He couldn't reach a supply of fresh water to wash them out. As ever more salt entered his eyes they began to puff up and his vision worsened.

With no running lights and no high-powered spotlight, Alvarenga was navigating not just blind but on pure instinct. The roll of the waves under his seat seemed chaotic but the waves had their own sophisticated sequence. They were slapping out a message, like

Morse code, against the hull of his boat. It was Alvarenga's job to decipher this rapid-fire pattern. Experienced navigators in Polynesia teach similar skills to their adolescent children by laying them on the sea and having them float on their back day after day for months as they learn to distinguish the subtle messages embedded in each wave. Polynesian canoe crews are thus able to read the waves and detect refraction patterns that indicate waves have struck land hundreds of miles away—a lifesaving skill when traversing swaths of the Pacific Ocean where islands are sparsely scattered over a huge expanse, like a few grains of rice in a swimming pool. Alvarenga had never conceptualized his navigation skills as superb or even special—his skills were so embedded they felt like intuition. But over the course of a decade at sea, he had commuted to work and back approximately 360,000 miles, equivalent to a trip from Mexico to the moon then halfway back to earth.

In the early-morning light, as the storm surged, Alvarenga became fixated on his compass and, though bashed by waves, remained confident and convinced that in four, perhaps six, hours they would be safely in port. The waves tossed surprise after surprise in his face, but with flourish and dexterity, he never lost the rhythm. The danger was constant but so too the adrenaline buzz. In many ways, this was the edgy challenge that made life at sea so exhilarating. Alvarenga abhorred walls. An office cubicle would have been prison. Bouncing through ten-foot waves, his eyes stinging and hand numbed from gripping the tiller, he felt free.

This was a dance he had executed dozens of times and he rarely stumbled. When professional athletes reach the highest levels of concentration, they describe being able to see the playing field in slow motion, hence the practically incomprehensible coordination of a soccer player diving and launching a perfect header into the corner of the goal. For Alvarenga, this onslaught of swells, crashing waves and wind was his playing field. In his head the whole glorious show was playing out and he was the star. Back at the *palapa* in Costa Azul, it would be yet another astonishing tale and a defining moment in his burgeoning career as captain.

Alvarenga's confidence was not shared by the increasingly terrified Córdoba, who was becoming aggressive and defiant, openly refusing Alvarenga's entreaties to bail the seawater. "I will see what I can do!" he shouted. Córdoba's fears were now fueled by a combination of crackling adrenaline and the paralyzing specter of sinking at sea. Alvarenga was enraged at the mutiny and responded angrily to the young mate. "When we get to shore, that's it. We are never working together again. Never."

Then Alvarenga took a different approach and tried to instill a bit of calm in the hysterical young man. "You like the money, eh?" Alvarenga taunted Córdoba.

"Yeah, I like the money," Córdoba admitted.

"Well then, get through this test. This [storm] is not my fault, this is natural and it happens to us all. Now it is our time to suffer but we are not going to die."

Alvarenga rued not having waited for Ray, his partner for the past year. The men were so close they called one another "*mi pareja*" (my partner), a phrase commonly used for married couples. It was a recognition of the day-in-day-out routines they shared. "We understood each other and I never had to tell him what to do," said Alvarenga, who imagined Ray bailing with both arms while providing a running commentary of jokes, stories and upbeat chatter. He could probably light a joint at the same time, thought Alvarenga.

Córdoba slipped further. He was now frozen, practically catatonic. Alvarenga couldn't release the tiller to bail but neither could he idly watch as the boat filled with water. Nearly a foot of water had collected, reaching up to his calf muscles. The water was unstable ballast that shifted with enough weight to slide the men from one side of the boat to another. The waves were now so large that when they broke into the boat the men were violently thrown about. On one wave, Córdoba was sent smashing down upon the edge of a bench. Alvarenga watched in dismay as his young shipmate was tossed across the boat. He grimly admired the man's stamina. Córdoba had survived four or five body slams that would have stunned most men. "It is all a matter of posture," Alvarenga thought. "He doesn't know how to position his body."

Alvarenga remained sitting, locked down to the motor, gripping the tiller tightly, determined to navigate a storm now so strong that harbormasters along the coast had barred any boats from heading out to sea. Emergency calls from shore ordered all boats to port— any harbor. Alvarenga never heard his radio; instead he was imagining the cheers he would receive when he docked inside the lagoon. Another grand entrance by Chancha! His fantasy was upset by another round of Córdoba screaming. The young, inexperienced man seemed to be losing his mind. He stood and howled into the wind. "Why is God punishing me?" Córdoba shrieked. "Why?"

For the next three hours, Alvarenga held a steady eastern course. He diagonally sliced through the waves. When he needed to turn farther north, he pulled the tiller toward his body, which would swerve the boat into a sharp curve to the left. Pushing the tiller an arm's length away from his body allowed him to cut a hard right turn, south.

Alvarenga kept the GPS monitor buried inside the bucket with his clothes—the eighty-dollar device was not waterproof. He checked the GPS infrequently but was rewarded with good news—despite the headwind and the northern currents, they had advanced forty miles toward the coast in the first hours. They were at least halfway to land, but the last miles would be the roughest. The storm, which had arrived with just a whisper of warning, was now taking full breaths—gathering strength on land and launching a wall of wind that literally blew the tops off waves.

The gasoline required to advance in such conditions was far greater than the manufacturer's estimated mileage per gallon. But Alvarenga had packed two extra fifteen-gallon containers. He had tapped backup gasoline stores on previous trips: to rescue a colleague, to search for a lost net or track a school of fish. "Some of the guys would go out with the minimum amount of gas. Later you would hear them on the radio, 'Hello, Boss, I ran out of gas.' They didn't plan on the return trip. That was their mentality."

Córdoba migrated from the safety of the stern to a perch on the bow. He was trembling, crying for help and acting so distraught that Alvarenga thought he was contemplating a dive into the sea. "He was out of his mind. Several times he hid inside the icebox," said Alvarenga, who described peering into the icebox to find Córdoba wide-eyed, half frozen in fear and piled like fresh catch atop a stack of shark carcasses.

As Córdoba wept and sought shelter, Alvarenga maneuvered the boat through ever-higher waves as he aimed for shore. It was hard to bail and steer at the same time, but Córdoba was useless, more deadweight than first mate. As one wave dropped them into a sickening fall, they landed with a hard thud—the impact felt like it had cracked the hull. "We were lucky that the boat had just been repaired," said Alvarenga. "A storm about a month before had bent and weakened a main strut. We had just recently repaired that with extra bond, so the boat withstood the constant pounding." While the hull survived, a plastic bucket holding the communications gear cracked along the bottom. Minutes later, when Alvarenga decided to call shore and report the deteriorating conditions and his new position, he found the bucket filled with water. Though wet, the radio functioned but the GPS unit was soaked and nearly floating. The device was ruined. It wasn't a matter of drying it out. Fortunately, they were approaching the coast, so Alvarenga would soon be able to navigate using landmarks from shore.

Running with the waves was a tricky and exhausting battle with the elements. By seven a.m. both men were running on reserve energy, so Alvarenga ordered a quick breakfast break. The waves had not let up and in retrospect the men were mystified by their own decision. What had possessed them to delay even for a single minute their race to the coast and the safety of land? But hunger does strange things to the human brain and somewhere in his multitasking mind Alvarenga decided the men could spare the luxury of a fifteen-minute breakfast break.

Alvarenga unpacked tortillas, onions and tomatoes. Four pounds of the blood-rich cow livers awaited in a plastic bag. He couldn't toast the tortillas as he might on a calm outing, but the cold corn tortillas wrapped around the chopped red meat still made a liver and tomato sandwich. Córdoba revived with the food and received a stern warning with his meal—Alvarenga needed his help and he needed him to bail now. The men ate rapidly as Alvarenga kept the motor running, idling the engine, and guiding the boat among the waves as he and Córdoba ate one stuffed tortilla after another.

Alvarenga finished breakfast, revved the motor and resumed a crashing course toward shore. He noticed a change in the visibility. The cloud cover was lifting: he could see miles across the water. No sign of land yet but he was slowly advancing. The mountains would pop up first, as splotches on the horizon, then slowly stretch up to reveal the promise of solid ground. Even if he couldn't make the safety of the Costa Azul lagoon, he knew at least six other spots where he could find shelter along the coast.

It was around eight a.m. when Alvarenga heard the first cough. It wasn't an outright burst of protest from the motor, but more like a hiccup or the soft growl of someone clearing their throat. The Yamaha had been running perfectly but it was the same motor that had failed earlier in the week. Within ten minutes, the motor's cough began to sound chronic.

Fishermen in Costa Azul treated newly refurbished motors with the skepticism given any new arrival to town. Before being taken to sea, these motors are typically mounted to a rack on land, revved up and left to churn. "We have to work them. Sometimes the pieces jam," said Alvarenga. "We always leave a repaired motor running for at least a few hours. That was something I did not do."

The motor's voice continued to change and the two men discussed the possibilities. Had water leaked in? They didn't think the spark plugs had been compromised—that would have produced a distinct sputtering that either man could fix in minutes by cutting the engine and cleaning the plugs with fresh gasoline, then continuing their journey. This cough was deep in the motor, and it was starting to steal power from the engine.

Around nine a.m. Alvarenga spotted the rise of mountains on the horizon. They were approximately twenty miles from land. Alvarenga pulled his head out of his jacket and looked for familiar landmarks. It wasn't necessary to use electronics now; he'd run this stretch hundreds of times. There was, he thought, just one last real danger: the vicious shoreline surf where breaking waves would be huge. Landing ashore during a storm was so dangerous that fishermen would perch on the rail of the boat ready to dive into the ocean, preferring to be flung ashore by the surf than be crushed to death by a flipping boat.

Alvarenga had barely savored the joy of sighting land when the motor's cough turned into a persistent hacking. Was the gas line pinched? Had something rattled loose? "I couldn't believe it. I could see the coast. We were fifteen miles off the coast and the motor started to die."

Alvarenga decided to cut the engine, perform a modest tune-up then continue toward shore. The risks of not checking the motor were clear. Three years earlier Alvarenga had suffered severe engine breakdown, the motor disintegrating until the propeller spun so slowly that he advanced at one mile an hour. It had been a numbing three-day crawl back to the coast. But after his ten-minute overhaul (including pulling and cleaning the spark plugs) the motor now refused to turn over at all.

It sounded like there was neither spark nor gas, nor any connection between the two. Increasingly agitated, Alvarenga yanked again and again at the outboard motor cord. Blisters formed on his index and middle finger. Like a guitar player switching out callused fingers, Alvarenga began using his ring finger. He ripped the cord until even his pinkie was torn and numb with pain. Finally the cord snapped. With no cord to start the motor, Alvarenga felt naked against the force of the storm. He pulled apart the motor and tried without luck to fashion a new ripcord. Then he erupted in anger. "I swore at the motor, I cursed it." He also immediately pulled out his radio and called his boss. "Willy! Willy! Willy! The motor is ruined," Alvarenga yelled into the radio.

"Chancha, Chancha! Calm down, man, give me your coordinates," responded Willy from the beachside docks in Costa Azul.

"We have no GPS, it's not functioning," said an increasingly frustrated Alvarenga. Realizing they were within sight of the coast, Willy came up with a simple solution.

"Lay an anchor," he ordered. Willy figured that Alvarenga could anchor down and ride out the storm. Being so close to shore meant a quick rescue mission could be sent to grab the men at the first break in the weather. In the worst-case scenario, they could save the crew and return later for the anchored boat.

"We have no anchor," Alvarenga said, speaking into the radio.

"Okay, Chancha. We are coming to get you. We are sending out Trumpillo," responded Willy.

"If you are coming to get me, come now, these waves are huge. We are taking on lots of water," said Alvarenga. "Come now, I am really getting fucked out here," shouted Alvarenga. They were his final words to shore.

Alvarenga redirected his attention to the storm and ordered Córdoba to adjust the sea anchor—the dynamics were vastly different on a boat with no motor, no thrust. Córdoba and Alvarenga were now alone in their battle against the storm. In this weather, it would be very risky to launch a rescue attempt—both men were in agreement on that point. Alvarenga gave Córdoba a crash course on survival. "I told him to scout the waves, to pay attention. To hold on to the boat. I tried to explain what was about to happen and what he should do."

As the waves thumped the boat, Alvarenga and Córdoba now began working as a team. A mutual survival instinct overcame fatigue. With the morning sun, they could see the waves approaching, rising high above them and then splitting open. Each man would brace and lean against a side of the open-hulled boat. Depending from which direction a big wave appeared, the men would jump to the opposite rail in an attempt to counteract the roll. But the waves were mad, slapping each other in midair, joining forces to create swells that raised the men to a brief peak where they could get a third-story view, then with the sensation of a falling elevator, instantly drop them. The men wore beach sandals that provided no traction. As the waves increased, Córdoba was tossed around like a crash test dummy. "He had a big bump on his head. It didn't bleed, but he really smashed his head," said Alvarenga. "He nearly cracked his ribs on another fall. I told him to hold on, that we had no doctor here, no medicine, no pills."

Alvarenga realized their catch—nearly a thousand pounds of fresh fish—was making the boat top heavy and unstable. With no time to ask or consult his boss, Alvarenga went with his gut: they would dump all the fish into the ocean. One by one they hauled the slippery fish out of the cooler. Most were less than fifty pounds and the men could each grab and toss a single fish overboard. But for the larger catch, including a pair of tuna and several sharks, the individual fish were seventy-five pounds apiece, meaning the men would grab head and tail simultaneously and swing the bloody carcass into the ocean. Falling overboard was now more dangerous than ever. The bloody fish were sure to attract sharks—it was as if they were chumming the seas to deliberately provoke a frenzy.

For nearly an hour the men strained against the wind and the shifting boat as they unloaded the catch from atop piles of ice. They often waited ten minutes for a break in the wave sets, then let go of the rail, rushed to the icebox and ditched a single fish. "We needed to get the boat higher in the water. That would give us more strength to fight the storm," said Alvarenga. They also tossed the ice and the extra gasoline. To further increase the stability, Alvarenga strung another fifty buoys. "It was the buoys that allowed us to survive that whole morning," said Alvarenga.

Around ten a.m. the radio died. The batteries ran out of power. Now they were unable to help organize a rescue. It was before noon on day two of a storm that Alvarenga knew was likely to have a five-day life cycle. Losing the GPS had been a minor inconvenience. The failed motor had been a disaster. Without radio contact Alvarenga was on his own.

The seesaw motion of being adrift made the men feel like they were going up and down more than in any distinct direction. Only much later would they realize how fast they were being blown northwest and pushed out to sea. They occasionally went into a spiral motion where the boat would spin several complete circles, then, pushed by the wind or aligned with ocean currents, would straighten up. Water was flooding over the rail and was two feet deep at their feet. The men bailed as fast as they could while keeping an eye out for changes in the wave patterns. Alvarenga's eyes were burning from the salty spray. Córdoba half crouched near the deck, held to the boat with one hand while trying to shovel water overboard with the other. When Córdoba stood, the water now reached nearly to his knees.

Around noon, a violent wave smashed the boat on the left side. The force of the wave reached under the boat, which lifted and tipped as if it would flip over, like a car going over a guardrail. Alvarenga, who had just begun to move from the stern to midboat, was tripped up and landed hard on the floor. Córdoba was swallowed in the deluge. He disappeared inside a surge of water.

"Everything washed out," said Alvarenga. Along with the lines, their water supply and the food, Córdoba was swept overboard. He managed to grab the rail with one hand, and with his body submerged to the chest, clung precariously to the outer rail of the boat. "He screamed and I didn't think he could hang on for long. I grabbed him by the hair and pulled him aboard. It was like landing a big fish."

Córdoba, soaked and terrified, was trembling on the floor of the boat as he silently thanked his captain. "He had water coming out his mouth, his nose," said Alvarenga. Nearly half the boat was filled with water.

Alvarenga stared in disbelief that he was now in a sinking boat. Córdoba remained motionless, paralyzed by the shock of nearly drowning. But Alvarenga quickly regained his survival instinct.

"Help me! Help bail," he shouted to Córdoba.

"It's better that we just go down," moaned Córdoba.

"Have faith," Alvarenga pleaded. "This is going to pass. It will pass!"

The storm roiled the men all afternoon as they fought to bail enough water out of the boat to keep it from sinking. The same muscles, the same repetitive motion hour after hour had allowed the two men to dump perhaps half the water. They were both ready to faint with exhaustion but Alvarenga was also furious. He picked up the heavy club normally used to kill fish and began to smash the broken engine in a fit of fury. Then he grabbed the radio and GPS unit and angrily threw the machines into the water.

The sun sank and Córdoba and Alvarenga succumbed to the cold. They turned the refrigerator-sized icebox upside down and huddled inside. When the wind whistled in at the bottom, they used the fiberglass outboard motor cover as a barricade against the most direct blasts. There was no spray from the sea. The men, soaking wet and barely able to clench their cold hands into fists, hugged and wrapped their legs around each other. But as the boat sank ever lower to the waterline the men took turns leaving the icebox to bail for frantic ten- or fifteen-minute stints. Each few gallons returned to the ocean was accompanied by heavy exhaustion and constant pain. Progress was slow but the pond at their feet gradually grew smaller.

Córdoba began to sob. "Don't be crying," Alvarenga yelled. "We need to bail, get the water out of the boat!"

As darkness shrank their world, the wind ripped straight off-shore and drove the men farther out to sea. Were they now back to where they had been fishing a day earlier—a hundred miles off-shore? With no GPS and only the stars as guides, they lost any means of calculating distance.

Alvarenga began to think of colleagues who had died at sea. El Indio. Vicho. La Celia. Pihasso and Richard. Many of them had left families behind and Alvarenga felt particular sadness for those who died young—if he died now, at least it would be with the knowledge that he'd fully enjoyed his life. For the first time he felt guilty that he had brought along young Córdoba. Just twenty-two years old, he'd barely graduated from adolescence. But Alvarenga assumed that a rescue party would be launched at dawn. He had participated in a similar mission years earlier. "There were some friends, their motor had died so they called on the radio," said Alvarenga. "I was onshore. I knew where they fished. I said, 'Let's go.' I stripped down my boat, just to basics, to keep it light and with lots of fuel. I organized the rescue and found them. We connected a cable and we dragged one of the boats back from the sea. Wow, they were excited—they screamed at me, 'Chancha, you did it!' God, were they happy."

Nighttime, however, brought a new set of dangers. With no light to highlight the incoming waves, the men were susceptible to being flooded or flipped. The wind blew cold across the water and survival seemed remote. Crouched on the floor of the boat inside the icebox, each man would unleash a frenzy of energy to bail the boat one last time. As they could no longer see the waves, they could not prepare for the hits. Like a cork bouncing around inside a washing machine they were catapulted first in one direction, then another. "People often forget that in the ocean everything is three-dimensional," says Luca Centurioni, an expert in ocean currents at the Scripps Institution of Oceanography in San Diego, California. "It is not a linear experience, it is often more like a pinball game."

Córdoba began to collapse. "Why do we have to move so much?"

"Follow my orders. Obey me, I am in charge," Alvarenga said angrily. "If you were in charge it would be different—we would be dead by now."

"Boss, don't get mad at me," Córdoba pleaded.

"Then obey and we'll get through this," Alvarenga said encouragingly. But privately he felt a rising sense of panic. "When will this end?" he asked himself. "And how?"

CHAPTER 4

Search and No Rescue

November 19, 2012, Costa Azul, Mexico

At nine a.m., when Alvarenga's SOS was received on the docks of Costa Azul, a debate erupted. Several fishermen wanted to launch an immediate rescue—send out boats and begin a search. Others thought it was too dangerous to embark. It was a moot argument; almost all the boats had gone out fishing that morning and were battling to return in the same stormy conditions. Two boats besides Alvarenga's were already missing. Ashore, there was only a skeleton crew available. The Coast Guard and port authority were notified but nobody expected much from those quarters. Their meager search-and-rescue resources were already tied up looking for yet another boat of missing colleagues who had disappeared in a storm two days earlier.

By noon, a desperate rescue plan took shape; a single boat would be launched. Trumpillo, a veteran helmsman, would take charge. Ray, Alvarenga's regular partner, volunteered to join the makeshift rescue operation. A boat was stripped of fishing gear and loaded with extra jugs of gasoline. The two-man crew donned foul-weather gear, packed a fully charged radio, food for two days, gallons of fresh water and heavy-duty line in case they needed to tow their companions to safety. The rescuers had only a rough guess of where they could find the stranded boat. Alvarenga—in his last radio broadcast and adrift with a dead motor—described seeing the mountains behind Boca del Cielo ("Mouth of the Sky"). This landmark indicated he was no more than twenty miles from shore. With exact coordinates it would have been a dangerous but direct operation. Without the GPS coordinates it was a guessing game. Was the lost boat fifteen miles from shore? Twenty-five miles? The difference added two hundred square miles to the search area—an area roughly four times the size of the city of San Francisco. With visibility marred by high seas, it would take almost a head-on collision for the two boats to find each other.

"It was brutal. The waves were huge—eighteen to twenty feet high," said Ray as he described the initial rescue mission launched at noon, roughly three hours after the SOS. "We got as far out as twenty-five miles but the waves were drowning us. Our boat was half filled with water. I thought we were going to sink," he said. "Trumpillo—the captain—said it was too dangerous, that we might die trying to rescue them. We turned back."

Trumpillo and Ray spent the day searching closer to the coast, then came back into the lagoon at nine p.m.; they entered alone, having failed to find Alvarenga and Córdoba. It was too late and too dark to do anything but wait for daybreak. Instead of celebrating Doña Mina's birthday and getting drunk, the men held vigil at the table in the beachside hut, attentive to the radio and the hope that Alvarenga might recover a few seconds of battery power. Perhaps his radio was just wet and would function again when dry.

Two other boats were missing and another four colleagues from along the coast had disappeared, never to be heard from again.

The crowd grew as the word spread. Versions of what happened to Chancha, or what might have happened, crossed the table. They laughed as one Alvarenga story after another was recounted. Lubricated by cases of Corona beer and piles of marijuana, the men avoided talking about him in the past tense—Chancha would surely be back to recount his latest tales of adventure and regale the crowd. The gathered crew lionized the missing fisherman with a series of greatest memories. "Remember when he was taking care of Salomon's house and they didn't leave him any money or food so he ate the dog food, you know those little square nuggets?" said Willy, laughing. "I saw him with a bowl of pellets and he poured milk atop it and was eating it like cereal. I told him, 'Man, you are going to get sick.' He looked at me and said, 'You don't see the dogs dying, do you?'"

No one doubted that Alvarenga had a chance to survive. When they held strongman contests, Alvarenga often won. He could lift the sixty-liter gasoline jugs overhead in a set of six repetitions. Who else had the ability to eat everything from raw raccoon to dog food? Drowning was unlikely, they thought, as Alvarenga was a strong swimmer. An expert navigator with a cool head, he had all the tools to survive a raucous storm at sea. "We heard him speaking on his radio and his boat had not sunk. That was a good sign," said Ray. "But I felt guilty that I had abandoned him. I was not with my captain when he needed me and he was out there with someone so inexperienced."

Alvarenga's contagious sense of humor had earned him many

fans, ranging from fisherman colleagues to a pair of fifty-year-old women, Doña Celia and Doña Mina, who regularly benefited from Alvarenga's generous gifts of fresh catch—mainly shrimp and fresh tuna. His kindly attention to Wendy and Indra, two children in the village whom he quietly furnished with coins to buy bubble gum, had not gone unnoticed. Nor had his solidarity with fellow fishermen. "When my sister—my little Carmelita, God bless her—was dying he was the only one to help," says Ray. "He gave me money so I could visit her. No one else would do that."

If most of the town considered Chancha a friend, his young mate Córdoba was a wild card. Few of the Costa Azul clan knew his story or had even met him. The fragments they began to piece together were not promising. Wolfman explained how he had patched together the unlikely duo of hardened Alvarenga and the rookie Córdoba. Wolfman had been working for a full year with Córdoba, who was a coastal lagoon guy inexperienced in the deep sea and just beginning to learn the ropes of the open ocean. Wolfman fancied himself a one-man training academy and had taken the young Córdoba under his wing. But he had doubts whether he could make a deep-sea fisherman of the skittish Córdoba. "He was a happy kid. No enemies. A mama's boy," said Wolfman. "But he was worried about a prophecy from a Christian woman [in his village]. She went on a fifteen-day fast and after that came out with a vision that Piñata was going to die at sea. He talked a lot about that."

Wolfman described how Córdoba had been stuck in a deep funk for the last several weeks. "Piñata was scared by the prophecy," says Wolfman. "I could see he was sad."

Córdoba was from El Fortin, a dusty village half an hour north of Costa Azul with fewer than two hundred inhabitants. Surrounded by mangrove jungles, El Fortin is largely cut off from the world and the pace of life remains a dusk-to-dawn routine, little altered by the arrival of electricity. It is a town that lives from the sea and a place where more homes have a motorboat than a car.

When Córdoba's concerned family members arrived at the fishing shacks in Costa Azul that night, they were already coping with a gruesome loss. One of Piñata's brothers had been stabbed in a street fight less than two years earlier. The blade severed an artery in his arm and he bled to death on the street. Now the Córdoba family was facing the possible death of Piñata. Córdoba's surviving brothers pressed Willy and Mino—the two highest-ranking fishermen—for an expedited search. Wolfman recalls it was a tense situation. "Córdoba's mother attacked me, she said it was my fault. That I had sent him to his death. My wife was worried; she said that his family was going to kill me. But I had nothing to fear. I hadn't done anything wrong."

Mino regretted not having more details about Alvarenga. He had no way to contact the lost fisherman's family. "He liked to talk but he was very reserved about his life in El Salvador and the things that he had left behind. He only talked about things that happened here in the ocean. About El Salvador? With me, at least, he never mentioned anything. He did not want to go back. He told everyone he was Mexican."

The fishermen ate, talked and drank throughout the entire night as they awaited daybreak. During the night, the owner, Willy, and his right-hand man, Mino, drove around the coastline buying up a stockpile of fuel. In the kitchen, Doña Reina, the in-house cook and Alvarenga's confidante, cooked extra plates of chicken, rice and fish. Alvarenga's colleagues imagined his suffering: bashed in the Gulf with no motor, no radio and an inexperienced mate.

Harbormasters along the coast had issued each fisherman a GPS chip. Many of the men attached the chip to a post on the boat, but the government never installed the antenna needed to track the signal. "The only real safety feature is a barrel that we bring on the boat. If the boat sinks, you can tie yourself to the barrel and float," says José Guadalupe, a colleague of Alvarenga. Like many fishermen, Guadalupe knows firsthand the dangers of fishing in the Gulf of Tehuantepec. "Every March 19, I remember my dad. He was lost at sea thirteen years ago and I was orphaned," he says. "My grandfather José Luis, he was also lost at sea. My uncle too."

At the first sign of light—5:30 a.m.—four boats prepared to launch, each with a two-man crew. The rescue team made final adjustments to their gear, stashed food for twenty-four hours and mounted a second outboard motor on two of the boats. Each boat carried 120 gallons of gasoline—the weight of the fuel sinking them inches closer to the waterline. No one was forced to join the rescue mission—it was an all-volunteer force and there were more than enough men to fill the eight spots. Loyalty to Alvarenga was fierce. Experienced captains, including Willy and Mino, would lead the way.

The weather on the second morning worsened—winds were forecast to top 60 mph and the waves fifteen feet. Yet no one balked at going out to find Alvarenga. Safety precautions in the zone were minimal. Despite the always-growing list of local casualties at sea, in the entire village there were barely a dozen life preservers and even those were rarely used. Some of the fishermen could not even swim. Heading out to sea at the peak of a Norteño was a huge gamble.

As soon as they left the sheltered lagoon and made it through the dangerous surf break the rescue party was assaulted from all sides. "The waves were hitting at an angle nearly parallel to us and we were trying to avoid the breaks," says one fisherman. "We were riding and avoiding the crashing waves and using the accelerator to keep from being rolled. These waves slap you and can sink you. I had to find the path to weave through. We were playing defense. It was difficult but I got out to forty kilometers [twenty-four miles]. The waves were four meters [thirteen feet]. Chancha's motor had died, otherwise he would have gotten out of the storm."

Alvarenga's last words weighed heavily on his colleagues— "Come now, I am really getting fucked out here!" It was a phrase uttered in despair and over the ensuing eighteen hours, there had been no further word from Alvarenga or any sign of his boat. It was as if the ocean had swallowed him, boat and all. "Usually you find the boat, or at least the gear," says Wolfman. "The bodies are always gone, they get eaten by the sharks."

As they searched throughout the day, the four rescue boats stayed in close radio contact both to organize which swath of ocean each boat would search and to respond urgently in case any boat flipped. "The waves were breaking here, breaking there," says Willy. "You try and avoid where it is breaking but they are crashing one after another. It is common for two to break together. It is all white and you are rising and falling. It is easy to flip." Willy and Mino searched for twelve hours, optimistic that they would find their colleague and baffled that not a trace of gear washed ashore or was picked up by the multiple patrols scouring the sea. When the varied crews gathered to compare notes, it was a grim summary: they had nothing.

In retrospect, Willy believes the greatest danger his men faced was not the weather but decades of overfishing. "Before, I went out to eighteen or twenty miles with nets. The fish were right here. Now we have to go out one hundred twenty miles. Before, there were more fish and they were closer."

After three days of harsh winds, the weather eased just enough for several of the fishermen to get up in a small aircraft. Operated by the local rescue authority in Tonalá, the plane had just finished the requisite three days searching (unsuccessfully) for fishermen lost farther south. Now the search shifted to a guestimate of Córdoba and Alvarenga's position. Given the winds, the currents and the uncertainty regarding their last known position, the airplane searched from Puerto Chiapas in the south to Salina Cruz in the north, a swath encompassing nearly the entire Gulf of Tehuantepec. "It was a small plane with two motors, I went up," says Mino. "It was ugly. The ocean was all very white and the turbulence was so bad it felt like it was going to take the plane down. It was a northern storm like I have never seen."

Being spotted by the rescue airplane was a long shot. "Each boat is so tiny, it's like a drop of water," says Rafael Gutierrez, a local rescue coordinator in Puerto Escondido, Mexico, pointing to a map of the coastline. The map was divided into rectangles, each one representing a block of vacant ocean sixty miles by sixty miles. Gutierrez has spent thirty years coordinating rescue operations in the Pacific Ocean using planes, helicopters, navy ships and the goodwill of fishermen. "From the air it is difficult. If there is much of a swell, you can't find anything."

Four days after Alvarenga and Córdoba's boat went missing,

Doña Reina commenced a tradition for missing fishermen. She bought candles and left them burning outside his beachside shack. She also left a glass of water, to quench his thirst. Mino bought flowers and a group of boats went to sea and held a ceremony in the open ocean. "They each throw a handful of flowers," says Mino. "I don't believe in any of that and Chancha knows it, but others said that I had to do it."

Such ceremonies are symbols of hope, not a capitulation. Fishermen lost in this part of Mexico have an unnerving habit of showing up months later with incredible stories. A passing container ship might find them adrift hundreds of miles from land and bring the starved men aboard. But these ships often continue their course, eventually dumping the castaways at the Canal Zone in Panama, in Long Beach, California, or Buenaventura, Colombia. Even after a rescue it could be weeks before a stranded crewman returned to Mexico. Some of the missing men never wanted to come home. "There are a lot of insurance scams with lost fishermen," explains Gutierrez. "When the fishermen disappear, sometimes it's because they are in another village with a lover or have immigrated to the United States."

Usually search-and-rescue operations continue for just three days, but in Chancha's case, when the weather permitted, a determined group of fishermen went out searching for nearly two weeks. But as the wind continued to rip from the north and the storm refused to relent, and as the gasoline bills surged, little by little the formal search ended. It was not that the colleagues had given up hope—quite the contrary. Of all the tribe, Chancha was considered the least likely to be found dead at sea, but the Norteño kept howling day after day. For sixteen straight days the wind whistled and the waves churned with menace. Little did the men know that their colleagues not only were alive, but had survived a storm so ferocious it had blown them out of the Gulf of Tehuantepec and into an unknown world.

CHAPTER 5

Adrift

 November 23, 2012
Position: 280 miles off the coast of Mexico
N 12° 47' 51.93" – W 97° 25' 39.14"
Day 6

After five days of careening waves and screaming wind the winds finally eased. Alvarenga and Córdoba were now approximately 280 miles offshore and well beyond the limited search-and-rescue capabilities of the Mexican Coast Guard. "They would have needed long-range aircraft," explains Art Allen, a search-and-rescue planner for the US Coast Guard. "As a radar object, these boats are pretty invisible, just fiberglass with an outboard motor. And only two people? That's not a big radar target. It's not surprising they weren't found. And there's also a thought process of 'How long do we search? What are their chances for survival? Are they even upright?' Twenty-meters-a-second wind is a pretty nasty wind. The Mexican Coast Guard may have presumed that the fishermen didn't last the [first] night."

Miraculously, the two men had not flipped. The sea anchor off the stern had aligned the bow to the oncoming waves and allowed

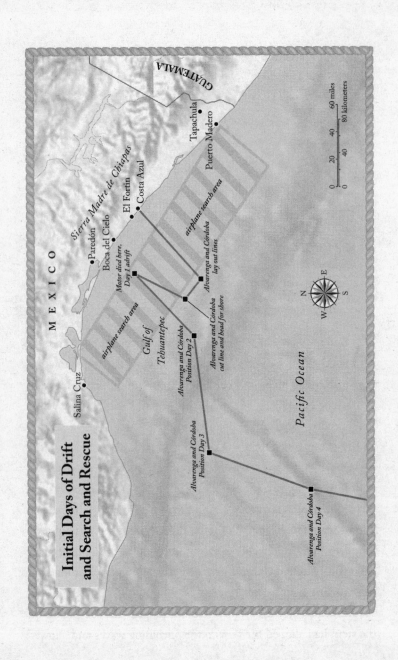

Initial Days of Drift
and Search and Rescue

MEXICO

Sierra Madre de Chiapas

Salina Cruz

Paredón
Boca del Cielo
El Fortín
Costa Azul

GUATEMALA

Tapachula
Puerto Madero

Gulf of
Tehuantepec

airplane search area

airplane search area

Motor died here,
Day 1 adrift

Alvarenga and Córdoba
lay out lines

Alvarenga and Córdoba
cut line and head for shore

Alvarenga and Córdoba
Position Day 2

Alvarenga and Córdoba
Position Day 3

Alvarenga and Córdoba
Position Day 4

Pacific Ocean

N
W E
S

0   20   40   60 miles
0   40   80 kilometers

the men to survive day after day bashing and crashing through incoming waves. Now the two men awoke to a freakish calm. As Alvarenga and Córdoba scanned the horizon, the lack of waves distorted their depth perception. The ocean's flat surface was stretched so smooth it made the sun seem closer and allowed the imagination to build the illusion of an edge to the ocean where an unlucky fisherman might just slip off.

In the open ocean, depth perception was tricky. A Styrofoam block just a half mile away could be distorted into looking like an aircraft carrier on the horizon. Objects a hundred feet deep were magnified and distorted by the water. With few points of reference every floating object was susceptible to the whims of imagination and the deceptions of wishful thinking. Like a traveler lost in a desert, Alvarenga and Córdoba had no certainty that what they saw or heard actually existed.

Puddles of seawater sloshed at their ankles, a reminder that despite nonstop bailing, Alvarenga and Córdoba had never fully emptied out the boat. The Yamaha motor lacked cover and cord—it looked naked. Nearly all the fishing gear was floating in the sea miles away and their fouled communications gear now lay at the bottom of the ocean. Taking stock of their tools and supplies was disturbingly quick: a long wooden plank, one gray bucket with some clothes, a battered fishing knife with a cracked handle, a trusty machete, a wooden club, the empty icebox (with lid), a pile of bleach bottles, a small pile of nylon rope, the useless motor and one red onion found wedged under a seat after the five-day tumult. Or had it been a four-day storm? Time was increasingly elastic in this world without clocks or calendars. A more primeval rhythm took hold: the warmth of dawn, the blistering daytime heat, the relief of sunset and the mystery of darkness.

Córdoba and Alvarenga had lost much of their body heat during the storm. The wind cut through their wet clothes. They had shivered and spent the four evenings clenched and entwined in what a US Navy SEAL trainer described as "a puppy pile."

———

Now on a cloudless morning, as the sun rose over the sea, Alvarenga rechristened his boat. The original name had been fairly generic— *Shrimper from the Coast #3*. After surviving a fearsome Norteño without a motor, nearly flipping twice and losing all his communications gear, Alvarenga decided his boat needed a more grandiose title. He began referring to it as *The Titanic*. His humble boat had survived one hit after another and Alvarenga was paternalistically proud. "My boat was more of a triumph than the other *Titanic*," he said. "That other one? It sank!"

As the morning sunlight comforted and warmed the men they hoisted a six-foot-long wooden plank from the floor, laid it across two benches that crossed the boat like central ribs and prepared a bed. The men stripped off their wet clothes and, clad only in underwear, stretched out to sop up the first glints of sunlight. Córdoba's shoulders and arms were so tired he could barely pull himself up. Bailing seawater had left his upper body collapsed. He had multiple bruises—many of them deep—after being flung from one side of the boat to the other. Córdoba felt a new loyalty to his captain. When he was swept overboard, it had been Alvarenga's quick reflexes that saved him from drowning.

That afternoon a plane buzzed overhead. "We could read the

letters on the side, T-A-C-A," said Alvarenga. "I thought, 'That one is going to Tapachula or Mexico City.' We tried to signal but they didn't see us." Córdoba felt like they were destined to a slow, painful death. "We are going to die, we are going to die," he moaned.

"What are you talking about? We are not going to die. Stop it!" Alvarenga scolded his companion. "Don't think that way. We are not going to die at sea. A rescue mission will find us, and we are going to be saved. We are going to get out of this."

"Ah, I am not so sure," Córdoba responded and began to cry in long sobs.

Fatigue, however, soon overcame them and both men collapsed into a deep sleep. Córdoba dozed with his head next to Alvarenga's feet. It was a balancing act for them to both fit on the same plank. When Alvarenga moved, Córdoba awoke. They slept intermittently throughout the morning, splashing water on their arms or legs to stay cool but never daring to dive into the water. The sun was burning hot and they loved it.

The men awoke with a painful thirst, but they had no fresh-water stocks. Coconuts were everywhere and the floating fruit tortured Alvarenga. He could see them swirl by, could almost taste the chilled coconut water. He spotted a solitary bobbing sphere. Then an entire clutch of coconuts, like huge grapes, drifted near and lured him; dared him to swim out. Alvarenga was not tempted. He was a confident and strong swimmer who often took an hour-long morning swim as he explored the lagoon near his palm-roofed hut. But here in the open ocean, Alvarenga knew the risks, even if he didn't actually see the fins of patrolling sharks. When a coconut was close, the swim from the boat to the coconut and back would take less than a minute. Maybe just thirty seconds. But Alvarenga feared it would take far less for a shark pack to hone in on his tell-tale thrashing.

Alvarenga had never seen a man eaten alive by sharks. But like the other fishermen from Costa Azul, he had heard the grisly details of the death of his former boss. Captain Gio had been a grouchy old-timer with a raspy, choking voice caused by the scarring from a bullet to the throat. Years earlier, Gio was churning home at a rapid clip in his launch when he smashed into a half-sunken log. The force of the collision launched Gio overboard. In the ensuing confusion, the boat veered off course and by the time the mate took over and circled back, a pool of blood and mass of fins confirmed that Gio would get no further burial. There were signs of a gruesome death but not a piece of Gio to be seen. Apparently sharks had been gathered under the log or nearby. The story of Gio plus Alvarenga's shark-fishing experience were savage reminders of the limited life expectancy of anyone swimming in these waters. No matter how much he longed for fresh coconut water and a bite of coconut meat, Alvarenga's sea smarts prevailed. He would wait until the coconuts were within reach.

On that first night of calm, their sixth day at sea, Alvarenga and Córdoba felt a bizarre combination of being trapped and also a sense of freedom. They were farther out to sea than either man had ever traveled, but without the barrage of crashing waves, with stars lighting the smooth ocean and no wind, it felt like they had arrived at a calm harbor. "We looked up and saw airplanes, saw those blinking lights," said Alvarenga. "We thought, 'How cool, those people are eating. They have lights and heat. They are relaxed and we are down here suffering.'"

Stretched out on the plank, in long bouts of silence, talking only briefly, neither of them stated the obvious: they were alone and adrift. They had heard enough tales of lost fishermen to understand that islands were few and far between. If they had stocked either a sail or a pair of oars, the men could have set a course, but lacking the tools, they drifted at the whim of the wind and ocean currents, swerving, looping and zigzagging across the wide-open Pacific. "A drifting boat gets these bursts of high speed due to a tidal current coming through and then you slow down," says Luca Centurioni, of Scripps. "You're always randomly pushed around . . . The ocean is not a river, so you're not going 'downstream' with the currents. This is stop and go, stop and go."

As they drifted west at approximately 75 miles a day, the nearest landmass in their path was a single, tiny blip on the map: Clipperton Island—a remnant of Napoleonic conquest, still under French rule but a lonely outpost 1,000 miles west. To the south, the closest islands were the Galapagos, 1,100 miles distant on the other side of the equator. NASA astronauts who flew over the Pacific Ocean in the Space Shuttle found it to be endless, even when traveling 17,500 miles an hour. "I never really believed that seventy-one percent of the earth's surface is covered with salt water until I flew over the Pacific," says Jerome "Jay" Apt, who flew on three Space Shuttle flights between 1991 and 1996. "Sometimes it took thirty-five minutes of our ninety-minute orbit to cross the Pacific."

As he watched the sunset, Alvarenga sensed they were in a different world. "I couldn't tell how far we were from shore. But the current really ripped us out," he said. "My ears started to ring after we passed two hundred miles from shore."

On the final day of the first week—November 23—Alvarenga awoke early. By five a.m. he'd surveyed the boat, taken stock (again) of the meager supplies and framed the outline of a plan. He had sufficient experience to realize that the only likely rescue was being spotted by another boat. But even that was difficult, as his twenty-five-foot craft sat low in the water. There was nothing like a mast that might provide a profile. The boat didn't have any glass that might flash reflections. From more than a half mile away, they were virtually invisible. The boat's white hull blended in so well with the sea it looked like a deliberate attempt at camouflage.

When Córdoba awoke he immediately began to pitch in. Despite his wailing and blubbering during the storm, Córdoba wasn't a man to complain about physical pain. Alvarenga explained the plan and, working together, the two men tied Alvarenga's T-shirt to the top of a wooden pole they had pulled from the ocean. They scoured the ocean for ships. Each man searched 180 degrees of horizon. The rising sun played tricks with shadows and as it glinted off the ocean it created a web of illusions. Faux ships dissolved into the clouds like mirages in the desert.

Alvarenga was sure they would be rescued soon, so he rehearsed and practiced. If a ship was seen, Alvarenga was ready to pull a small cigarette lighter from his pocket (where it was protected from the salt and water) and set the shirt afire. Córdoba would hoist the flaming shirt and the fire would send up a cloud of smoke to alert the passing ship. At night the chance of the flame being spotted was far greater, but it was going to be a random encounter.

After nearly a full day and a dozen false alarms they finally heard the growl of a ship's engine. It was late afternoon when the vibrations came up through the hull. The men scanned and squinted but couldn't see anything. Córdoba placed his ear to the deck and confirmed the rumble of a far-off motor. Then they spotted it. Far to the north, a container ship was approaching. They could not see individual containers or read the ship's name. It was little more than a Lego block on the horizon. They calculated that the container ship was not going to pass even within a mile of them so when the two ships were closest, Alvarenga held the T-shirt while Córdoba set it afire. The shirt wouldn't burn. It was damp, laden with salt and the small puffs of smoke were less a distress signal than a pathetic reminder of their predicament. Alvarenga shouted and waved his other shirt. Oblivious, the container ship chugged along. The men had no flare gun, no searchlights and their only mirror was so small it barely served for shaving. They flashed light from the mirror in the boat's direction but watched in frustration as the Lego block marched steadily across the horizon. "That's when I had a first lump of fear. We were very, very far from the coast," said Alvarenga. "A place where no fishermen go."

As Córdoba began to panic, Alvarenga tried to calm his novice mate. "We are lost but we are going to live." Córdoba pestered Alvarenga with his fears. "Where will we get our water? And our food?"

Alvarenga distracted his distraught mate by ordering him to keep watch on deck. Alvarenga was busy trying to design a shelter from the wind and sun. He flipped the box on its side so that he could sit in the shade and still scan the ocean while he brainstormed.

"Just the fact that he saw a box he put fish in, and was able to take that and turn it into a shelter, shows that he is wired well for survival," suggests Joseph "Butch" Flythe of the US Coast Guard. "There are people in this world who would have sat in that boat and complained that the sun was cooking them. There are even people who are in a survival situation for quite a while and they have a cell phone in their pocket and don't use it."

The sun was now insufferable. The combination of salt, sweat and blistering heat made it feel like they were being cooked alive. Gusty winds were gone and the clouds far away, like distant drawings. The two men huddled in the shade of the tiny structure and prepared to nap as a school of palm-sized triggerfish gnawed at the fuzzy green mold growing on the hull, their clacking and crunching a background sound track to an otherwise overwhelming desolation. "I found it comforting, it reminded me we were not alone," said Alvarenga.

Alvarenga insisted that rains would soon arrive and provide drinking water. Córdoba was impatient. "I can't take it, I am so thirsty," he complained. Córdoba could see no salvation. Without even a distant shore to feed his dreams, he was sure they would both die.

The sea was so calm it was unnerving. The temperature soared above 90 degrees Fahrenheit and the dry air teased the remaining moisture from their bodies. When Alvarenga swallowed, the spittle seemed to bump and rattle down his throat. He worried that his throat might swell and cut off access to his stomach. Was this the way he was going to die? Córdoba's lips were swollen to twice their normal size and, sucked dry by the sun, began to crack. Red welts, caused by salt blocking up his sweat pores, began to pop out along his arms and legs, breaking the layers of skin that were now shrunken and tight. It felt like his skin would pop open and lay bare the muscles and tendons beneath. Fat reserves that offered a chance to extend life were being converted to basic life-support energy. But without sufficient water and carbohydrates, their bodies began to lose the capability to break down fat. Lethargy laid siege to Córdoba's normal functions. Alvarenga, accustomed to days without food or water, fared far better.

Finding fresh water became the men's obsession. "You are drying up, you feel desperate," said Alvarenga. "You are surrounded by water and you are going to die of thirst, what a punishment." They began to identify and track clouds on the horizon. They begged the clouds to gather force and churn into a thunderstorm. Still it didn't rain. The clouds would bunch up, thunderstorms ripped on the horizon, lightning sliced down, wisps of wind a sign rain was imminent, but it never rained. The close calls began to haunt the men. How could storms and rain be all around them and yet they remained as dry as a desert? Was it bad luck? A curse? The two men were dumbfounded. Alvarenga's experience at sea had long ago taught him the dangers of drinking seawater. Despite their desperate condition and longing for liquid to slosh in their mouths they each resisted swallowing even a cupful of the endless salt water that surrounded them.

November 25, 2012
Position: Approximately 500 miles off
    the coast of Mexico
N 12° 35' 35.09.89" – W 99° 20.21"
Day 8

The men passed another full day without water. They had now lost the ability to conserve body heat. "We could climb inside [the icebox] and though it was tight, we could both huddle inside; one of us could stretch his legs up the side and we were protected from the wind, and if we hugged," said Alvarenga, "we could maintain at least some warmth. My face swelled up. My tongue was dry, I had no saliva."

Again and again the men searched the boat but could not find a single fishing hook. Alvarenga remembered the moment when the wave had crashed over them. If he had only grabbed the toolbox, he would have saved an invaluable supply of hooks, lines, thread, a pair of knives and a sharpening stone. But it had gone sliding over the rail as he'd watched bug-eyed and held on tightly.

Alvarenga's *Titanic* was now headed southwest, a fortunate deviation that allowed him to avoid the Equatorial Countercurrent—an enormous ocean eddy that would have hijacked his westerly course and spun him into a circular, counterclockwise loop—perhaps not letting them free for weeks. As he drifted, Alvarenga was shocked by the amount of trash and flotsam in the water around there. Abandoned fishing lines migrated with the current. Riddled with hooks, nooks and crannies, these "ghost lines" became the nucleus of an organism that provided a home to crabs, small fish and turtles.

"I was so hungry that I was eating my own fingernails, swallowing all the little pieces," said Alvarenga, who began to grab jellyfish from the water, scooping them up in his hands and swallowing them whole. "It burned the top part of my throat," he said, "but wasn't so bad. I ate two of the purple jellyfish, those burn more." But jellyfish did little to satiate his hunger so he began to fantasize that he could eat his own finger. "I needed a piece of something." He was right-handed so it would have to be on his left hand. The pinky was the most useless. It would be the first to go. Alvarenga prepared for a gruesome operation. He would hack off his pinky with the machete, stanch the blood flow and then dice up his own finger and eat it. The amount of meat was minimal, probably a few bites. Hunger was teasing the sensibility out of his mind. But his plan had a potentially fatal flaw: he might bleed to death. Alvarenga was not convinced that he could stem the blood flow from his own finger. "I would have died, bled to death or got halfway through and stopped because of the pain."

As they drifted southwest, Alvarenga eyed the small triggerfish—seven inches long—that had been chewing on his boat the night before. Known as "sea piranhas," the triggerfish practically sanded the bottom of the boat clean with their teeth. Staring into the clear water, Alvarenga identified other members of a growing retinue. With a flat squarish head—like a miniature sperm whale—and an unmistakable green skin that passed in a flash, the prized game fish mahimahi zipped by in schools of a dozen.

While the fish activity under their boat increased, so did the prevalence of sharks. "I needed hooks. Or a net to catch fish. Or a harpoon," said Alvarenga. "I could see the fish go by and in my mouth I tasted them. With a harpoon I would have been set. But I didn't have it so I had to imagine what to do. I had a pole and tied a knife to it and tried to spear them. I speared two fish but didn't land them. I dove into the water trying to grab them with my hands." The fish got away.

Alvarenga invented another strategy to catch fish. He kneeled alongside the edge of the boat—eyes scanning for sharks—and shoved his arms into the water up to his shoulders. With his chest tightly pressed to the side of the boat, Alvarenga set a trap for the fish. He kept his hands steady, ten inches apart. When a fish swam between his hands, he smashed them shut, digging his fingernails into the rough scales. Many escaped but soon Alvarenga mastered the tactic—"Sometimes after the triggerfish finished eating they would just float for a minute and I would grab them"—and he began to snatch the fish and toss them into the boat while trying to avoid the teeth. "The triggerfish teeth are terribly sharp and they nipped off the end of my fingertips or small pieces from the palm of my hand," said Alvarenga, who was able to capture as many as thirty of the small fish in a single session. "They would bite me but I hardly felt it. Who cares if they bit, I had caught them."

The men set up a mini fish-processing plant. Alvarenga would snare them, and with the fishing knife, Córdoba expertly cleaned and sliced the flesh into finger-sized strips that were left to dry in the sun. When Córdoba dumped the bloody innards of the palm-sized triggerfish into the water it was rarely more than a few minutes before mako and blue sharks feasted. The four-foot sharks scraped their rough skin along the bottom of the boat, sending up a jolting blow and a noisy reminder of how little separated these two worlds.

Alvarenga ate fish after fish. He stuffed raw meat and dried meat into his mouth, hardly noticing or caring about the difference. He was famished after days without a meal, yet his body was still in a state of adrenal overdrive that allowed him to ignore basic human needs like sleep in order to focus on the more crucial task of finding water.

Alvarenga began to drink his urine. He wasn't embarrassed and he encouraged Córdoba to follow suit. It was salty but not revolting as he drank, urinated, drank again, peed again, in a cycle that felt like it provided at least minimal hydration to his body. But urine, being filled with salts, throws the body's internal equilibriums off balance and requires the body to consume even more precious water in an attempt to flush out the salts. Drinking urine, both men realized, was a desperate measure. They needed protein, calories and hydration, so they scanned the ocean surface for food and tools. Vegetation was extensive, ranging from the trunks of palm trees to mats of seaweed.

Alvarenga and Córdoba divided their time between scanning the horizon for ships and inspecting the nonstop parade of floating garbage. They became astute scavengers and learned to distinguish the myriad varieties of plastic that float across the ocean, littering the surface with a permanent mark of the petroleum age. Garbage was so prevalent that trash became a constant source of possibilities. Alvarenga and Córdoba grabbed and stored every empty water bottle they found bobbing in the water. Nearly every day they could see dozens of the floating bottles, and when they drifted nearby they used the flagpole with the burn marks from the T-shirt to snag them. At least now if it rained, they had a plan. They would clean out one of the plastic indentations on the boat, eliminate the salt and gunk and then transfer the collected water into the plastic half-liter bottles. Their plastic bottle collection, which grew almost daily, formed the basis of their first line of defense against thirst. Trash was now a tool.

When a stuffed green garbage bag drifted within reach, the men snared it, hauled it aboard and ripped open the plastic. They forensically inspected every item in the bag. A crust of bread would have been heavenly; a tortilla, the Holy Grail. When the men found a wad of prechewed gum, they divided the almond-sized lump, each man feasting on the wealth of sensorial pleasures. Underneath a layer of sodden kitchen oil, they found riches: half a head of cabbage, some carrots and a quart of milk. It was half rancid but still they drank it. It was the first fresh food the two men had seen in a week. They treated the soggy carrots with reverence befitting a Thanksgiving dinner. "We didn't eat it quickly at all," recalled Alvarenga. "Instead we chopped it up very fine and prepared an entire meal." With the precision of diamond dealers, they enthusiastically divided the loot. "I found a plastic bottle of soft drink floating in the ocean with just a little drop inside, but ahhhh! How sweet! I imagined that I was back in the world," said Alvarenga. "What a pleasure it was."

The two men hauled aboard every batch of seaweed within reach. Sometimes a crab or small fish could be found tangled in the spiderweb of plants. The men were at the epicenter of a newly hatched ecosystem—the few square yards of ocean under the drifting boat's hull now a petri dish where barnacles, crabs and fish began to congregate.

Tuna fishermen in this area of the Pacific are known to dump tree trunks into the ocean, then return in two days and circle the area with their lines. "Fish in the open ocean tend to aggregate under anything that provides any sort of structure. A boat that is floating for a long period of time acts as a magnet for fish," says Daniel Cartamil, a shark expert with the Scripps Institution of Oceanography, who describes the rapid buildup of a food chain in which the smaller fish "would act as a magnet for predators," including sharks. "Once sharks have found food, they will pretty much hang around all day," says Cartamil. "They won't leave."

The two men could see that food was plentiful and nearby. Seabirds dove into the water to scoop up sardines. Tuna fish flashed under the boat chasing smaller fish. Birds landed on the prow of *The Titanic* to swallow a recent catch. The birds soiled the deck with syrupy excrement that smelled horrendous and which the men feared might foul any freshwater stores. The two men shooed the birds away, cursing the fact that their boat was a landing pad. A pea-sized drop of excrement could foul an entire section of the boat that might later fill with rainwater, thus the men's vigilance to scare away the birds and prevent them from landing. They considered building a scarecrow. Without realizing it, they were becoming experts on the behavior of these frequent visitors.

After nine days of minimal water and only a few servings of dried fish, milk, cabbage and carrots, Alvarenga and Córdoba were so desperate that they began searching for minuscule microdroplets. The men divided the boat in equal halves, from bow to stern, with an imaginary line running down the middle of the hull. Then they crouched and began licking the entire surface of the boat, especially the molded indentations, which tended to hold a few drops of morning dew. "Like cows," said Alvarenga, who discovered and explored the secret contours of his boat with a slow and desperate intimacy.

November 27, 2012
Position: 520 miles off the coast
of Mexico
N 12° 02.57.25" – W 100° 55' 06.14"
Day 10

Alvarenga was so thirsty and hungry he began to imagine a new source of food. He had a vision of pure nutrition: sea turtles. "I was taking these short half breaths, and wanting water and not having water. I thought I would die from the anguish," said Alvarenga. "My breaths were getting short. I started to suffocate. It felt like I was drowning. I couldn't get the oxygen; it was horrible. I thought a turtle might save me."

Finding a sea turtle would not be difficult as the Mexican coastline was host to coastal marine sanctuaries that included sea turtle conservation and hatchery programs. From September through January, tens of thousands of sea turtles come to nest and lay their eggs. These eggs are then fenced off, allowing tourists to photograph the hatchlings as they crawl back toward the surf to face the odds. "They say the [sea] turtles are in extinction, but we go forty kilometers [twenty-five miles] from here and they are everywhere—like rocks on a mountainside," says Mino, Alvarenga's supervisor. "You have to swerve this way and that to avoid them and sometimes 'bang!' You hit a turtle at God-knows-how-many revolutions per second. Sometimes they are half sunk so you can't see them. We are talking thousands of turtles out there."

Thousands of these turtles are caught every year by fishermen and sold for fifty dollars apiece on the black market. Although "Fresh Turtle Steak" is rarely printed on the menu, the savvy gourmet along the Mexican coast never has to search far to find a local restaurant willing to serve up the illegal delicacy. Despite the threat of fines and public awareness campaigns, turtle meat finds its way into household cooking pots and commercial kitchens all along the coast.

Sea turtles in the open ocean dive when boats appear. It is common, however, that when a boat is still, the sea turtles approach. Attracted to floating objects that might serve as a rest stop or source of food, sea turtles along the coast routinely swim *toward* a stationary fisherman's boat and make a racket as they try to climb aboard.

The first turtles Alvarenga and Córdoba found were dead. "They fill up like a balloon and turn purple," said Alvarenga. "The smell is terrible, we couldn't eat them. It was impossible."

But in late November—roughly ten days after losing their engine—Alvarenga heard a "thunk" in the night. He thought a log had bumped the boat. Climbing out from under the icebox, he was surprised to see an eye. Then a second eye. He grabbed the two-foot-long turtle by the back and tossed him aboard.

"Let's eat the turtle," Salvador told his stunned companion. "We can drink the blood! If we are really this thirsty, we drink blood!"

"No. No. No. That would be a sin. Let's catch fish," Córdoba replied, shocked by the radical proposal.

"Sin? What are you talking about? A sin?" said Alvarenga. He prepared his knife.

Alvarenga's mouth was dry and his tongue swollen. He did not hesitate. "I killed the turtle with the knife and there were some tubes coming off the motor. I sliced a piece of tubing off the motor and used it like a straw." Turtles were gorged with a thick merlot-colored blood with hints of violet. If thirst was the problem, Alvarenga reasoned, then turtle blood was the solution. He slurped pint after pint of the liquid blood and later ate the congealed blood that formed into a Jell-O-like consistency.

"Eat it, eat it!" Alvarenga pleaded to his companion.

"No. No. I can't," Córdoba said, balking at the thought.

Then Alvarenga began to carve up the meat. He began with the flippers. Cutting into the thick skin was wrenching and slow work. To crack open the shell and reach the thick meat in the tail took an hour of work. Inside the turtle's stomach he found a collection of garbage including plastic bottle caps as well as clams and barnacles.

Laying out the turtle steaks, Alvarenga tried to kindle a fire. His lighter was long since dead, so he tried with his mirror. He had used a turtle shell as a frying pan before. Wood could be shaved off the plank they slept on. But with his lighter dead and the mirror useless in creating a flame, Alvarenga settled on the sun to warm up his fresh meat. But his patience was limited. Less than an hour after laying out the thick purple meat he was slicing finger-long strips of raw turtle meat and chewing it with glee. He smiled as he savored the luscious flavors. Nothing about the meal made him retch; to the contrary, he felt feted by the sea.

Lying awake inside his icebox home after his first day of turtle food, Alvarenga felt his body surging to life. His thirst temporarily quenched by blood, his appetite sated by raw turtle steaks, he gave thanks for the turtle and for his good fortune. Alvarenga saw the turtle as a venerated gift, handed to him by a benevolent sea.

Once he began scouring the open ocean for turtles, Alvarenga found they were as common as sharks. When a turtle came up for air, the head and nose rippled the surface and sometimes the animal would float, as if sunning on the surface. "A resting turtle at the surface would not be expecting any danger from a big chunk of flotsam," says Blair Witherington, a research scientist with more than twenty-five years' experience in sea turtle biology and conservation. "Turtles often like to hang out around stuff that floats. And it could be they just saw Alvarenga's boat as just flotsam out there. . . . Some of these turtles may be diving deep for food and the water down there is cold. By the time the turtle comes up, it might want to soak up sun."

Alvarenga's entire day mutated into an obsessive turtle hunt. Córdoba was also an eager hunter even if he refused the nutrients and energy contained in the blood. Despite no rain and intense sun, turtle meat kept the two men alive and they began recovering strength.

At every meal, Alvarenga divided the blood and meat with a solemn equanimity but Córdoba ate only the meat; he resisted the blood, so Alvarenga was drinking double portions. Alvarenga began to stockpile food—he caught three turtles and penned them up in a small pool of water on the deck. The turtles climbed and tumbled around, creating a racket day and night and a counter note to the crunching of triggerfish.

Alvarenga's taste for turtle was not limited to the blood and meat. "I would pull out the eggs. Córdoba did not like the meat but he ate it, but when he tried an egg he loved it. Then he ate many, many turtle eggs. There were lots and lots of turtles around there. I would catch them, kill them and then put my hands in and pull out the eggs."

Invigorated by the food, the men planned to escape. Using the turtle shells, they decided to row across the Pacific. "I had a turtle shell in each arm and for two hours rowed and rowed," said Alvarenga. "Then I thought, 'This is impossible, what am I doing?'"

CHAPTER 6

Hunter Gatherers

 November 30, 2012
Position: 550 miles off the coast
    of Mexico
N 11° 44' 18.06" – W 101° 26' 6.47"
Day 13

A lvarenga was resting inside the icebox, a bucket of turtle scraps next to the wooden plank that was his bed, when he heard, *Splat!* Another bird, another mess, he thought. *Splat . . . Splat . . . Splat.* The rhythm of raindrops on the hard roof of the icebox was unmistakable. "Piñata! Piñata! Piñata!" Alvarenga screamed as he tilted up the icebox and slipped out. His crewmate awoke and joined him. Rushing across the deck, the two men deployed a jerry-rigged rainwater collection system that Alvarenga had been designing and imagining for a week. Córdoba scrubbed clean the bottom of the gray five-gallon bucket and positioned its mouth skyward. Alvarenga balanced the plastic housing to the outboard motor on the deck, jamming it at an angle to collect rainwater.

After days of drinking urine and turtle blood, licking up droplets of freshwater, munching turtle eggs and nearly dying of thirst, a storm finally bore down on the men. Dark clouds stalked overhead. The stormy weather came on fast and the men opened their mouths to the falling rain, stripped off their clothes and showered in a glorious deluge of freshwater. The men lapped up spoonful after spoonful of water as it dripped into the bucket. The growing swells rocked the boat, the water sloshing in the bucket a measure of their riches. Within an hour the bucket had an inch, then two inches of water. The men laughed and drank every couple of minutes. As water collected in the outboard motor housing they poured it into the gray bucket. After their initial attack on the water supplies the men vowed to maintain strict water rations. "What if we go another ten days without rain?" Alvarenga asked Córdoba.

The storm picked up. Swells now reached eight feet and swung the boat around and around. They had little ballast, no rudder and only the makeshift sea anchor dragging behind them to align the bow with the surging waves. Besides having no control over the boat, the men were half frozen. With the rain came a deep chill as their rehydrated bodies were still incapable of generating or holding body heat. Then too the men had not planned on wet clothes and their obsession with collecting water hadn't included plans for keeping clothes dry. Their clothes sodden, the men shivered and entered the icebox, although it was daytime. Nearly naked they hugged.

Alvarenga and Córdoba tried to escape the water gathering at their feet by sitting on the plank, then for much of the stormy day they sought refuge in the box. When the rain poured down in sheets, visibility was little more than a hundred feet. The whistling wind played tricks with their minds. As darkness swept in, the men heard chilling screams. A voice—like taunting laughter—emerged from the ocean depths. Alvarenga was not sure whether this was a hallucination or a nightmare. Was he going mad? Were they going to be eaten alive?

After a day, the rain let up and as the sun began to cut through the thinning cloud patch, a calm silence returned. The men took stock of their new reality. They had transferred water from the indentations on deck to completely fill the five-gallon bucket with fresh water. It was enough for at least a week if rations were kept to a minimum. Though their thirst was sated the men's hunger grew, as if the arrival of water had primed the body for the promise of food. Alvarenga began to attack the stock of three turtles—each one represented three full days of food.

Using his authority as captain, Alvarenga made an executive decision. He ordered Córdoba to eat. But instead of screaming or forcing the issue, Alvarenga instead seduced his mate into eating by presenting the turtle steaks as a gourmet delicacy. After cutting the meat into thin strips and dripping salt water for flavoring, he toasted them on a part of the outboard motor housing heated by the sun. Alvarenga sliced each strip into tiny squares and using the vertebrae of the triggerfish created what looked like a fancy appetizer. The turtle shell served as a plate and to the surprise of both men, Córdoba began to enjoy turtle meat. His body immediately overruled his mind—rich in fat, vitamins and protein, turtle meat was exactly what a starved human body required.

"It was really common for European sailors to gather sea turtles and turn them upside down in the holds of the ship, and tie their flippers together," says Witherington. "The turtles would stay alive without any food or water for weeks and weeks and weeks."

Alvarenga and Córdoba began a ritual of eating together as they slowly consumed equal-sized portions. "One myth about survivors is that people think you're so starved that you bury your face into the food and it all tastes the same. It's not that at all," says Steve Callahan, author of *Adrift*, his memoir of survival at sea for seventy-six days aboard a tiny raft after his sailboat was sunk by a whale. "I would fantasize about all these subtle differences in flavor between different parts of the fish. I would hang the meat until it got really dry and it was like 'Ahhhhh, that's like toast, nice and crunchy.' The liver was sweet, so that was dessert. . . . It's not like you're walking through the grocery store and you look at a package of fish for sale, you buy it, throw it in the cart, take it home, cook and eat it with absolutely no consciousness that this was an actual creature that had a life. Instead, you are connected to all that richness in a very close way."

Turtle meat staved off the worst effects of starvation but there was never enough food. Salvation came in the unlikely form of a shark pack. "I would see stains—dark shadows in the water—as schools of fish passed by," said Alvarenga. "The sharks were chasing them and the water boiled. When the sharks started eating them, the fish would slide up to the side of my boat and I would be scooping them out until the sharks left."

The shark pack and feeding frenzy didn't surprise Alvarenga, but Córdoba was stunned by the spectacle. He kept far from the waterline and brandished a wooden pole when the sharks launched an attack. "They banged and crashed around as they hunted," said Alvarenga. "I would watch the sharks and tell them, 'Someday we are coming back for you. All this torture you are causing us? We will be back.'"

Alvarenga was also talking to the outboard motor. He was

still stunned by the machine's betrayal. "I was very angry with the motor. I found some branches in the ocean and began smashing the motor. I was swearing. I smashed it with my machete and the wooden poles," said Alvarenga. "Later I asked for forgiveness and I took it apart to try and make hooks. There was lots of metal inside."

 December 2, 2012
Position: 650 miles off the coast
    of Mexico
N 11° 03' 43.81" – W 102° 10' 52.20"
Day 16

As he picked apart the motor, Alvarenga tried to decipher the cause of the engine failure. A single screw? A cracked motor housing? Wet spark plugs? Whatever lay at the root of this motor's premature death, Alvarenga was certain it was something mundane and simple. Fixing the motor was beyond his limited mechanical capabilities, and anyway, weeks earlier they had watched as all their fuel containers sank beneath the waves, presumably to rest on the ocean floor. Alvarenga dissected the outboard motor in search of a sharp piece of metal he could fashion into a tool or a weapon. When he removed a foot-long rod it took him less than a day to shave one end into a sharp point and to fashion a makeshift harpoon. He needed only to anchor the harpoon system to the boat via a thin line of fishing filament and the men would have a reusable weapon capable of supplying them with fish. On the first toss the filament snapped. His handmade harpoon sank into the depths.

Alvarenga continued to strip pieces from the outboard motor in an effort to craft tools. Most of the motor was locked up by bolts and screws but through a combination of bashing the motor and prying it apart, the two men removed a second strip of metal, this one as long as a man's forearm. Alvarenga placed the metal on the rail of the boat and using his heft bent it into the shape of the letter J. He imagined the curve of a gaffing hook. After half a day of exertion, Alvarenga had done it. There was no barb, but by scraping the metal along the edge of the propeller for hours he shaped a sharp tip.

Alvarenga was a lifelong hunter who always ate whatever he caught. The sport of hunting never appealed to him; it was food he was after. He began to experiment with his new weapon. Leaning over the edge of the boat, he would first grab triggerfish then cut them up and chum the water with blood and pieces of flesh. The bait attracted more triggerfish and the flat-headed mahimahi. His hands in the water, Alvarenga positioned the hook as deep as possible. Córdoba tossed more bait—including turtle entrails—and waited. Alvarenga's plan was to position the hook under the soft underbelly of the mahimahi, then whip it up, in the hope of snagging the fish deep enough to haul it aboard before it wriggled free.

Two decades of hunting had taught him patience. He had vast experience killing raccoons with a slingshot and shooting birds out of the sky with a shotgun. Several times Alvarenga had mahimahi flirting with his bait, nearly lined up with the handmade hook. Still he waited. Even the slightest movement of the hook spooked the curious but cautious mahimahi. Finally, Alvarenga lined up a two-foot mahimahi. Snapping his arm up, he ripped the hook with such force that it cut through the fish. Writhing and in shock, the mahimahi fought but was aboard *The Titanic* in seconds. Córdoba smashed the fish in the head with the propeller, which he had removed from the motor. Alvarenga watched the beautiful creature's chameleon death performance. Bright greens, brilliant blues, the fish seemed almost magical as it changed colors while dying. Alvarenga too was in shock. He had planned the whole sequence, no surprise there. But having a fresh fish as long as his arm changed everything. Córdoba was proud of his captain. The bounty felt communal.

Alvarenga prepared the mahimahi with obsessive attention to detail. He rescued every nugget of meat and added to each man's portion one kidney and one eyeball. They didn't divide the heart or liver for fear of losing precious drops of blood, so each man slowly chewed an entire organ. Their feast felt like a six-course meal. They even had extra meat, which they balanced atop the outboard motor housing to dry in the sun.

After the meal, Alvarenga went back to the hunt. Catching the second fish took less than an hour. Then Alvarenga got careless. When a third fish was within range he yanked the hook into the fish, a bit sideways but deep. The mahimahi lashed out and slipped the hook from Alvarenga's grasp. He watched as the fish, trailing a stream of blood, darted away, the homemade hook impaled in its belly. "I felt like crying. I couldn't believe it. It was gone," said Alvarenga, who was back to fishing with his hands. They rationed the meat from the two mahimahi and cut it into nuggets the size of a kernel of corn. They savored each bite. "Sometimes I would just hold the piece in my mouth for five minutes, letting the flavor leak out," said Alvarenga.

December 10, 2012
Position: 920 miles off the coast
of Mexico
N 9° 48' 30.06" – W 106° 58' 49.17"
Day 24

The two men were living off survival rations of three cups of water a day, piles of fresh turtle eggs and portions of dried turtle meat. Although they would collectively eat up to a dozen triggerfish every day, the men were extremely dehydrated. They maintained a strict ration of one cup of water in the morning, one cup at lunch and one in the evening. When Alvarenga licked his lips, at least he could celebrate that he no longer tasted salt. The rain had washed his body clean and the calm sea meant he was no longer constantly doused in salty sea spray. But his throat remained swollen and felt brittle. Could the skin be flaking off inside? Or was this just another creation of his ever more fertile imagination?

Córdoba was in worse shape. He pleaded with Alvarenga, "Oranges, bring me oranges." Alvarenga stood above the prone man and assured him food was close. "Okay, I am going to the store, I will see if it is open, to bring you some food," he said with conviction as he pointed to the horizon. "I will get tamales, oranges and shrimp." Alvarenga strode with confidence for the few seconds it took to cross the length of the boat. After waiting for five minutes in silence, he strode back with bad news. "The store is closed, but don't worry, they open in an hour and they have fresh tortillas." To his surprise, the scheme worked. Córdoba stopped moaning and fell asleep. The game of visiting the store bought Alvarenga a few hours of respite from the cloud of fear that had seized Córdoba's mind and rarely loosened its grip on the despairing young fisherman.

Despite brutal thirst and aching hunger, Alvarenga maintained a reserve of goodwill, and in an effort to humor his ever more despondent shipmate he made frequent visits to the grocery store. Alvarenga's trick solved several deep psychological wants, including Córdoba's need for a roadmap outlining a solution. Alvarenga's clarity, purpose and determined explanations soothed much of Córdoba's anxiety. Waiting for tamales, even imaginary tamales, was bearable.

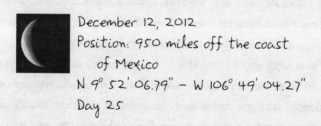

December 12, 2012
Position: 950 miles off the coast
     of Mexico
N 9° 52' 06.79" − W 106° 49' 04.27"
Day 25

Alvarenga began to look forward to his strolls to the store—it not only calmed Córdoba but also allowed him to imagine life on land. Dr. John Leach, senior research fellow in survival psychology at the Extreme Environments Laboratory at the University of Portsmouth, England, suggests that by nurturing his sick mate, Alvarenga was building a foundation to maintain his own mental health. "If you've got a task to do, then you're concentrating on that task, which provides a degree of meaning in your life. That's one of the reasons that people like doctors and nurses have quite a high survival rate in concentration camps during wars," says Leach. "If you're a doctor or nurse in camp, you've got an automatic task, you've got a job that gives meaning to your existence, which is looking after others."

Before long, Alvarenga began taking his own imaginary journeys. He had never owned a car, but aboard *The Titanic* he imagined owning a brand-new pickup truck. He polished the chrome, tuned the booming radio, admired his jacked-up cab and the flirtatious looks he received as he cruised around Costa Azul, ripping up the dirt roads with knobby tires. Like Córdoba's vision of a nearby grocery store, Alvarenga entered another dimension—although in his case as a result of deliberate self-hypnosis. Alvarenga spun ever more elaborate tales and whether it was a meal, a woman or an imaginary cold beer, his invented world provided a platform from which he could taste the myriad pleasures he so craved.

"The thing about survival is that there are moments when you have to be active in order to survive," says Dr. Leach, who works frequently with prisoners and survivors of hostage situations. "But there are also times when you have to be passive. And it's on those occasions that people will quite often retreat into their own head. What tends to happen in long-term survival is that there are changes in your memory structure . . . some aspects are improved because they are being exercised. Quite prodigious feats of memory can be performed by people who are isolated. The caveat is that it's okay living inside your own head provided it doesn't slip into psychosis."

Alvarenga and Córdoba had no way to track time. They had no watch, no clock. But as a young boy, Alvarenga had been taught by his grandfather to mark the months by following the cycles of the moon. It was a skill that he picked up early and never abandoned. This ingrained habit allowed him to calculate their time at sea. They had left shore with nearly no moon, seen it grow during the storm and following days, and now its light was waning. The men had been adrift for roughly three weeks.

December 15, 2012
Position: 1,000 miles off the coast
    of Mexico
N 9° 25' 29.34" – W 107° 39' 59.79"
Day 28

One evening as the men rested inside the icebox, a slight thump startled them. Then another thump. And a third. Emerging from a light sleep, the men found three flying fish flopping on the deck. "They whistled through the air and fell on the boat," said Alvarenga. Córdoba defined the gift in religious terms, a delivery from heaven for which he thanked God. Alvarenga had long considered church just another landlubber's scam. For him, the arrival of fresh fish was a reminder that food was bountiful and reinforced his belief that more than anything else, survival was his job, not God's.

Except for the turtles, the two mahimahi caught with the hook, dozens of triggerfish grabbed from the sea and the gift of three flying fish, by the middle of December the men hadn't eaten more than the equivalent of a single meal a day. The constant sun and limited supply of fresh water pulled their skin tight, an abnormal Botox-like shrinkage. Combined with the pallor from their malnourished blood, it made the men look like starved, haunted prisoners. "You have an invariable loss of about one and a half liters of water a day. Essentially you are a leaky bag," explains Professor Michael Tipton, a survival physiologist with the Extreme Environments Laboratory at the University of Portsmouth, England, and coauthor of *Essentials of Sea Survival.* "Because your blood volume is reduced—and of course it's your blood that is delivering oxygen around the body and to the brain—you have a decreased oxygen supply. That's when you get things like hallucinations, delirium and finally death . . . dying of thirst is a pretty nasty way to go."

Córdoba's shirt hung loose. He was falling out of his clothes. He was shrinking, especially around his eyes, thought Alvarenga, who couldn't avoid noticing the similarity between the skull and crossbones insignia stamped on Córdoba's hoodie and his ever more bony face. Alvarenga's girth too was several sizes smaller and his strength was ebbing away, but his mind remained sharp.

Córdoba was burning through his physical and mental reserves. He submitted himself to what he believed was a fate chosen by

God. "I don't want to suffer," the skinny lad said. It was a phrase he repeated like a mantra. Córdoba had a vision of a heavenly palace complete with pearly gates. Alvarenga, who harbored a stubborn optimism, tried to humor him: "Even a random corner of that palace is good enough for me," he said. "I don't necessarily need his temple. Give me a street corner with golden skies and crystal oceans. Any old corner as long as it gets me out of this hell."

Fifteen years older and a veteran of countless misadventures at sea, Alvarenga maintained an indefatigable will to survive, but ravaged by thirst and hunger he recognized their collective health was slipping rapidly. Yet all around them the sea teemed with life. Alvarenga felt he was in a cage where food was showcased tantalizingly close, just barely out of reach. Above their boat, the sky was dotted with the angular wings of gliding seabirds. On the horizon, fish chased by predators leapt out of the ocean. At sea level, islands of refuse washed by. Alvarenga—always a skilled hunter on land— began to stalk the seabirds. He imagined they were wild ducks and plotted to capture one to determine firsthand how much meat was stuck to its legs, breast and wings. "They would get away when I tried to catch them. It was impossible. For three days they all escaped. I was angry and hungry," said Alvarenga. "I was trying to rush them and snatch them out of the air. It was a brute force attack, but they were too fast. I never even touched one." Alvarenga spent fruitless—and meatless—days unsuccessfully hunting birds. "I stopped and tried to figure it out. How do you catch a bird? I told myself: think like a cat."

Crouched flat like a soldier crawling through a battlefield, Alvarenga waited for a bird to land. When it first perched, the bird was attentive for several minutes, swinging its eyes, surveying the scene. Alvarenga didn't move—instead he waited until the bird's defenses relaxed. When the bird busied itself eating fleas, lice or whatever parasites lurked deep inside its plumage, he inched across the deck of the boat. Alvarenga avoided eye contact as he stalked his prey. When he crept closer, the bird snapped to attention so Alvarenga froze still and the bird resumed preening. When his prey was within reach, Alvarenga slid his arm up the side of the boat, his fingers clenched in a fist. Then he extended his fingers in slow motion, careful not to scrape the side of the boat. With a snapping motion he trapped the bird's foot. A stinging pain ripped across his knuckles as the bird pecked and escaped. Studying the bloody welt on his hand and his overall strategy, Alvarenga noted a single flaw—he would have to ignore the pain of that first beak strike. If he could grab the bird's neck with his other hand, he would have a solid meal and the beginning of a strategy for long-term survival.

It took several more attempts. Often the birds flitted into the sky while Alvarenga was still several feet away, and once he touched a bird but felt its legs slip between his fingertips. Then he did it. "Before I thought about what to do, I had the bird's neck in one hand and a leg in the other." The trapped bird shrieked and fought. Wary of stories that wild birds aim for the eyeball, Alvarenga kept the thrashing bird—which he called a duck—at arm's length until a short crack confirmed he had broken its neck. Examining the bird, Alvarenga decided to fillet it like a chicken. He sliced open the chest cavity and, after plucking the feathers one by one, peeled off the skin to expose a skinny carcass that seemed to have already been stripped of meat. What could you eat? All that effort for this? Alvarenga was disappointed his hunt had culminated with such a miserly harvest.

An expert with a knife, Alvarenga felt like he was showing off as he cleaned the meager catch and laid out strips of glistening flesh. He added his only condiment—drops of seawater—onto strips warmed in the afternoon sun. He and Córdoba sat down to eat, if not enjoy, their first full meal since the flying fish. "In my mind, I prepared a feast with cilantro, onions and tomatoes," said Alvarenga. He popped a sashimi-sized chunk of raw "duck" into his mouth and chewed with gusto.

Córdoba made a costly mistake: he smelled the seabird meat. Unlike Alvarenga, who conjured gourmet flavors, Córdoba revolted at the stench, like that of rotten fish. He wouldn't try a bite. For four days Alvarenga alternately threatened and cajoled Córdoba to eat raw bird meat. Finally, the despondent mate took a tentative bite. Hunger had vanquished revulsion.

"See, I told you," Alvarenga gloated. "Thought you didn't like bird, eh?"

"Yeah, I like bird," Córdoba admitted.

———

Now in their fourth week adrift, the two men abandoned traditional modesty and walked naked, squatted on the rim of the boat next to the motor to defecate into the sea and then washed their butts with seawater. To pee they stood and urinated into the ocean. From roughly ten a.m. to four p.m., the men escaped the sun by living inside the icebox. It was crowded, stinky, uncomfortable and flat-out painful to wedge two bodies into the box—Alvarenga developed constant lower back pain from being scrunched up. But there was no other way to avoid being burned by the sun. "Once you get sunburn over about five percent of your body surface, then that starts to impair your ability to maintain your body temperature," says Professor Tipton. "How important was it that they created shade and stayed under it, minimizing the solar heat load? It was critical."

Despite the boredom of long hours during the hottest part of the day cramped inside the icebox, the men recognized that this inconvenience mattered little compared with the shelter it provided from the harsh sun. Yet even with the shade, they were still sunburned and their skin was covered in blisters that erupted into a full-body rash. The salty spray became painful. But the icebox kept them from being toasted alive.

After the first successful capture of a seabird, Alvarenga and Córdoba became accomplished "duck" hunters. The two men hunted wild birds in earnest. "Catching a bird standing on the side of the boat was difficult as they often flew away," said Alvarenga. The easiest way to catch the birds was at night. Alvarenga lay on his back, under the pole where the birds liked to perch. He waited until the birds were comfortably settled or even asleep. Then in a one-two move, he grabbed a leg with one hand and the neck with the other. If he planned to eat the bird immediately, he broke the neck with the casual familiarity of a man popping open a can of beer. Sometimes he even used his body to trap the birds. "They would always land on the boat to rest so I learned their strategy. I would hear them circling so I would stand still and they liked to land on my head. I was afraid they would take out my eyes," Alvarenga said. "Then I would grab them off my head."

When it was time to eat, they divided up the catch, an equal number of birds each. A path to survival was now mapped. "I would eat the feathers, the bones, even the feet," said Alvarenga. To pass the time, Alvarenga would sometimes kill two birds and then chop them up like ceviche. "I would not kill them and just stuff them in my mouth. I chopped them and chopped them into very fine pieces, then placed them in a bucket and used fish spines like toothpicks to serve it up. That was one way to pass the time, eating each piece, one by one."

Steve Callahan, reflecting on the seventy-six days he spent drifting alone in the Atlantic Ocean in 1982, says, "People think you just sit around, and wait to wash up on something. And I have always pointed out to people that survival is not a passive activity, it's an active pursuit. If you don't work at it, you are screwed. I have a pet theory that one of the most dangerous things you can do in life is try to minimize all risks. You never fall on your face, nothing happens, and so when something big happens, you're totally unprepared, you have no tool kit."

Inside the icebox, Alvarenga noticed that his hearing was becoming sharp. "I could tell the size of the bird by the sounds. Sometimes I would hear a deep whoosh sound, and I knew it was a big bird. The birds flew low over the icebox on the first loop. Then looped again a second and a third time, then landed on the icebox. 'Yes!' I would say. 'Now I am going to eat duck.'"

When the wind and temperature permitted, the two men spent hours at night outside the icebox creating games with the sky, inventing competitions to see who could call out a shooting star first. They fell asleep counting stars—it was a game that Córdoba usually won: "He passed a thousand stars," said Alvarenga.

"Sometimes when we were both in the box and heard a bird, I

would hold up the edge, he would creep out. He was good," said Al-varenga with pride. "The icebox would not bump down on the deck and scare away the bird." While Córdoba became a skilled hunter, he still retched at the sensation of swallowing raw bird meat. Al-varenga, however, went native. His brain, set on survival and long accustomed to raw food, ranging from iguana to crabs, adapted to whatever might provide nutrition.

At night, before going to sleep, the men set fish traps. They sliced a hole in the side of five empty bottles of bleach—previously used to float their fishing line. For bait they stuffed feathers and chunks of bird meat into the bottles. A pair of intact Clorox bottles with screw-on caps kept the traps floating near the surface. The men trolled their traps, attached to the boat by one of the few pieces of solid twine available, behind them. Occasionally they found small fish trapped in the bleach bottle and even if the traps were empty, the thrill and possibility of a catch helped bolster the dream of a more steady food supply.

December 23, 2012
Position: 1,200 miles off the coast
   of Mexico
N 9° 20' 46.92" – W 110° 34' 49.43"
Day 36

Watching the moon grow bright, Alvarenga calculated Christmas was near. Traditionally he would have feasted on roast turkey or chicken mole—roasted chicken bathed in a thick chili pepper sauce. The sauce includes a dollop of chocolate, allegedly a frantic effort by Mexican nuns attempting to impress a visiting bishop with their rich cuisine. Alvarenga and Córdoba would be lucky to have a few bites of raw fish and sun-roasted strips of meat, peeled off the skinny "ducks."

In order to avoid arguments over who received a bigger portion, one man prepared the food and the other chose which serving to eat. Alvarenga diced four entire birds for their big meal. He had now learned not to pluck the feathers but to expertly peel the skin off the birds. A full bird, including the gut, provided as much meat as a hamburger. The saltwater flavoring helped mask the stench, but the men noticed that at night, inside their icebox refuge, they too were starting to smell like the flesh of seabirds—a rank and rotten odor like that of dead fish.

On the evening they estimated was Christmas Eve, as the men chatted, cleaned the birds and commenced their traditional meal—if there can be anything traditional about slicing, dicing and eating raw sea "ducks"—Córdoba coughed. "My stomach," he groaned as his eyes bulged like he was going to be sick. Bubbles and liquid dribbled from his mouth.

Alvarenga, who had waded through his companion's fears, tears and complaints, realized this was no exaggeration. A sudden, wrenching pain convulsed Córdoba's body. Alvarenga handed him a half-liter bottle filled with rainwater and, ignoring their rations, Córdoba sucked the bottle down and then spat it out. Whatever had taken hold of his gut held tight and the pain intensified.

The men dissected the intestines of Córdoba's "duck." Often the stomach and intestines brought surprises like plastic bottle caps or entire sardines. This time the men found a six-inch, articulated skeleton. The skin had fallen off and most of the meat was gone, but enough remained for them to identify the remains of a venomous, yellow-bellied sea snake.

"Chancha, there's a snake inside here!" Córdoba exclaimed.

"Yeah, and you already ate it," responded Alvarenga.

"Oh shit, I am going to vomit," stuttered Córdoba.

As Córdoba screamed and spewed white bubbles from his mouth, Alvarenga wondered if the poison had entered his mate's bloodstream. Was it fatal? How did it kill its victims? Watching as, drop by drop, a bubbly foam leaked out of his companion's mouth and listening to his guttural groans, Alvarenga considered his own fate. Had he also been poisoned? Was the venom going to hit?

Alvarenga didn't get sick and after four hours of retching and coughing, Córdoba stabilized. The men huddled, looking for subtle signs of improvement—aware the poison might have spread to other organs. The men tried to recall cases of bites by the yellow-bellied snake. But they had only heard thirdhand versions and their only firm conclusion was that even the most hardened fishermen gave the snake a wide berth and tried to decapitate it with a machete.

The venom was not fatal, and Córdoba made a full physical recovery within two days. But in the realm of psychological terror, the poison possessed Córdoba. He retched at the thought of eating another raw seabird and withdrew from the world of food. Never again would he feast on one of Alvarenga's "ducks."

CHAPTER 7

A Fight for Life

January 1, 2013
Position: 1,500 miles off the coast
        of Mexico
N 8° 23' 04.00" – W 114° 29' 53.79"
Day 45

A week after the disastrous Christmas Eve dinner, Alvarenga and Córdoba tried to guess which evening of a nearly full moon was New Year's Eve and which sunrise the launch of a new year. On January 1, 2013, drifting alone in the open ocean, approximately 1,500 miles from shore, the lost fishermen were fortunate not to know the full breadth of their isolation. If they continued on the same southwest course, the next solid land was Australia 8,500 miles away. A few random rocks, atolls and cays were lightly strewn along the way but the two fishermen had now drifted into a rectangle of ocean twenty times the size of California yet holding a total population of fewer than twenty thousand people. Bordered by Hawaii to the north, Central America to the east, French Polynesia to the south and Australia to the southwest, they were far from heavily trafficked global shipping lanes. Alvarenga and Córdoba were in the marine equivalent of a roadless area in a vast, uncharted desert.

The constant appearance of floating garbage, however, reminded them that somewhere, far out of sight, civilization existed. Alvarenga made it a point to try on every one of the sodden sneakers floating by in hopes of finding a pair of size 7s. He found a black size 8 sneaker for his left foot and proudly stomped around the boat, one foot shod, one bare, enjoying the novelty. Before tossing the useless shoe back into the ocean, Alvarenga tore the padding out of the sneaker and stored it as gauze in case of a medical emergency. Years earlier he nearly severed a fingertip with an errant machete chop while out at sea on a fishing expedition. He had flushed the wound in the salty sea, then bound the damage with black electrician's tape. Adrift at sea, he understood that any medical emergency would have to be treated using a homemade first-aid kit assembled from scraps and trash pickings.

With the New Year came a change in weather. The storms of the coast were replaced by a surreal calm. Their speed slowed to 1 mph. Walking would have been far faster. Day after day they sat, dead in the water—stalled on a flat landscape. Sailors in the eighteenth century named this stretch of ocean the Doldrums and considered it a death sentence. Sailing ships regularly spent weeks in the Doldrums, sails flaccid and the crew dying of hunger as their food stock disappeared and their boat drifted without a breeze. English poet Samuel Taylor Coleridge left a haunting description of this phenomenon in "The Rime of the Ancient Mariner":

> Down dropt the breeze, the sails dropt down,
> 'Twas sad as sad could be;

And we did speak only to break
The silence of the sea!
Day after day, day after day,
We stuck, nor breath nor motion;
As idle as a painted ship
Upon a painted ocean.

But the Doldrums are also notorious for being among the wettest areas on earth, with fierce and sudden thunderstorms. "Sailors, when they only had sailing ships, did not want to go into the Doldrums: first, because there are a lot of storms, and second, because the winds are unpredictable. It's hard to get out," explains Shang-Ping Xie, a climate researcher with the Scripps Institution of Oceanography.

Known to scientists as the Intertropical Convergence Zone (ITCZ), this narrow band of low-pressure air just north of the equator produces storm cells that have been described as "seeds" that can later erupt as full-blown hurricanes. Explorers describe this area as the world's "freshest ocean" and being so awash in intense precipitations that the rain actually forms a brief layer of "sweet" water that floats on the salty ocean surface. Xie describes the ITCZ as "the place with the heaviest rainfall on earth."

Storms in the Doldrums begin as a colossal convection cycle where intense sunshine near the equator warms the surface ocean water to 85 degrees, producing massive evaporation that rises as clouds. Unlike many storm systems that march forward, these storms initially are stationary. Like a giant steam engine in neutral, huffing and puffing but going nowhere, these storm cells spin off enough energy to power the earth's dominant weather patterns.

Like the proverbial butterfly that flaps its wings in Africa and causes a Caribbean hurricane, these convection cycles near the equator expand and explode to determine the severity of typhoons in Korea and the arrival (or not) of droughts in South America. Alvarenga was drifting in the epicenter of global weather, a dynamic and rapidly changing zone of the Pacific Ocean now at the center of scientific efforts to understand global weather and global warming. In awe of the raw power and prodigious energy production, climate scientist Xie considers the Intertropical Convergence Zone, where Alvarenga now floated, as "the beating heart of the planet."

When the storm clouds gathered force and blotted out the sun, Alvarenga and Córdoba could do little. Anything that could blow away had long since been sucked into the ocean. Bailing water was now a question of activating muscle memory. The fishermen were prepared for four hours, eight hours, even twelve hours of bailing. They had survived nearly a week of storm early on and memorized the drill. Pounding rain ceased to impress them. But in the first week of 2013 they saw something totally different—Córdoba spotted the waterspout first. Approximately four hundred yards away, he pointed and Alvarenga stared at the towering tornado of swirling water. The waterspout sucked up the ocean as it pulled them closer. His boat vibrated like it was being shaken by an earthquake. "It was a wall of water, like a skyscraper. You could see it going up and up," said Alvarenga. "I saw black things spinning around in the middle. It looked like fish being sucked out of the water."

Within minutes, the waterspout dissolved. The whole episode carried such a ghostlike appearance the men questioned whether it was real. Had they conjured the entire scene? Then a second waterspout formed. And a third. Spinning off the edges of a gusty thunderstorm, the tempest raged on all sides. The fishermen were cut off from any sense of distance and place—visibility narrowed to a hundred yards. Spray and ever-higher waves then limited visibility to a few boat lengths in every direction. As the sun's muted glow sank, their world shrank into a cloak of terrifying darkness.

The storm lasted five days. Bailing day and night, Córdoba and Alvarenga stopped only for the occasional meal of fish strips, now waterlogged from the spray. Water was so plentiful they abandoned rations and drank quart after quart from an open bucket.

The increased rainfall allowed the men to rehydrate their bodies and facilitated bodily functions including blood circulation and digestion. "What you can afford to eat is dependent upon your fluid availability," says Professor Michael Tipton. "When you eat protein this creates ammonia in your body, then urea, which is poisonous to your system. To eliminate urea you need liquid to produce urine. So if you eat a lot of protein you raise your fluid requirements . . . these things are intimately related."

The heavy rains provided a moment to stock up on freshwater. The men took the cap off each plastic bottle and balanced them like bowling pins throughout the boat. It was a test of patience as the men watched water collect drop by drop and fill each bottle. The temptation to grab a bottle and chug a half liter became irresistible. When Córdoba saw the growing stash of water he would finish off two bottles in quick swigs, ignoring Alvarenga's pleadings to be more prudent with their limited water supply.

With Alvarenga providing the backbone of resolution and experience, Córdoba began to resume his duties as helper and the men developed a daily routine. By five a.m. on most mornings, Alvarenga was awake and sitting on deck. Mornings were the calmest time of the day. "It was joyous because the sun rose up in the east and I knew that somewhere back there was land. That was where my world lay." He hauled in the traps, curious to see if any fish had been caught overnight. Regardless of the haul, he always waited for Córdoba to awake before dividing the meager catch in an offer of equal portions. If the morning was cold or rainy, breakfast was eaten inside the icebox. Naps followed, then for most of the day they sat entombed in the icebox.

When it rained, the two men would leave the icebox to sit in a drizzle or shower in a downpour and celebrate the novelty of clean skin. If a breeze picked up the combination of wet and windy was too cold for comfort so they stayed cramped in the icebox telling stories, imagining a return to land and counting down the hours till daybreak. "I would wrap myself up in a ball and cry. I was asking God for the night to be over soon so that I could warm myself in the sun," said Alvarenga.

If the following day's food had not been caught they took turns hunting. "At night it was harder for me to sleep. I would wake up because of the sharks bumping into the boat or to hunt the birds that sometimes landed," said Alvarenga.

Córdoba was less active at night. He snored loudly. "A small roar," said Alvarenga, who awoke frequently to find his sleeping companion trapped inside a nightmare and screaming aloud. "I could never understand what he was saying but it was ugly." Despite the fights they endured during the first days of their odyssey Córdoba and Alvarenga now treated each other as friends. Astronauts in space often develop lifelong bonds of friendship with their fellow crew despite years of petty rivalries. A similar phenomenon is well known among soldiers under enemy fire who then become a "band of brothers."

February 1, 2013
Position: 2,100 miles off the coast
  of Mexico
N 7° 59' 24.206" – W 124° 16' 23.62"
Day 76

When they had several days' worth of backup food and especially after they had caught and eaten a turtle, Córdoba and Alvarenga forgot the torment and found solace in the magnificent scenery they alone observed. "We would talk about our mothers," Alvarenga said. "And how badly we had behaved. We asked God to forgive us for being such bad sons. We imagined if we could hug them, give them a kiss. We promised to work harder so they would not have to work anymore. But it was too late."

Like adolescents on an adventure, the two men would lie down at night, faces skyward, and doodle with the stars. Night after night they tried to outdo each other as they invented constellations, each man trying to create a more fantastic drawing. The men commented on the occasional satellite that drifted across the night sky. They fantasized that the planes they tracked across the heavens had been sent to rescue them. Córdoba, who had sung in his church choir, launched proud renditions of his favorite hymns in a powerful voice. Acoustics were better inside the icebox—like singing in the shower—so Córdoba commenced a solo concert and his muffled voice reached Alvarenga on deck, who then started singing with him. Not knowing all the words, he hummed along and for a few brief chords a chorus enveloped the men in a moment of total distraction. "I loved to listen to him sing," said Alvarenga.

Alvarenga had grown up in Central America and as an adult in Mexico lived astride the cult of a benevolent Jesus. Catholic Mass is so common in his native El Salvador that shopping malls set aside lower-rent spaces for chapels. In rural Mexico, ceramic figurines of the Virgin of Guadalupe are lashed to the hood of the family pickup. None of it made sense to Alvarenga, who maintained a healthy distance between himself and the entrance to any Catholic church. He had defiantly replaced that belief system with Santa Muerte, the grim reaper death saint whose image he had tattooed on his arms, its claws on his back.

Though dubious of the promises of Christianity and at times antagonistic to Catholicism, Alvarenga had always taken care never to insult the gods. He saw religion as a commitment and one he was far from accepting. "I had never been in a church," said Alvarenga in a notable divergence from the majority of his colleagues who regularly flocked to Mass. "I saw these guys come out of church then get drugged or drunk, and soon they were back in church. I watched that and said, 'I am never going to do that. They are making fun of God.'" Alvarenga figured he was in the clear "as long as I didn't make fun of him and didn't offend him."

Córdoba meanwhile was obsessed with his regrets and the sensation that he had squandered his few years as an adult. Córdoba also felt haunted by the prophecy told to him weeks before the fateful trip by a member of an evangelical church. In her dream, "Brother" Ezequiel died at sea. She saw it. She warned him. Córdoba felt haunted. "He said this journey adrift had to happen," said Alvarenga.

———

As they floated in the Pacific Ocean, Córdoba was sure he had tempted fate when he ignored the warnings of his own demise at sea. "I am going to die. I am going to die. I am going to die," he repeated. "No one will ever find us."

"Calm down, have faith," Alvarenga urged.

"You are crazy! No one will ever find us," Córdoba screamed.

Córdoba confessed to Alvarenga that his sins had hastened his fate. He begged Alvarenga to avoid the same trap, to seek redemption. They sang promise after promise to the sky, repeating the prayers. Córdoba even organized a religious fast. Instead of eating they prayed for their souls and resisted hunger for twenty-four hours.

Alvarenga began to internalize the hymns and prayers. He had few other tools at his disposal and given his predicament, could see no downside. "I had faith that God existed and that I could ask him for things," said Alvarenga. "After all, you aren't going to ask the Devil for favors. How would that work? So I asked for a miracle: that someone would find us. I couldn't understand why I was being forced to live this hell. Why was I chosen to suffer?" asked Alvarenga. "Why me? Why not someone else? Why so long? I realized

I would never know my daughter, as she grew older, and so I asked God to take care of her. I cried and cried thinking I was never going to know my daughter."

Alvarenga's vision of Fatima, his thirteen-year-old daughter, was completely imaginary. He had not seen her since she was less than a year old. If she heard about the storm and the reports of his lost boat, she would assume he was dead. Alvarenga felt a surge of anger. Giving up was not his style. He promised that if he survived he'd go straight back to El Salvador as soon as he was rescued. It didn't matter that there were people there who might murder him in retaliation for a decade-old feud. It didn't matter that Fatima was as likely to receive him with a slap across the face as a hug. He was determined to seek reconciliation. "I asked God to get rid of these bad thoughts and asked him to forgive me. That I would be his soldier—all of that."

"Most people don't start praying to God, they try to strike a bargain with God and that's different," says survival psychologist John Leach, deconstructing the oft-told myth that extreme survival is accompanied by a religious epiphany. "The usual form is 'Dear God, I'm in a mess here. I'll tell you what, if you get me out of this mess, I'll be good from now on' or something similar. . . . It doesn't last very long." Leach acknowledges the power of religion to help castaways. "Prayer itself can work because . . . it slows down your breathing. . . . It's also using up residual capacity in the brain, which otherwise might be taken up with anxiety and fear components."

Joseph "Butch" Flythe, who spent decades in the US Coast Guard and taught at the national academy, believes that while "faith is not a guarantee [for survival], it has been shown in a lot of situations to be the deciding factor." Flythe cites examples of American soldiers held prisoner in Vietnam: "They'll tell you that 'my faith kept me alive' or 'my faith that I would get back to my family kept me going.' You see a similar line of thinking with Alvarenga. He talks about keeping his mind on his family, he thought about God, something higher than himself. Even though he is alone, he is taking comfort in the fact that he knows there is a higher power there."

Despite his temporary bonding with God, Alvarenga's true faith remained attached to one of his core beliefs: optimism. "I never thought in the negative, I remained positive," he said. "I told myself I was going to survive, to be brave, have faith, not fall down. I knew that I was adrift, but I was thinking about surviving. I was always thinking ahead, planning. I was brainstorming inside the icebox. How did I do it? I imagined solutions."

With two decades' experience at sea, Alvarenga was in an environment that felt like home. Córdoba was confused and lost. The back-and-forth swells and rocking were driving him mad—could they just be still for a minute? When the waves passed three feet, and especially when the wind made them choppy, he began to vomit. It was a crude symptom of his overall physiological collapse. "We know that people who get seasick are nearly always the first to die in a sea survival scenario," says Professor Michael Tipton. "When you look at the fatal accident inquiries, when you look at the stories from the life rafts, the person who got seasick is nearly always the first person to die."

While the previously incredulous nonbeliever Alvarenga gathered strength from a higher power, the more devout Córdoba was locked in guilt, terrified of this strange world and convinced he was the ill-fated protagonist in a deadly prophecy. Though they shared the same boat, the two men were veering off on different trajectories.

 March 1, 2013
Position: 2,600 miles off the coast
    of Mexico
N 6° 22' 21.99" – W 131° 36' 02.84"
Day 104

Even with the stock of water and a more reliable food supply, Córdoba sank deeper into depression. Despite two years as an assistant in shark hunts, he had always felt unnerved when he lost sight of shore. His entire world was spinning on an axis he couldn't fathom. Both men were now fully hydrated but since the fateful dinner with the poison snake, Córdoba had maintained his steadfast refusal to eat raw birds.

"You eat them," he told Alvarenga. "I will stick to fish."

When Córdoba mentioned the poisoning incident, he suggested it was a plot by Alvarenga. "What *bad luck*," Córdoba would recite in a voice heavy with irony. "I got the poison duck."

"I didn't give it to you, you picked the birds," responded Alvarenga, who had allowed Córdoba to choose his own ration that day. "There were four birds, two each."

Now, when fresh meat arrived on the dinner table, Córdoba directed Alvarenga to open the gut of any animal they planned to eat.

A Fight for Life

Never again did they find a snake inside a bird, but Córdoba balked at bird meat, usually eating just a bite and only after enticements or threats from Alvarenga. Like a veteran nurse stuck with a surly patient, Alvarenga began to make the best of a difficult case. As captain, Alvarenga maintained the coercive power that came with rank, but it was his nurturing skills that convinced Córdoba to eat at least tiny portions. Alvarenga's empathy for Córdoba's burgeoning paranoia and his quick reflexes—like yanking Córdoba aboard by his hair—cemented the rules and roles of their relationship, one life-affirming and decisive, the other slumping into the depths of an unrelenting depression.

Alvarenga offered to eat his own meal an hour early—breaking their vow to eat together—to demonstrate that the food was not harmful. But Córdoba remained stubbornly fixated on the possibility of being poisoned. Food was dangerous. It was a concept he couldn't shake, and as he grew thinner, he clung to that vision. Despite his constant hunger, he tried not to complain of pain and seemed bewildered as he told Alvarenga, "I'm drying up! Chancha, I am drying up."

As Córdoba withered and shriveled, his arms began to look like sticks; his thighs were reduced to the size of a forearm. "His face was sucked in. His eyes were ugly. Like a skeleton," said Alvarenga.

"Are you going to eat me?" Córdoba asked.

Alvarenga told Córdoba not to worry, then joked that his mate was so emaciated that there was hardly any meat left. And besides, said Alvarenga, they had a stock of three live turtles, a small flock of birds and dried strips of fish. To keep the captive birds from flying off Alvarenga would break the bones in one wing. It was a cruel measure, he noted, but an essential part of his survival. Alvarenga's bird-hunting techniques were now so effective he was eating a bird every day, sometimes two, and his weight had stabilized. Córdoba tolerated the occasional turtle meat and fresh triggerfish but there was never enough to slow his overall deterioration. Fear of food had become his new mantra. He asked Alvarenga to make a promise.

"Don't eat me," Córdoba begged. "If I die, put my body up on the prow, tie me to the front of the boat."

"Stop talking nonsense, no one is dying," Alvarenga replied, though he suspected this was no longer true.

Córdoba imagined it was better to die in the ocean than starve to death in the boat. "I don't want to suffer," he groaned.

"Me neither, but God will get us out of this," said Alvarenga, hoping the reference to faith might stir his moribund companion.

Córdoba then concocted a kamikaze plan: he would wait for the shark pack to thicken, and then jump into the water. When the sharks were gorging on bird entrails, he moved near the edge of the boat.

"Good-bye, Chancha," he said and prepared to throw himself over the rail.

Alvarenga grabbed the skinny young mate. They fought and wrestled but Alvarenga overpowered Córdoba in a bear hug, dragged him along the floor and stuffed him into the icebox. Córdoba began to bang and thrash, but the icebox alone weighed close to a hundred pounds and with Alvarenga climbing atop, Córdoba found it impossible to tilt the box to one side and escape. Córdoba was trapped. Alvarenga refused to let his enraged mate out. "You need to stop thinking about killing yourself or drinking seawater or throwing yourself into the ocean," Alvarenga yelled through the walls of the icebox.

A Fight for Life

When Córdoba calmed, Alvarenga slid off the top of the icebox, lifted the edge and crawled inside. The two men talked. Alvarenga listened to Córdoba's arguments that their death was inevitable, and then in response he outlined a recovery plan. They just had to hold out, to maintain reliable access to shade, water and nourishment. "This is such a story—and we can tell it. We have to fight! To tell our story," argued Alvarenga. He imagined the rewards. "If I get out of this," he told his friend, "I am buying a car."

"You are crazy," Córdoba retorted.

Córdoba's defiance resumed. He angrily demanded the opportunity to end his own life. When Alvarenga again restrained him inside the box, Córdoba began to beat his fists against his face and slam his head into the wall. "He was desperate. He smashed his head against the boat. I would try and calm him. I was battling to save my life and battling to save his life. He was out of it. But I had to help him, he was my companion," said Alvarenga, who watched as his partner rolled into a fetal ball, cried loudly, screamed, yelled, then fell asleep. When the two men awoke, Córdoba was hungry but unwilling to eat. "I gave him food in his mouth, small pieces on a fish spine," said Alvarenga. "It was like feeding a child."

Alvarenga realized that few patients get well when they are depressed. Using stories to distract his weak mate, Alvarenga invented tales of life on land. For hours he would sit next to Córdoba and describe plans and future adventures. Health, optimism and food began to occupy the heart of Alvarenga's stories. When Córdoba became animated the two men vowed to stick together onshore. In their fantasies, they designed and built a Mexican bakery business. Alvarenga had worked in El Salvador at a *panadería* and was accustomed to kneading out five hundred loaves before sunrise. He'd be the baker. Córdoba would save up money, buy a bike and pedal around town selling fresh bread.

Alvarenga now hallucinated more frequently and began to live inside his own stories, talking aloud to his imaginary audience. Former girlfriends visited him for nights of passion in his hammock back at the Costa Azul lagoon. He scored goals in soccer matches at his favorite beachside pickup field. He scripted the reunion with his long-estranged daughter, Fatima. They'd walk on the beach, dad, daughter and grandparents, the complicated tentacles of extended family eased by a stroll in the sand. He imagined the preparation of elaborate feasts. "I was eating raw birds and had no cilantro and wanted chicken soup, so I started to imagine I was putting tomato, cilantro and salt on my chicken," said Alvarenga. "I plucked 'the chicken.' I cooked it. I imagined chopping it all up. In my mind I was having dinner with my friends."

Alvarenga had slowly hypnotized Córdoba and without realizing it, also launched his own mind into a fantastic alternate reality. It was a skill long used by Steve Callahan, who in 1982 survived seventy-six days on an inflatable life raft in the Atlantic Ocean. "In dreams rarely can you be aware of any smell or taste. But I could taste stuff. I could smell food in my dreams. . . . At first I really resented it. Because then you wake up and it was like, 'Ah, shit, there's nothing here. How disappointing.' Then as time went by, I came to really prize those dreams because it was the closest I could get to food."

The yarns worked. Although Córdoba still refused to eat bird meat, he would savor the fish eyeballs that Alvarenga offered, each gelatinous sphere speared on a fish vertebra, as an enticement. From a distance it looked like a plate of black olives with toothpicks. Neither of them realized that it was actually medicine. The concentration of vitamin C in fish eyeballs has long been sought out by shipwrecked sailors seeking to fend off scurvy.

———

One day Córdoba made a drastic decision: he began to refuse all food, except for fresh turtle, which was a rare delicacy and less frequent the farther they drifted from shore. He gripped a plastic water bottle in both hands but was losing the energy—and interest—to put it up to his mouth. Alvarenga offered tiny chunks of bird meat, occasionally a bite of turtle. Córdoba clenched his mouth. Depression was shutting his body down.

"I am going to die this month," Córdoba said.

"You are going to die for sure if you follow that plan," answered Alvarenga. "I am going to live. I am surviving this and we are going to show the world. We will be an example."

"I don't believe any of that," Córdoba answered. "We are going to die."

"Don't think about that. No one is going to die. You have to fight," said Alvarenga.

The two men made a pact. If Córdoba survived he would travel to El Salvador and visit Alvarenga's mother and father. If Alvarenga made it out alive, he'd go back to Chiapas, Mexico, and find Córdoba's devout mother, who had remarried an evangelical preacher. "He asked me to tell his mother that he was sad he could not say good-bye and that she shouldn't make any more tamales for him, they should let him go, that he had gone with God."

March 15, 2013
Position: 2,900 miles off the coast
        of Mexico
N 5° 58' 57.69" – W 135° 28' 12.00"
Day 118

"I am dying, I am dying, I am almost gone," said Córdoba one morning before breakfast.

"Don't think about that. Let's take a nap," said Alvarenga as he lay alongside Córdoba.

"I am tired, I want water," Córdoba moaned. His breath was rough.

Alvarenga retrieved the water bottle and put it to Córdoba's mouth, but his mate did not swallow; instead he stretched out. His body shook in short convulsions. He groaned and his body tensed up.

"Don't die," said Alvarenga, who suddenly panicked. He screamed into Córdoba's face, "Don't leave me alone! You have to fight for life! What am I going to do here alone?"

Córdoba didn't reply. Moments later he died with his eyes open.

"I propped him up on the bench to keep him out of the water. I was afraid a wave might wash him out of the boat," said Alvarenga. "I cried for hours."

Alvarenga awoke the next morning, climbed out of the icebox and stared at Córdoba in the bow of the boat, sitting on the bench like a sunbather. Alvarenga queried the corpse, "How do you feel? How was your sleep?

"I slept good, and you? Have you had breakfast?" Alvarenga answered his own questions aloud, as if he were Córdoba speaking from the afterlife.

"Yes, I already ate, and you?" continued Alvarenga, talking to Córdoba.

"Me too," he then answered as if he were Córdoba. "I ate in the Kingdom of Heaven."

The conversation continued as if they were two chatty mates eating a leisurely breakfast. Alvarenga decided the easiest way to deal with losing his only companion was to simply pretend he hadn't died. Throughout the day, Alvarenga treated the corpse like a friend with whom he could share fears, thoughts and stream-of-consciousness stories. "Why don't we go to Tonalá [the Mexican city where fishermen from their region regularly partied], have some beers, a great dinner. First, I'll take a shower. I have my clothes ironed and ready. I have good shoes too."

On the second day after death, Córdoba's body turned purple as the conversations unfolded. During day three, his skin began to cook in the sun. Like dry leather it developed a crusty edge. "I touched him and he was solid," said Alvarenga. "He never smelled; he just dried up in the sun. It did not disgust me at all. It seemed normal. I hugged him."

By the fourth day, Córdoba was nearly black and Alvarenga had fully incorporated the corpse into his daily routines, saying *Buenas días*, *Buenas tardes* and *Buenas noches* (Good morning, good day and good evening). Then Alvarenga began to sing hymns to the corpse. He was certain that Córdoba was listening and watched intently to see if the body moved.

Alvarenga began hours-long storytelling sessions with his motionless friend. He invented elaborate tales of survival. "How is death?" Alvarenga asked. "I want to know, my friend. Tell me about death. Is it painful? Is death easy?

"Death is beautiful. I am waiting for you," Alvarenga answered as if Córdoba were speaking aloud.

"I don't want to go," retorted Alvarenga. "I am not going there, not headed that way!"

This soliloquy with the corpse wreaked havoc on Alvarenga's sanity. He started to go mad. He couldn't imagine surviving alone on the boat. Despite their fundamental character differences, the men had worked as a team, hunted together, suffered for months and shared a common fate. Maybe death was not such a dark path, Alvarenga thought as he spent hours staring at his dead mate.

Six days after Córdoba's death, Alvarenga sat with the body on a moonless night, in full conversation with the mummified corpse, when, as if waking from a dream, he was suddenly shocked to find he was conversing with the dead. "I tried to throw his body into the ocean but I couldn't." Later in the evening he tried again. "First I washed his feet. His clothes were useful, so I stripped off a pair of shorts and a sweatshirt. I put that on. It was red, with a little skull and crossbones. And then I dumped him in. And as I slid him into the water, I fainted."

CHAPTER 8

Swimming with Sharks

March 23, 2013
Position: 3,100 miles off the coast
   of Mexico
N 5° 16' 56.38" – W 139° 05' 44.44"
Day 126

Alvarenga awoke with a headache—a small lump on the back of his head confirmed he'd fainted and fallen backward as he slipped Córdoba's emaciated frame into the Pacific. He couldn't remember seeing the body hit the water, and given the preponderance of hungry sharks, not remembering was better. How long had he been unconscious? Alvarenga felt it was just minutes, yet his entire world had vanished. The landscape felt hostile. Instead of nursing his dying friend, instead of talking to the desiccated corpse, he was alone, a tiny speck in the vast Pacific. "Have you ever seen a leaf spinning around in a puddle?" said Alvarenga. "That was me."

A half-dozen captive seabirds and two live turtles walked and crawled at their end of the boat. Taking stock of his new solitude, Alvarenga was terrified. For the first time in his life, a problem at sea trumped his worst experience on land. Seeking refuge at sea had always been Alvarenga's escape hatch. Sea life was easy. He genuinely enjoyed the taste of turtle blood and had been munching raw crab since his tenth birthday. Now, his trademark enthusiasm was scrambled. "I spent the morning staring at the spot where I dumped his body," said Alvarenga. "I didn't want to suffer anymore so I put a knife to my throat. It felt like I was having my hand pushed. Who was that," Alvarenga asked, "the Devil? It was an anguish of suffering, hunger and thirst. I was in the fires of Hell.

"I climbed inside the icebox and started to cry," said Alvarenga. "What could I do alone? Without anyone to speak with? Why had he died and not me? I had invited him to fish. I blamed myself for his death."

"Thoughts of suicide are not uncommon," says Dr. John Leach. "Because you get to the stage where you see this as being your life, and although you might be surviving, you're not living. It's that balance of what you're prepared to accept. In certain tribes, people actually accept that once you've decided the balance of life has gone the wrong way, you just go off and kill yourself."

Alvarenga, haunted by his mother's belief that God never forgave a person who took his or her own life, now rejected taking his own life. Suicide, he feared, might launch him into an eternal Hell. "I asked God to be more powerful than the Devil. I didn't want the Devil to take me away. And I told myself, 'Don't be a coward. If you die, you die, but not this way.'" Alvarenga dropped the knife. "I promised God that I would not try to kill myself. If I died it was his will but I was not going to kill myself."

It took only a few days for Alvarenga to discover the benefits of solo travel. "I could catch a bird and eat it. With Ezequiel, we had to divide the bird and the organs, part of the liver for him, part of the liver for me. We were always dividing up. After he died I could eat as much as I wanted, could drink water in my own style. When he was alive we had strict water rationing, just a cup. A cup for him and a cup for me so that it would last. Everything was planned and distributed. After he died, I could do things my way. The water lasted longer, the food lasted longer."

A flock of birds huddled in the bow of the boat and Alvarenga hunted in earnest until he had twenty-five birds aboard. Now Alvarenga was assured of a food supply and companionship. As he slept in his icebox, the birds fought, cooed and rustled. In the morning, he exited his icebox to confront a platoon of hungry shipmates. "I woke up one morning and saw two eggs, bigger than a chicken egg. I wondered, are these going to hatch? I started questioning the birds. 'Who is the daddy here? Which one of you is mom?' Then I ate the eggs."

Hunting distracted Alvarenga from his daily isolation. So did the fantasy of being rescued. Alvarenga was so convinced that a ship was likely to pass nearby that he tied the remnants of a T-shirt to a pole and fashioned a ragged, pirate-style flag. Even on tiptoes, he could get the flag no more than ten feet above sea level, yet his confidence brimmed to the point that he now worried that when the inevitable rescue ship approached, he needed extreme caution to avoid being ground up by its propellers.

A wild beard curled off his face in all directions and the small shaving mirror's value now was to document his evolution into a wild man and, perhaps, as a signaling device. Amplified by his optimism, Alvarenga imagined that the light flashing off his handheld mirror would alert distant ships. To this end he continued practicing flashing sunlight off the mirror.

Alvarenga sat on the fiberglass bench and scoured the ocean's surface, searching for ships. Sunrise and sunset were best as blurry shapes on the horizon were transformed into neat silhouettes and the sun was bearable. With his eyesight fine-tuned, Alvarenga could now identify a tiny speck on the horizon as a ship. As it approached, Alvarenga identified the type of boat—usually a transpacific container ship—as it growled by. These sea barges plowed the sea effortlessly, and with no visible crew or activity on deck, they were like drones at sea. Every sighting pumped Alvarenga with an energy boost that jolted him to wave, holler, jump and flail for hours. Approximately twenty separate container boats paraded across the horizon yet the maddening ship-tease still excited Alvarenga.

With Córdoba alive, Alvarenga had felt divided between "What should I do?" and "What do I have to do?" Often he subjugated instincts and natural reactions to attend to the needs of his dying friend. Alvarenga was now alone—except for his rotating stock of wild but soon-to-be-eaten birds—and he began to build his idea of what a home should look like. Sharing the icebox had been unwieldy in almost every dimension—psychological, physical and logistical. With twice the space, Alvarenga appreciated the luxury of an uncluttered home. When he saw a lightbulb floating by, he grabbed it, studied it and tried to figure out the meaning of this gift from the sea. Then he hung it from the inside roof of his icebox. The bulb swung from the ceiling. At night Alvarenga would reach up to the wall and switch his lamp "ON." Before he closed his eyes to rest he reached up and imagined the click as he turned his lamp "OFF."

It was just after breakfast when Alvarenga spotted a boat. It was still a dot—initially no different from so many other maddening encounters. But this dot was headed directly toward him. It was miles away but Alvarenga was sure their paths would cross. He spent the entire morning fixated. The boat drew closer. He yearned for a single flare. The deck came into view and Alvarenga saw three large red crosses on the side of the boat. The boat cut across the horizon a half mile from Alvarenga, and though he screamed and waved his arms, the ship churned across his bow, raising a wave but not slowing. Alvarenga collapsed. Jumping, signaling and screaming was more a reflex than a sign of hope. Safety and rescue, he bitterly concluded, would come not from sea but from land.

Two nights after the boat with the red crosses rumbled across the horizon, he heard a sound like a turtle thumping into the hull. Quickly and quietly Alvarenga slipped from the box and stalked to the water's edge. A blue barrel the size of an oil drum was floating and had smacked into the side of the boat. Alvarenga hauled in the empty barrel. Sealed with a screw cap, it had none of the telltale green fuzz or barnacle colonies affixed to objects drifting for months. He guessed it had been tossed from the ship with the three red crosses. "Immediately I thought I could use it to store water. I put it up on the bow," said Alvarenga. "Then every time it rained, I stored water. I had a tube to suck the water out and I could pour it in as well."

With a self-imposed ration of one cup of water at breakfast, one at lunch and one in the evening, Alvarenga had solved one of his primordial tasks. "I was always measuring the water. I was always worried, what happens if it doesn't rain? When it rained, I drank the fresh water from the [indentations on the] boat and didn't touch my stores. When I had to use the stored water I was very careful, I went very slowly." From a single storm Alvarenga could gather enough water to raise the level of the barrel a full twelve inches, equivalent to two weeks of water if rations were tight. "That barrel changed my life."

A month after Córdoba's death, Alvarenga made another stunning find. His eyes zeroed in on a pattern. Birds—a flock of them—were perched on a dead whale floating ahead. As he drifted closer, he saw that it wasn't a whale, but some sort of object with dimensions the size of his own boat. Whatever it was, the birds were attracted and to Alvarenga's hunter-gatherer mentality a concentration of birds meant food. Momentarily forgetting his decision to avoid swimming with sharks, he dove overboard and stroked away from his boat. He tired immediately. His arms were floppy and his legs weak. Alvarenga sputtered to a near stop after twenty yards. It took him several minutes to regain his buoyancy. His muscles had not been exercised for months and he fought to gain a rhythm but soon was swimming through the water, slow but steady. Halfway to the object, Alvarenga realized he was completely wrong. This was no boat-sized anything—the object was smaller, the birds were crowded side by side.

Swimming with difficulty, Alvarenga was twenty feet away and still couldn't identify the object. Scared, the birds squawked and rose, escaping this suspect predator. Alvarenga could now see the object unobstructed—a piece of Styrofoam, one foot thick and the size of a twin mattress. He now realized he was dangerously far from his boat. Anxious and fearful, he panicked. He slithered up the side of the Styrofoam, stretched his arms wide and began to paddle back to *The Titanic*. Alvarenga stroked hard but he could not get both arms in the water at the same time. The Styrofoam was too wide. He slid back and began kicking, his arms clenched to the Styrofoam. Alvarenga cut the distance to *The Titanic*. Five minutes later he was aboard his boat, panting and terrified. He triumphantly propped the Styrofoam up against the icebox and studied his trophy.

In a flash, Alvarenga was furious at himself for his risky swim. What had motivated him to dive into shark-filled water? Was it a barely disguised suicide mission? That night Alvarenga could not sleep. He questioned if he was losing his mind. Suicide was not an option, and he had vowed to fight for life. During months adrift he had maintained a solid grip on his instincts and behavior. How had he so blatantly abandoned common sense? Sharks were attracted to anything that floated; thrashing on the surface was like catnip to the predators he knew lurked under his boat. "My God," Alvarenga thought, "what have I done?"

Alvarenga then focused on his catch. He wedged the Styrofoam against the motor and searched for a solid piece of fishing line—he couldn't afford to lose this new gift to a gust of wind. He found a length of nylon rope that had come aboard entangled with a turtle's flipper. The rope was half rotten but he salvaged a section and tied down the Styrofoam. "I set it up by the motor and from above the birds could see the white. As soon as I had that Styrofoam set up, the birds landed. It was the difference between watching them and eating them."

Alvarenga balanced a pole atop the icebox and tied the other end to the remnants of the motor as he built a perch for tired birds, who could see the white expanse from high in the sky. Migrating birds, exhausted from a transpacific flight, half collapsed when they landed. Soon Alvarenga was capturing as many as five birds a day. His hand-eye coordination was better than ever. "I didn't even have to think about grabbing a bird. By the time I thought about it, I had already broken its wing," said Alvarenga. He maintained a flock with dozens of captive birds as a guarantee against starvation. When it was time to prepare a meal, Alvarenga fixed his eyes on a single bird, waded in and grabbed it. The flock scattered at the onset of the assault then counterattacked, drilling their sharp beaks into the flesh on Alvarenga's calf or slicing a toe with a well-aimed beak strike. Alvarenga shrieked when pecked. The beaks were as long as his finger and powered by supple neck muscles that allowed the birds to wind up for the hit, like a cobra striking its prey. In a rage, Alvarenga struck back, snapping the neck of the most aggressive bird. He later lamented his rash reaction. If he didn't eat the flesh immediately it would dry up—depriving him of valuable water and nutrients.

May 1, 2013
Position: 3,700 miles off the coast
of Mexico
N 4° 59' 37.48" – W 147° 40' 58.74"
Day 165

It was well past midnight when Alvarenga's dream of being rescued arrived. First he heard the music. Then the echo of human voices

José Salvador Alvarenga with his newborn daughter, Fatima, in Garita Palmera, El Salvador.
(ALVARENGA FAMILY)

Alvarenga in El Salvador prior to leaving the country for Mexico.
(OSCAR MACHÓN)

The blue cooler box that protected Alvarenga and Córdoba from the sun.
(MATT RIDING)

Ezequiel Córdoba in one of the few known photographs of the young fisherman and soccer star.
(JAMES BREEDEN)

Though battered and green with mold, Alvarenga's boat was salvaged by a local family and kept in their front yard. (AFP)

Ebon Atoll, where Salvador Alvarenga washed ashore in January 2014.
(OLA FJELDSTAD)

First-known picture of Salvador Alvarenga after he hit solid ground. He had been ashore for less than forty-eight hours when this photo was taken. (IONE DEBRUM)

Alvarenga making his first radio calls from Ebon Atoll, where he washed ashore. Alvarenga was eventually patched through to rescue officials and family members.
(OLA FJELDSTAD)

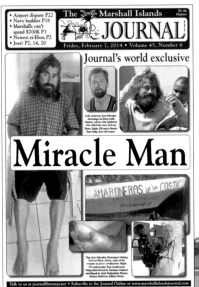

The front page of the *Marshall Islands Journal* on Feburary 7, 2014.
(*MARSHALL ISLANDS JOURNAL*)

(Above) Alvarenga being interviewed on the patrol boat *Lomor* by Norman Barth, deputy chief of mission for the US Embassy in Majuro, Marshall Islands. *(Left)* Alvarenga shuffling ashore after a twenty-four-hour journey from Ebon Atoll to Majuro, the capital of the Marshall Islands.
(US EMBASSY, MAJURO)

Alvarenga was treated by Dr. Franklin House, a physician visiting from Texas who was fluent in Spanish. (FRANKLIN HOUSE)

Fatima, Alvarenga's daughter, upon learning that her father is alive, Garita Palmera, El Salvador. (OSCAR MACHÓN)

Alvarenga's first haircut in a hotel room hideout in Majuro. (MATT RIDING)

Alvarenga in the ambulance on the way back from the airport in San Salvador, El Salvador. (AFP)

Alvarenga's reunion with his daughter, Fatima, in Garita Palmera, El Salvador. (AFP)

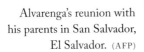

Alvarenga's reunion with his parents in San Salvador, El Salvador. (AFP)

Alvarenga completed his promise and visited Ezequiel Córdoba's mother, Ana Rosa, to personally describe the agonizing death of her son. (AFP)

Alvarenga and author Jonathan Franklin in Garita Palmera, El Salvador. (OSCAR MACHÓN)

José Salvador Alvarenga one year after returning home.
(OSCAR MACHÓN)

Alvarenga walking the beach with his daughter in
Garita Palmera, El Salvador. (OSCAR MACHÓN)

and the cacophony of competing noise—motors, machinery and the banter of conversation. It sounded like a party. Alvarenga was sure he had drifted to land. Convinced his suffering was over, he told himself, "I am saved. I am free!"

Sliding out from under the icebox he saw bright lights. The celebration grew louder, like a discotheque packed with a carousing crowd. It was as if someone had cranked up the volume. But Alvarenga was confused. The party was moving. The music and lights slid by as he stared in shock. A cruise ship? A yacht? It motored away as Alvarenga yelled—*"Ayuuuuuuda! Ayuuuuuda!"* ("Help! Help!") He smashed the propeller on the side of his boat and stamped his feet to make noise but there was no response to his desperate cries in the dark. Alvarenga began to sob. "It was the opportunity of my life. I had been out there so long, only looking at water and sky."

As the party motored on, Alvarenga watched his plans to begin life anew flicker away. He had no idea if any islands lay ahead but after nearly six full cycles of the moon his close encounter was so disheartening that he finally quit. It had been a phenomenal run, he told himself. For nearly half a year he had survived thirst, hunger, storms and the death of Ezequiel, but now his energy to live was finally exhausted. "I watched the sharks circling the boat and thought I should throw myself into the water. I could be their food. I dive in and they eat me," said Alvarenga. "I threw some garbage into the water and the sharks went into a frenzy. They were anxious, as if they knew that maybe I would dive in. I knew how fast they eat the chum and they would have eaten me before I hit the water. I wouldn't have taken even a second breath. Like piranhas they would have shredded me. 'I can end it right now,' I thought.

There is only so much suffering you can endure. I couldn't stand the solitude; it was too much." Alvarenga was consoled by a savage understanding: "It won't take long."

But he held out. Alvarenga found strength from the long-abandoned relationship with Fatima, his now thirteen-year-old daughter. "I started to think about her for entire days. How is my daughter? Will I know her? Am I going to die never seeing her again for even a single day? I cried so much," said Alvarenga. "I dreamed that she was screaming 'Papi!' and that made me so happy."

Along with his resurgent will to live, Alvarenga also developed a raging case of cabin fever. His psyche required a change of scenery so he devised a radical plan: ditch *The Titanic* and float off in the cozy icebox. The icebox would float faster and no matter how far away land awaited, the journey would be quicker. He could collect water when it rained and trap birds on the roof. Common sense then prevailed. He recognized the suicidal nature of his plan to downsize.

Instead Alvarenga chose to expand his world by swimming in the water astride his boat. But the water was teeming with sharks. One shark "came up and over the edge. Then I could hear as he dragged and scraped his whole body along the bottom of the boat," said Alvarenga. "I told him I wasn't going to be eaten, then I clubbed him and still he came after me." Alvarenga discovered that stomping his feet—creating an underwater echo—could derail the attacks for fifteen minutes. "He wanted to destroy my boat. He would collide at full speed. And I would attack him with a pole. He would do a half turn, open his mouth, and come back with his teeth twisted up."

Alvarenga designed a shark detection system that permitted him to take brief swims in the water under his boat. First, he tossed a half-dozen bird's feet into the water near his boat. As the feet sank, Alvarenga watched and waited to see if the water roiled. If no sharks appeared, he lowered himself into the water feet first and—trying to make minimum splash—went for a refreshing albeit nerve-racking swim. "It was my bath," said Alvarenga. "I liked playing with my hair. My huge hair covered my whole face. I would look into the water, that was my mirror, and I was like a monster. God was I ugly."

Alvarenga knew it was foolish to try to spot a shark. Instead he relied on the reactions of the smaller fish that lived under his boat. When they were relaxed he was relaxed, and when they panicked he prepared to scamper aboard. Alvarenga was adopting a strategy used by savvy airplane passengers who, during violent turbulence, closely monitor the body language of cabin attendants. As long as the attendants acted normal, so too did the frequent flier. A twitchy or nervous attendant, however, was always cause for deep alarm.

Swimming became a joyous escape. Once every few weeks, Alvarenga ventured into the deep and swam free. He pried clams and barnacles off the bottom of his boat and added shellfish to his diet. He could live for two complete days on a large serving of the barnacles. "I would imagine I was at the beach with my friends going for a swim. Getting off the boat allowed me to relax, even if it was for five minutes."

Alvarenga also ran brief safety inspections of *The Titanic*. "I would judge the current to make sure that I wouldn't drift away from the boat, then I would run my hand the length of the boat to make sure it was solid. I had to pop my head underwater and see if all was okay, to make sure there were no weaknesses."

Despite watching the moon ebb, grow and glow for seven full cycles and having drifted more than four thousand miles, Alvarenga remained as isolated as ever, on a drift to nowhere. Jason Lewis, who spent thirteen years conducting the first human-powered circumnavigation of the earth, and spent weeks in a tiny paddleboat crossing the Pacific, describes the area Alvarenga inhabited as "the quietest place on earth" with a silence both eerie and bizarre. "Because it's totally quiet, theoretically it's a beautiful place. If you planted a little desert island there with palm trees, it would be paradise," wrote Lewis in his explorer's diary. "There's sun, the water is absolutely translucent, you can see straight down for hundreds of feet, and see nothing. And the absence of wind meant the silence was deafening. Like someone pulled the plug and the world around had ground to a halt, my body being the only thing left switched on."

Despite his physical and geographical solitude, alone on his boat, Alvarenga found a deep happiness living "without sin, without evil, just myself with no problems, no one to accuse me of anything. I was tranquil, and adapting to the ocean. This was my new life."

Alvarenga had solved his principal challenges of shelter, water and food yet he was still a prisoner. But instead of a tiny cell, he was adrift in a gigantic ecosystem. Hundreds of miles from the nearest island and stripped of every modern convenience he existed in a state best described as "solitary unconfinement."

CHAPTER 9

Encounters with a Whale

 June 1, 2013
Position: 4,400 miles off the coast
of Mexico
N 6° 24' 00.85" – W 159° 21' 22.34"
Day 196

The rasp of a heavy brush raking the hull awoke Alvarenga. The shaking and scraping continued for ten seconds. It was a unique sound, unlike anything he had previously experienced over the course of half a year adrift in the Pacific Ocean. Had he run aground on an island? Alvarenga slipped out from under the protection of the icebox to investigate. As he emerged, a carpet of gray skin rippled past. A deep-sea creature, so immense he could see neither head nor tail gliding by. It was several times longer than his boat. A monster from the depths had come to swallow him, thought Alvarenga, who described the beast as having "a [dorsal] fin that looked like the wing of an airplane." On the second pass he saw the beast's huge eye, an orb as big as his own head. Alvarenga fled to his icebox.

Throughout the night, Alvarenga huddled inside the icebox,

his knees tight to his chest, his dangling beard around his arms, wrapped like a shawl. Nervous and confused, he devoured four dried triggerfish as he awaited the security blanket that was daybreak. Would this huge beast upend his tiny *panga* boat? Was this the kind of monster that attacked? Would it knock him into the water and eat him?

Streaks of pink preceded the first comforting blast of sunshine as Alvarenga exited the icebox to inspect the ocean. Less than thirty feet away, the monster floated. Its gray skin was speckled with white dots. It was the world's largest fish: the whale shark. Alvarenga had seen whale sharks off the coast of Mexico but never so close or so large. The average whale shark weighs 25,000 pounds, but this one was larger than the coastal whale sharks he had seen, likely weighing more than 30,000 pounds. "My boat rode low in the water so I touched it," said Alvarenga. "The skin was rough like a metal file or sandpaper. If he had jumped out of the water, the wave would have sunk me."

During the morning, as the huge animal floated passively beneath Alvarenga's boat and nuzzled the rail, his fear evolved into curiosity. What did the massive creature want? He studied the fish's enormous, oval-shaped mouth, which, lacking visible teeth, looked inviting, like an escape hatch. "I can fit in there," he thought.

On their second day together, Alvarenga discovered, then celebrated, that the whale shark was a food magnet, the epicenter of its own ecosystem. Black and white pilot fish preened the animal's brushlike mouth. Flat-headed remora stuck to its belly and ate parasites from the skin. Alvarenga's food chain merged with a new cluster of aquatic life—fishing was better than ever.

The massive whale shark dove out of sight and Alvarenga

watched in awe as the shadow melted into the deep. The mighty animal returned as it chased schools of fish to the surface, pinned them against the bottom of Alvarenga's boat and swept through— mouth agape to swallow the entire pod. Recognizing that the whale shark had a mouth filled with bristles that looked like a huge comb, not with teeth that might rip his arm off, Alvarenga joined the harvest. He placed both arms into the water alongside his boat, submerged to his shoulders. His hands poised, Alvarenga traced with his eyes individual fish as they lurched and darted away from the looming mouth. When they neared, Alvarenga snapped his powerful arms shut. It was like catching triggerfish, but each fish rewarded him with several pounds of fresh fillet. Raw or sun-baked it was pure energy. Each fish also carried a prize: a liver as big as his fist. Fish liver was a blast of healthy living that Alvarenga savored like chocolate bonbons. "I could eat fish liver all day," he said. "I prayed and prayed, 'When, God, oh when will I get fish liver?'"

Alvarenga launched into hours-long conversations with his new guest. He told stories to the whale shark. He touched its spotted skin at every opportunity. Just as he had created two-way conversations with Córdoba's corpse, Alvarenga now held animated chats with this mammoth fellow traveler. The joys of companionship, even with a whale shark, fertilized Alvarenga's fantasy world. No longer was he alone, and he slept better when he heard the splashing of the whale shark. Alvarenga felt a deep kinship and imagined his own revitalized life if he could ever make it home. He would be a family man with a clutch of children and a field full of animals. Alvarenga had no desire to live on land, the ocean was his calling, but he felt ashamed that he had abandoned his family. He begged to the heavens for a final chance, an opportunity to salvage the relationship with his daughter, Fatima, and his parents. Giving up fishing was not negotiable, it was his passion, but from Mexico he could make the trip back to El Salvador several times a year, spend storm season with his daughter then head out to sea the rest of the year.

Friendship and fantasy with the shark were instantaneous. Alvarenga imagined that he and the whale shark were each a character from the Bible. Alvarenga chose Jonah and inhabited his role with hallucinatory gusto. Perhaps the whale shark was a test of his religious faith. Was it here to swallow and rescue him? "What about I get on your back? And you take me to shore," Alvarenga queried the colossal fish. Desperate to change his scenery, Alvarenga asked the whale shark to take him anywhere—to land, the ocean depths or a jaunt around the world. "I asked him to swallow me, but I didn't want to get bitten, so I asked, 'Do you bite?' I was not going in there if he told me that he was going to chew me up. But if he agreed not to bite me? Then I was thinking of going in."

Alvarenga was so eager to find salvation that he imagined the whale shark providing assurance that he would not be eaten. But timing the jump into the mouth proved impossible. The whale shark's mouth never opened up at the right time and was often far away, so Alvarenga began to plan another entry. He would jump into the water, swim into the mouth and glide down the throat. But with so many sharks Alvarenga abandoned his Old Testament re-enactment. He feared being chewed apart before even having the opportunity to experience life inside the belly of a whale shark.

The giant fish allowed Alvarenga to overcome the terror of solitude and the madness of still being trapped in the Doldrums. He craved a companion to spark up conversation, listen to his laments or console him during the explosions of lightning that felt as if they would crack open his world.

Jason Lewis remembers his thirty days in the Doldrums as terrifying. "The lightning comes down to the water," wrote Lewis in a journal he kept while at sea. "You'll see these thunderstorms developing, and they'll be very dark and foreboding. You watch them for hours, rolling toward you. Everything happens very slowly. It was an awful, awful place to be emotionally. Terrible days of hopelessness and despair. Every day out there feels like a week of normal time, and every week feels like a month, a month felt like a year."

After a week of joint traveling with the whale shark, Alvarenga awoke to find he was again alone. His companion had migrated during the night. The disappearance of the gentle giant left him in a shock of loneliness. All his stories bubbled up, but there was no audience. His depression, however, was brief. Soon after, a baby whale shark arrived—the offspring, concluded Alvarenga. The young whale shark was ten feet long, rowdy and rambunctious. "He was an unruly child," said Alvarenga, "not like his dad."

The young whale shark used the thick skin on his back to scrape barnacles off the hull, and then circled back to swallow the harvest. "At night he would crash into the boat every twenty or thirty minutes. It was constant harassment," said Alvarenga, who was unable to rest night after night. "I wanted to sleep but I feared the boat would be shoved up out of the water, would flip over and I would be dumped into the ocean."

Then the current picked up, at times doubling to two miles an hour, and the smaller whale shark disappeared. "He was someone to talk to," said Alvarenga. "The time passed more quickly. When I was alone the days were longer, I was bored. When the baby whale shark was there I cried much less, we could talk things out."

———

Alvarenga was now advancing as fast as three miles per hour as he floated into the heart of the world's largest marine sanctuary. This section of the Central Pacific is home to some of the healthiest shark populations left on earth and is one of the few remaining areas where sharks are free to reproduce as they once did in all the world's oceans. Although sharks are demonized as man-eaters the equation is actually the other way around. For the roughly ten annual fatal shark attacks on earth, the world's fishermen slaughter approximately twenty million sharks a year, many of which end up as shark steaks on a dinner plate. Severe overfishing has produced the literal decimation of shark populations (only 10 percent remaining) in the last half century, making contemporary shark science akin to extrapolation from the survivors of a global genocide.

Thus shark researchers from around the world travel to the Central Pacific to study sharks from a station on Palmyra Atoll, a remote 680-acre island described by marine biologist Jacob Eurich as "a predator-dominated system. They call it top down, because there are just so many predators. And since there are so many predators out there, they're going to be more hungry, since there aren't as many resources for them."

Eurich, who spent months scuba diving off Palmyra Atoll, a GoPro camera strapped to his head, described an environment in which "a lot of the sharks did look very, very thin—as far as sharks go."

Unbeknownst to Alvarenga, he was drifting directly toward Palmyra, which, like many Pacific islands, is rutted with the flotsam and jetsam from US-Japanese military battles during World War II. An abandoned runway at Palmyra was overrun by thousands of boobies and other birds that found the heated asphalt an ideal nesting ground and converted the blacktop into a giant incubator. Rusted jeeps line the coast and the jungle has overgrown warehouses still stocked with surplus aviation fuel and World War II food rations. If Alvarenga could wash or swim ashore to the island, he'd be saved. Research vessels went out almost daily and might spot the floating fisherman. Scientists on Palmyra were wired to the world and maintained a mini health clinic. But the odds of an encounter were slim. Palmyra Atoll is so flat that even from two miles away it blends into the horizon. Although he could not see land, Alvarenga sensed it was nearby—the bird life was suddenly more diverse, the water a lighter blue and packs of reef sharks cruised beneath his boat. He scoured the horizon as he studied the sudden wealth of bird species. Sooty terns, brown-footed boobies and black noodies all added variation to his diet and fed his curiosity. But he never saw the atoll and drifted right by. Continuing west, his next best chance of hitting land was Papua New Guinea, 3,700 miles distant, and just north of Australia.

———

At night, as he cruised due west at a lively clip, Alvarenga lay awake on deck staring into a darkness regularly shattered by bolts of lightning. Veteran sailor and environmentalist Ivan Macfadyen, who has crossed the world's oceans numerous times, describes the Central Pacific as a tumult of explosive storms. "The sky lights up with sheets of lightning and blinding rain coming down and you're standing out there knowing there is nothing else out there for the lightning to hit for the next three or four thousand miles. You just have to dig deep inside yourself, because if something goes wrong, there's no one coming to help. You're on your own. And to a large degree, I don't let my head go there. If you start to imagine saber-toothed tigers in the corner of the room, then suddenly they're all over you. The fear factor is overpowering."

Alvarenga's years as a fisherman had prepared him for the on-slaught of coastal storms, but now he was at the mercy of tropical storms forming in the Central Pacific. It was the beginning of an active storm season. Tropical cyclones and typhoons develop in this area, then track west toward the Philippines and Korea. Long before these nascent storms are tracked by anxious governments in South-east Asia, thirty-foot waves and 80 mph winds churn the open ocean.

Alvarenga had ample time to study the anvil-shaped cloud formations that exploded on the horizon. Intracloud lightning illuminated the innards of these towers of clouds that rise so high commercial jets flying at 36,000 feet regularly alter their course to avoid contact. Air France flight 447, which crashed off the coast of Brazil in 2009, attempted to negotiate a bank of these clouds in the Atlantic Ocean and fatally underestimated the power of these equatorial storm cells. One sailor navigating the area described "dark gray menacing clouds coming toward us like something straight out of a horror movie." Alvarenga looked at the rapidly rising clouds and remembered his years in El Salvador as a baker. He imagined massive balls of dough, packed with yeast and rising.

Alvarenga knew these mischievous clouds could instantly flip a sunny afternoon into a raging storm. There was so much rainfall that Alvarenga soon felt he was more likely to rot than die of thirst. The weather followed a predictable schedule: clear mornings, rising cloud banks at noon and then drenching afternoon rains. Occasionally the storms hit after the sun went down.

Sport fisherman Jody Bright has spent hundreds of nights drifting and fishing in the Central Pacific Ocean. He describes the scene as otherworldly: "When there's no moon, with black water and black sky, you can't see anything. So if you've got an ecosystem building around your boat, then you've got different animals coming up at night. They'll breach, jump and splash. If they are cetaceans they'll blow."

Riding the storms at night was like being in a combination roller coaster and bumper car ride with the lights turned off. Alvarenga was jolted from one side of the boat to the other. Anchored by the weight of the motor he spun in circles. The waves crested and usually he would slip over the peak and slide down the backside and slam into a trough where it felt like he would be swallowed by the ocean. If the moon was visible, Alvarenga could measure the distance between waves and fix his eyes on the incoming set. But without the moon, and especially if it was raining, there was no visibility, no way to prepare for the next wave. Zigzag lightning bolts flashed a millisecond of light, and then exploded on the surface. For a moment he was glad not to have a mast. Hiding in the complete darkness of his icebox, Alvarenga saw flashes of light so bright he feared that he was no longer on earth.

Alvarenga questioned if his journey was a life lesson sent by God. By all reasonable standards, he should have been dead long ago. Was he being allowed to live for a reason? The only answer Alvarenga could articulate was that he had been chosen to bring messages of hope to those considering suicide. He began to recite the lessons aloud: "Don't think about death, if you think you are going to die, you will die. . . . Everything will work out . . . don't give up hope, remain calm." It was the very mantra he had unsuccessfully attempted to impart to Córdoba. Now he was using it as a guide for his own psychological survival. "What could be worse than being alone at sea? That's what I could tell someone thinking about suicide. What further suffering could there be than this?"

Despite his positive preaching, Alvarenga was beset by suffering. Headaches never ceased. A gooey white pus dripped from his left ear. The throbbing pain forced him to chew on the opposite side of his mouth. His throat was swollen from the ear infection that overloaded the lymph nodes in his neck. He could barely swallow due to the pain. Then Alvarenga remembered a traditional home remedy from El Salvador. He peed into a bailing bucket and poured the urine into his mouth. He swished the salty yellow liquid around like mouthwash as he waited for it to warm. Next, he dribbled the liquid into his cupped hand and, tilting his head to the right, filled his infected ear with warm urine. He repeated the process at sunrise, at noon, and at sunset. After six sessions he was cured. "My mother had done that to us as children," Alvarenga explained. "Urine helps to clear up ear infections caused by water getting in there."

Alvarenga's eyes were also suffering. The sun blinded him. Regardless of which way he looked it was like a spotlight aimed at his eyes. Every swell and small wave reflected the light and shot it back into his face. Alvarenga clenched his eyes shut and lamented the loss of his sunglasses. Alone at sea, the value of simple possessions was magnified. A pack of matches would have upgraded Alvarenga's menu from subsistence hunter-gatherer to Mexican gourmet. A hat could have shielded his eyes and protected his face. And a pillow! What wouldn't he sacrifice for a soft spot to rest his head? Seaweed worked as a pillow until the bugs crawled out. He had pulled a tiny crab from his ear and could never fully relax knowing his cushion was alive with a dozen miniature species crawling, slithering and stinging their way into his dreams.

The average temperature was now 90 degrees when the sun was out and 85 degrees at night. Humidity ranged to 90 percent and Alvarenga was often drenched in sweat. Like being in an oven, thought Alvarenga, who was born and raised in a tropical environment. As a child in El Salvador he had been accustomed to an average annual temperature of 75 degrees. But it was one thing to live in a leafy fishing village where the average temperature flirted briefly with 90 degrees, and quite another to be endlessly exposed, like a piece of leather left out to dry. The only relief came when the skies opened and raindrops froze on the miles-long journey down. Chunks of hail smashed into tiny ice fragments on the deck. Alvarenga collected and savored them one by one as they melted in his mouth.

To avoid being roasted, Alvarenga rarely left the icebox for more than fifteen minutes during the day. Unable to fully stretch out, he propped his legs up the side, a painfully uncomfortable position made worse as three vertebrae had been wedged out of alignment by the awkward posture. These three slipped vertebrae pinched the nerves branching off his spinal column and radiated a hot burn. His lower back pain was constant and at times so debilitating that Alvarenga could not walk. Instead, he crawled along the deck of the boat, scraping his knees and desperately trying not to bend his back.

In the open ocean, sea turtles were now scarce. A key cornerstone of Alvarenga's food pyramid had disappeared. No matter how many triggerfish or raw birds he consumed there was no equivalent to the energizing and nutrient-rich blast provided by a half gallon of fresh turtle blood. Then the arrival of birds became erratic. They had arrived in flocks, with up to four simultaneously landing on the boat, but then the visits slowed, even stopped. Alvarenga assumed this trend would get worse so he experimented with new fishing techniques. He tried to build a hook from one of the metal bands that he had found on the flipper of a turtle tagged by scientists. But he couldn't bend the tiny chunk of metal into the correct shape or file the edges to make either a sharp point or a barb long enough to keep a hooked fish from thrashing free. He imagined that there was still enough metal inside the outboard motor to fashion a harpoon but after tiresome hours of prying and exploring, he couldn't strip anything of substance from the green hunk of metal. Now the outboard motor's primary function was to absorb sunlight and serve as a rustic hot plate to toast fish.

The prevalence of shark packs, especially smaller sharks that he could catch, helped replace Alvarenga's loss of turtles. Sharks became a key source of protein and medicine. It was an uneven harvest—the average shark he grabbed was no longer than his arm and sometimes it would be a week between shark packs—but every catch signified a feast.

Alvarenga had never seen such dense shark packs. At times there were fifty circling sharks around his boat. "They would start hitting me on this side, on that side, bouncing me around," Alvarenga said, describing the sensation of living at the epicenter of a coordinated shark attack. "From the back of the boat, they tried to jump in. They knew someone was inside. I had this big pole and I was poking them and trying to stab them and that made them furious. They would circle and circle my boat then cut in and attack."

Back in Mexico, Alvarenga had impressed colleagues by hauling live sharks straight out of the ocean with his bare hands. The easiest way to pull off this attention-grabbing stunt was to cruise slowly in the motorboat and wait for a shark to swim abreast at the same speed. Then in a single motion, he would grab the shark by the fin and flip it aboard. But drifting slowly, without the motor to accelerate, Alvarenga could only watch as the sharks zipped past. His hand-eye coordination was superb but the sharks were too fast. Using several cups of feathers and bird blood he came up with a new hunting strategy: he would slow down the sharks.

Alvarenga waited until nighttime, when he knew sharks would be more active. He dumped a splash of bloody innards into the water then waited. Sharks flocked to the spot, snapping up the offal. They were too deep to grab so Alvarenga positioned the bait just inches below the ocean's surface. Suspending the entrails and blood in a bleach bottle roughly a foot deep, Alvarenga could now lure the sharks directly alongside the boat. When they slowed to eat, he had a chance.

The moonlight was strong and Alvarenga could see deep into the clear water as mahimahi blasted through and stole his chum. Sharks prowled the perimeter. Any shark longer than Alvarenga's leg was too heavy and too dangerous to capture with bare hands. He waited for a small shark. Twenty feet away one broke the surface, swaying its head from side to side in a predatory approach. A triangular fin cut the water and as it hit the bait Alvarenga seized the thirty-pound fish by the dorsal fin and wrestled it over the rail. Quickly he backed off and watched as the confused shark flopped on the deck. "I was hungry," recalled Alvarenga. "I wanted to eat it, so I smashed it in the head." The shark snapped, rows of teeth looking for a solid bite.

Normally Alvarenga kept a club the size of a baseball bat aboard the boat, but he had lost it. His machete had also fallen overboard; sometime after the death of Córdoba it disappeared. Normally, it would have been quick and straightforward for Alvarenga to kill a flailing shark. Now his only weapon was the propeller that Córdoba had unclipped from the motor. He used it as deadweight and dropped it on the shark's head. As he retrieved the propeller his hands were uncomfortably close to the shark's flailing teeth. He was nearly bitten in the leg. After a half-hour battle, Alvarenga knocked the shark unconscious with the now bloody propeller and sunk a knife deep into its brain. Though he was out of breath, hunger called. He sliced open the shark's belly, spilling blood and organs onto the deck. Headed for the liver he made an unusual discovery: two yellow eggs, the size of those from a chicken. With his knife he carved a small hole in the eggshell. "I thought maybe they would poison me, like Córdoba, but told myself, 'Nah, that's impossible,' so I ate them." Continuing on his culinary quest he dug out the liver. "It was two feet long and inside was soft, like butter."

The liver inside a shark is huge—accounting for a quarter of the entire bodyweight—and rich in vitamin A, omega-3 oils and immune-boosting nutrients. Oil extracted from shark liver is sold as a nutritional supplement in health stores worldwide. Japanese fishermen use it to cure wounds, treat cancers and fend off the common cold. *Samedawa*, the Japanese word for shark liver oil, is roughly translated as "cure all." Shark liver oil is most prized when taken from deep-sea sharks—exactly the type that Alvarenga found so delicious.

"People who have been in survival situations seem to end up

craving the parts of the bodies of the animals they are eating that are rich in vitamins," notes Professor Michael Tipton, the survival physiologist. "The people who end up doing that do not necessarily have a good understanding of the nutritional content of the different parts of animals they are eating. But they end up going to that area because of it tasting good, because they are in need of it."

Alvarenga's digestion had been painfully uneven—the fish scales and bird bones he was swallowing caused sharp abdominal cramps. The rough diet and limited water rations blocked his intestines. The pain was so intense he sometimes doubled over as if he had been punched in the gut. His stomach was solid like stone and he could not defecate. "Like having rocks in my system," he remembered. But shark liver, he discovered, was a laxative and allowed him to wash out the feathers, bones and accumulated grit from his system. Like changing the oil in a car, everything ran better after a massive serving of shark liver. Alvarenga ate serving after serving of the oily liver, and dried a stash for his ad hoc first-aid kit. "If I had too many bones and spines [inside me] and I was bloody and in pain, I would chew on dried liver. It was like a medicine." Alvarenga then invented another use for shark liver. Thinking he could use the thick, blood-rich gelatin as sunblock, he smeared it on his skin. "It is dark so I put it on my legs, my face. But it smelled rotten. After a few days the smell was unbearable."

"I even ate the skin of sharks," recalled Alvarenga as he pantomimed the force needed to shred the nearly unbreakable skin. "I put the shark skin behind my teeth on this [left] side and yanked." The constant friction filed away the ridges and indentations on his molars until they were worn down to a fraction of their original size and became smooth, like polished marble.

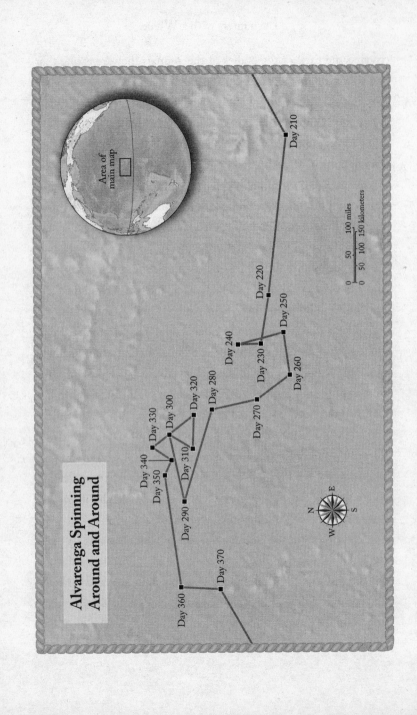

Alvarenga Spinning
Around and Around

Area of
main map

Day 210

Day 220

Day 250

Day 240

Day 230

Day 260

Day 270

Day 280

Day 320

Day 300

Day 330

Day 340

Day 310

Day 350

Day 290

Day 360

Day 370

N
W   E
S

0   50   100 miles
0   50 100 150 kilometers

CHAPTER 10

On the Road to Nowhere

 June 24, 2013
Position: 5,000 miles off the coast
    of Mexico
N 5° 40' 54.14" – W 166° 29' 50.44"
Day 218

As he rested inside the icebox shelter, a nauseating stench startled Alvarenga. He climbed out to the deck, glanced around his boat and surveyed the horizon, looking for the source of the overwhelming stink. Had a dead fish splashed aboard? Had one of his captive boobies died? He saw a flurry of movement barely visible amid the intense midday glare. A thick flock of birds circled and dove. "Probably a school of tuna," thought Alvarenga, who immediately went into hunting mode. Without a harpoon or a net, his chances of hauling in a dazzlingly agile swimmer like a tuna were slim, but tuna ate smaller fish that might be snatched by hand. Feeding tuna produced enough bloody leftovers to attract packs of predators so Alvarenga was careful to keep his hands out of the water and an eye out for shark fins at the surface. As he drifted closer to the hubbub, the odor became unbearably thick, almost sticky. His eyes watered. He wanted to retch.

Then Alvarenga saw the commotion—a floating whale. A chunk of flesh the size of his boat had been pecked from the floating carcass and the feeding frenzy gave him a chill. The decomposing giant was being pecked and pulled apart by hundreds of birds. Like an iceberg, the bulk of the whale floated below the surface and Alvarenga was sure dozens of sharks were ripping from below. The whale seemed to vibrate from the nonstop attacks, as if it were being disassembled by a hundred mini jackhammers. The death of the whale was less upsetting than the pace at which it was being consumed. The feast was accompanied by a raucous sound track. Fighting birds squawked and shrilled as they battled for access to the booty.

Alvarenga was desperate to get upwind and past the gruesome spectacle until he realized the spillover effect. "The birds were eating the rotten flesh, then came to my boat to rest. I caught many of them but I wasn't sure if I could eat them they stunk so bad," Alvarenga said. "I had to wash the meat over and over to get rid of the stink."

The bonanza of birds from the dead whale launched a new round of bountiful catch. In the late afternoon and evening, birds, including small black terns, landed on the boat to rest then sleep. Alvarenga ambushed them again and again until he had filled his boat to maximum capacity: thirty birds, including boobies and a host of other species he had never seen before. It was a living pantry. The noise, smell and commotion of this thirty-member flock made life aboard the boat as chaotic as life inside a chicken coop, but the chattering flock also added a dose of civility to his lonesome world.

Without the need to constantly hunt, Alvarenga spent hours observing the birds. "They were all different sizes—big, small and even a tiny bird the size of my pinky," he said. "I ate them all."

Alvarenga talked incessantly to his captive flock. "I would say, 'Speak to me; I have no one to talk to!' They would cock their heads and look at me." Alvarenga asked the birds how they could be such idiots "flying out here in the middle of the ocean when land was over there?" Then he offered advice. "If I were you, I'd be staying onshore."

Alvarenga also attempted to build a message delivery system using the legs of the birds he considered most likely to fly to land. Without pen or paper he had no way to write a formal message so instead he scratched his name onto the tiny metal bands that he had taken from the turtles as well as three birds that arrived already wearing metal ankle "bands." He bent the metal rings back onto the birds' legs and instead of breaking a wing to keep them hostage, implored them to leave, to visit faraway lands and summon forth a rescue. He was never confident that the birds would deliver his cryptic scratching but the sight of a messenger bird flapping into the distance always kindled hope.

Alvarenga next invented games with the animals. He used a dried puffer fish as a soccer ball and tossed it midship, which became "midfield." Because it was covered in spines the birds could not puncture the balloonlike fish, but due to their hunger they struck it again and again, flipping the "ball" from one end of the "field" to the other. To stir up action Alvarenga tossed chunks of fish and bird entrails across the deck, then watched as the captive birds attacked and chased the puffer fish. He named one bird Cristiano Ronaldo, another Rolando and put Maradona and

Messi on the same team. Alvarenga spent entire afternoons as both fan and announcer, immersed in this world of bird football. His favorite matches were Mexico vs. Brazil. In this world, Mexico always won.

When a brown bird the size of a goose but with thick legs arrived it was a rarity to Alvarenga, who was studying birds like an obsessive ornithologist. "He was so beautiful with a black head, that's why I didn't eat him. The other birds were ugly, really ugly, but he was unusual, he was one of a kind." The flock ostracized the newcomer and Alvarenga began to cultivate a relationship with the bird he called "a sea duck." He lured it closer with food and found it so social that he began to domesticate the wild bird. "If I banged my finger he would come over. I would pretend I was speaking to a person and would talk with him for hours. He was an animal that was alive, like me."

Alvarenga and his "sea duck" lived inside the icebox together. "He sang all day and I learned to copy his song," Alvarenga said. "When I fed him, I would sing to him." He named the bird Francisco, which he shortened to Pancho. Alvarenga let Pancho sleep inside the icebox with him at night. "He didn't try to escape. Inside the icebox, I fed him small pieces of fish. I gave him water in a turtle shell. I used to ask him when he was going to get married."

———

Alvarenga had now drifted five thousand miles—the distance from Rio de Janeiro to Paris—at an average speed of one mile an hour. Had a baby been crawling alongside, Alvarenga would have been left behind. Researchers at the US Coast Guard's search-and-rescue unit as well as experts at the University of Hawaii have now re-created Alvarenga's drift using a model of his boat, ocean currents and known wind speed. For the first eight months he likely tracked on a westerly path with the small deviations like the rise and slump of rolling country hills. But in July 2013, his path went haywire. First north, then east, west and south. Like a child drawing a five-pointed star, Alvarenga zigzagged erratically in every direction. He was trapped in a huge circular current known as an "ocean eddy." Fortunately, the lack of forward movement was accompanied by a bountiful environment rich with sea life and new food possibilities.

One of the maxims of open-ocean commercial fishing is "follow the eddy." Fishermen don't guess where fish are, they plot points on the map where fish will soon gather, explains sport fisherman Jody Bright. "If you look at the drift chart, which is almost a current chart, you'll see there are a lot of eddies and back eddies, and things like that. That's where the fish will tend to congregate as long as that eddy is spinning. What those eddies do is congregate all sorts of life together as it swirls around. And so everything finds each other. The commercial boys will watch that with their satellites and all their technology and they'll see the eddies form, and sometimes get there before all the fish. And as the eddy builds and it strengthens, they're in the right place at the right time. That's the key to commercial fishing nowadays."

As Alvarenga swirled aimlessly, adrift at the mercy of surface wind and the ocean currents, he was stalked by his fear of the ocean depths. The deep ocean shrouded and sheltered giant beasts that emerged, especially at night. Sea monsters existed; Alvarenga had heard their roars. The splashing. The grunts and howls. He had tracked the streaks of light, like underwater rockets. "What tends to happen at night is you get phosphorescence in the water. So if there are dolphins or anything around they look like torpedoes," explains environmentalist Ivan Macfadyen, describing the biolu-minescent bacteria that produce a tail of light behind moving ob-jects. Alvarenga delighted in seeing his boat's wake alit at night, looking as if a path had been drawn through the endless contours of the ocean, and he imagined a route home. But he was terrified by the sounds of these huge unseen animals—whales perhaps—as they rumbled up from the depths. Their invisible splashing felt like an attack launched by forces hiding thousands of feet deep and di-rectly below his boat.

Sixteenth-century explorers populated the open oceans with so many sea monsters and serpents that as early as 1545, Norwegian scientists published a Sea Monster Chart depicting sea serpents and horned fish with an appetite for ships of all sizes. In one illus-tration, a twelve-foot lobster is seizing a sailor in his left claw as he appears ready to devour the man. Nearby, a green and orange beast like a wild boar with sharp fangs emerges from the depths, plumes of water erupting from twin blowholes like steam from a locomo-tive, while giant squid, with the face and whiskers of a cat, prowl the surface.

Not all the stories were fables. Leatherback turtles cruising the open Pacific weigh up to two thousand pounds with front flippers eight feet long. A giant squid caught in the Pacific had an eye that measured sixteen inches across. Most of these animals surface at night in a cacophony of grunts, splashes and, according to Alva-renga, piercing shrieks.

Alvarenga's clothes were now shredded. The sun, salt and wind wore away his shorts. His T-shirt looked like a dirty rag. Only the skull and crossbones sweatshirt—stripped from his mate's withered corpse—protected Alvarenga against the sun. From the waist down he was naked except for a pair of ratty underwear and yet another random floating sneaker snatched from the sea. Atop his head a burled mane of copper-colored hair rose in coils and was held in place by hairpins made of fish vertebrae. From his face a thick beard exploded outward then tumbled down to mid-chest. Alvarenga's mouth was shrouded by a convulsion of hair. Burned by the sun, the tip of his nose glowed red. Multiple bites from triggerfish left his fingertips bloodied and small chunks of flesh had been torn from the palm of his hand. His forearms were pockmarked with scabs that bore witness to the risks of hunting wild birds with sharp beaks. Despite the nonstop suffering embedded in his daily routines, survival was no longer a goal but a way of life.

Alvarenga had passed through fear, despair and terror to find peace and the mental space to experience "inner qualities such as humility and empathy" akin to what Jason Lewis felt when he traversed the Pacific Ocean and first suffered then found a deep peace. "Feeling compassion towards all things seems easier out here than it does on land," Lewis wrote in his journal. "This is a threshold point at which the drowning element is finally suffocated. The sensation of panic is replaced by a warm, cozy feeling like a return to the womb."

———

Alvarenga's reflexes and entire body were now honed for hunting. He could identify a leaping sailfish hundreds of feet across the flat ocean. His sense of taste was hyper-sensitized to the distinct flavors of turtle hearts, triggerfish livers, sea turtle kidneys and shark brains. His fishing techniques were also an efficient and established routine. Every morning he hauled in the ever more tattered line and inspected the bleach bottles that he had converted into fish traps. When he found fresh fish, which happened three or four times a week, Alvarenga delighted in playing chef. He spent hours slicing the meat, drying it in the sun and then storing the sun-baked fillets.

As he prepared meals, Alvarenga chewed the edible organs and lapped up drops of fresh blood. He chopped up the brain, the eyes and the intestines and stored the ceviche in an empty Clorox bottle. Dried bird's feet were snack food that he kept next to his bed in the icebox. Hunting and gathering for food now consumed roughly five hours a day—a huge improvement over an earlier stage of his journey when an entire day of hunting often yielded nothing. A green trim of mold sprouted under the seats and blossomed. Bird bones littered the deck and feathers were stuck between shards of turtle shells and a pile of bird beaks that Alvarenga used as back scratchers and unsuccessfully as musical instruments as he tried to drum out rhythms on the fiberglass seats.

Thanks to the circular eddy that congregated life, the ecosystem beneath his boat surged. An entire food chain flourished and regenerated beneath the confines of his boat and its accompanying underwater growths. Bobbing atop this vibrant habitat, Alvarenga felt he was king of his own food pyramid, though he was the first to admit it was an empire in which there was little permanence in the roles of hunter and hunted.

Alvarenga tossed feathers into the ocean to measure the current and watched as they hardly budged. Impatient, he began pestering the ocean with questions.

"Are you going to take me to shore or out to sea? I want to know," he pleaded.

"To the shore. Only a few more days, don't worry," he imagined the response.

"How about tomorrow? Send me a signal that you are not lying," pleaded Alvarenga.

"I am alive," the ocean replied. "And I don't lie, I speak the truth."

"Show me you are not lying," ordered Alvarenga. "Send a signal so I can trust your words."

"Very soon there will be a signal, a perfect signal," replied the ocean. It was a comforting response that allowed the beleaguered fisherman to relax.

The frequent but brief cloudbursts and the two-day storms drenched Alvarenga. He now maintained three separate stocks of water, including approximately sixty half-liter plastic bottles, the gray five-gallon bucket and the half-full fifty-five-gallon barrel. He estimated that he could survive for many weeks without rain.

His icebox shelter was waterproof and undamaged. The edges were cracked but the roof didn't leak, the walls were solid and when he climbed inside, wind and rain were largely kept out. He considered scratching messages or a count of full moons on the inside of his home but both ideas felt like capitulations etched by a dying mariner. Alvarenga planned on telling his survival story in person.

When the rain stopped or when he passed through the eye of a storm, Alvarenga was able to marvel at the natural wonders of his lonesome world. He imagined the sea was decorated with glittering diamonds and stared in wonder at the stars. He could scan the sky and instantly spot the moving dots, including satellites, airplanes and shooting stars.

With food, water and shelter established, Alvarenga was increasingly adapted to his new world. He no longer felt a desperate desire to escape. He ate more and suffered less. "My mind had adapted. I didn't feel lost. It all seemed normal. I was not asking, 'What do I do tomorrow?' I knew. When I was first lost, every day was a mystery about how to survive. Now I asked God to bring me enough turtles, birds and fish to survive until I hit land or someone found me."

The maddening spiral drift was now more obvious than ever. Sometimes the sun would rise off his bow, other times directly aligned with the stern. Alvarenga's fantasies turned to the sky. "I imagined taking the wings off the birds and attaching them so I could fly home. Tie them to my shoulders and fly home."

Alvarenga had many hours that he considered "free time." Daily life became not only bearable but oddly enjoyable. Using the central spine from the fin atop a triggerfish as his needle, he began to sew. His black facemask was falling to pieces but individual threads were strong, so he unraveled the strands and used them to repair Córdoba's tattered skull and crossbones sweatshirt. The hood was in danger of falling off and he needed shade on the back of his neck. Sitting on the fiberglass bench—now cracked, buckling and frayed around the edges—he sewed neat lines of stitching back and forth in a losing battle to preserve the frayed union between sweatshirt and hood. Sewing allowed him to relax so he started designing a pair of sharkskin moccasins. The skin from sharks was rippled with what felt like thousands of invisible barbs. Placing the skin side toward the ground, Alvarenga measured then cut around his foot as he designed shoes. Strapped on like sandals, his rough footwear covered the sole of his foot, left his toes exposed and allowed water to slosh out.

For a pillow and chair he used a round buoy the size of a soccer ball rescued from the gathering force of the giant ocean swirl that tended to drag in trash and flotsam. Made of a hollow metal ball and covered in chipped paint, the buoy was his favorite piece of deck furniture. Propping his head on the buoy and his feet on the bench, Alvarenga rested his aching back, stretched his legs and allowed his mind to be mesmerized by a galaxy of brilliant stars. The moonlight glared off the surface and beneath him he could see the silhouettes of tuna, sharks and turtles, and mysterious shadows that swirled deeper in the black sea.

From his captured birds, Alvarenga removed the most exotic tail feathers then stuck them into his bushy crown of hair. Using the water as a mirror he designed a collection of feather headdresses. When he needed shade on his face, a bowl-shaped turtle shell became his sombrero, providing relief and a dash of style.

In an attempt to rebuild muscle mass, Alvarenga instituted a physical fitness campaign: sit-ups on deck and forced marches back and forth two hundred lengths of the boat—which measured eight paces. But a gym routine was too much for his unsettled mind. Leisure and downtime felt like a reward for becoming an expert hunter and he quickly lost interest in adding gym classes to his daily routine. With a stable, then growing, food supply, Alvarenga's weight loss stabilized; his core health improved. A thin layer of body fat rebuilt upon his gangly frame. The religious fasts that he had held with Córdoba were a bygone ritual. Alvarenga greedily feasted. "I ate up to eight little birds a day. Twice I got very sick as I ate too much. I gorged myself and had to go on a diet. I was just eating too much so I started to schedule my meals. Instead of eating all day, I would have three meals a day—breakfast, lunch and dinner. At the proper hours."

Although Alvarenga was unaware, he carried the optimum body type and precise age for an extreme survival situation. He was exceptionally strong but not too tall or muscled to require massive caloric intake, and at thirty-four years old near the perfect vortex of maximum strength and maximum experience.

In a trick to maintain mental health, Alvarenga traveled deep into fantasyland. He cleaved his identity into two personas who might have been dubbed "Alvarenga the Victim" and "Alvarenga the Storyteller," and while his body habituated the former, his mind migrated to the latter.

He spent entire evenings chatting with the ocean. He pleaded with the sea—which he always addressed as feminine—"to just dump me off" and cheerfully berated his hostess. "When, oh when, are you going to get me out of here?" Alvarenga laced his soliloquy with irony: "I must be a bother, toss me ashore. . . . I am so heavy, you don't deserve this. . . . You have been carrying me for oh-so-long, you must be bored. . . . Don't carry me any longer, I am not even paying you."

"Humor is a signature characteristic of survival. And in a survival situation, it is the first thing that goes and the last thing that comes back," says Dr. John Leach, the survival physiologist. "We've got an expression: we talk about somebody having a 'sense-of-humor failure.' So if you've got a survivor that shows a proper sense of humor, then that person has adapted."

Suffering from an acute case of physical isolation and emotional deprivation, Alvarenga sought shelter by living inside his own custom-designed virtual reality. He had an abundance of free time and a deficit of the most basic pleasures. "I didn't see a living plant or tree," said Alvarenga. "I didn't talk to another human being." He invented tales of beautiful women and honed his abilities to dream while awake. His stories became shields.

Psychologists describe this technique as a combination of self-hypnosis and self-delusion. For Alvarenga it was a method to graft pleasures onto a world overflowing with horrors. Steve Callahan describes his mental state during his ten weeks lost in a life raft in the Atlantic Ocean as one of permanent instability. "Your ups are the greatest highs you will ever have. You make some little repair to something that was a real challenge and you think you're the king of the world," he says, describing his emotions during his seventy-six days adrift. "And then you suffer some teeny, teeny little setback, and you're just crushed."

Alvarenga imagined an alternative reality so believable that he could later say with total honesty that alone at sea he tasted the greatest meals of his life and experienced the most delicious sex. "In my mind," he said, "I brewed fresh coffee every morning."

In the US Navy SEALs, "self-talk is using positive affirmations, positive terms to yourself," said one trainer. "We're talking to ourselves all the time. Sometimes we're critiquing ourselves, sometimes we're subvocalizing what the bad things are around us. . . . There's a lot of goodness that comes from that. It also helps you resist those temptations to resort to a state of fear or panic."

Alvarenga was mastering the art of turning his solitude into a *Fantasia*-like world. He started his mornings with a long walk. "I would stroll back and forth on the boat and imagine that I was wandering the world. In my mind it was a highway, so I would climb inside my car and go for a drive. Other times I would take out my bicycle and go for a bike ride. By doing this I could induce my mind into the belief that I was actually doing something. Not just sitting there, thinking about dying."

But just as a bountiful autumn leads to a stingy winter, in the open Pacific feast and famine followed sequentially. As the new moon rose, Alvarenga was suddenly tossed out of the eddy and sent again on a westerly course. It had taken him an eternity to escape the swirl. His forward motion during this eternity that was five full cycles of the moon was minimal. During the course of two full lunar cycles he actually drifted east—back toward Mexico. But now he was churning west at a brisk two miles an hour. Alvarenga admired his wake but quickly made an awful discovery—leaving the eddy meant leaving the bounty. Food began to disappear. He was back in the desert.

CHAPTER 11

A Year at Sea

 November 18, 2013
Position: 5,500 miles off the coast
of Mexico
N 7° 42' 01.23" – W 173° 55' 51.64"
Day 366

O n the one-year anniversary of his journey adrift, the moon was full and José Salvador Alvarenga became the first person in history known to have survived an entire year in a small boat, lost at sea. Alone in the ocean, Alvarenga imagined a birthday cake and piñata. He envisioned a party at home in El Salvador with his family. As he drifted into the record books, back in Costa Azul another boundary was crossed. Having been lost for a year, both Córdoba and Alvarenga could now be legally declared "missing and presumed dead."

A pair of simple funeral services were held in and around Costa Azul. At Alvarenga's beach hut, Doña Reina, the chef to the fishermen and confidante to Alvarenga, renewed his shrine with a fresh glass of water, religious candles and flowers. "The candles never burned all the way down, they always left a chunk of wax," she said. "If he had died, they would have burned away, like the candles for Ezequiel Córdoba. Those candles burned and were gone but with Chancha, the candles never totally disappeared. That made me happy."

Alvarenga's friends solemnly placed two bottles of grain alcohol at his doorstep yet refused to accept Chancha was dead. His simple one-bedroom living space was not given away to a new fisherman; no one was allowed to move in. "I always looked for him when I went out fishing," says Wolfman, who years earlier had mentored the younger Alvarenga in the ways of shark fishing. "We didn't find the boat, the buoys, the gas, nothing. I thought that was a good sign, a sign he was still out there. That he was alive."

Under the code of fishermen's rights, Córdoba's and Alvarenga's families could now "presume death" and collect death benefits. After the funerals, Córdoba's mother, Ana Rosa, asked Willy and Mino for twenty thousand Mexican pesos ($1,800), the going rate for a lost fisherman. "They blamed me for his death and kept asking for more and more money," says Mino, who paid the family's cash requests but was never convinced that his hardy worker, the irrepressible Chancha, had perished. "Chancha spoke to me in my dreams. I dreamed about him three times. I never told anyone, but he talked to me and when I woke up, I felt he was alive."

Unable to communicate with the Alvarenga family, Mino had no idea where to send money to Alvarenga's next of kin. But Alvarenga's father received the news of his son's presumed tragedy. The grapevine of coastal fishermen carried a message from Mexico hundreds of miles down the coast to El Salvador, where Ricardo Orellana, who worked in a humble flour mill, received word of his son's disappearance. It was a pain and loss he suffered in silence.

Fearing the news might kill the lost fisherman's mother, Maria, who was ill with diabetes, Orellana never told his wife that their son was lost at sea and presumed dead. His granddaughter Fatima, who continued her daily routines in third grade, already harbored doubts that her father was alive. "My mother told me that my dad was dead, that he had been eaten by a shark," says Fatima, recounting a conversation years before her father was lost at sea. "But I didn't believe her. I used to dream that he had arrived and I would awake and go outside. I saw a shadow, but when I chased it around the corner it was gone."

Alvarenga's dreams overflowed with travels back home to reunite with his family in El Salvador. "My friends would be there saying, 'Salvador, how are you?' or 'You are back!' I would cry and tell them, 'I am fine. I am fine but bring me food! Bring me food, bread, everything!' That allowed me to relax. The hallucinations made me comfortable because I was with my people, I was able to be in my hammock. My father was there and I would say, 'Dad, my boat is floating away!' And my dad would say, 'Forget about the boat. You are saved, let that damn thing go.'"

With his lively entourage of family, friends and lovers, Alvarenga built a wall of insulation from his bleak reality. Calm seas also cheered him. "I would laugh aloud when I awoke and the ocean was calm and flat. It made me so happy. I knew I could catch more fish and stay dry." Awakening to the memory of Fatima, his abandoned daughter, was harder to confront. The guilt tortured him but also provided a bedrock of motivation. He latched onto the yearning to be a good father. Fatima might never forgive him, but he was determined to earn her love. The thought of dying at sea and leaving behind a daughter he had never supported fueled Alvarenga's resolve to never give up. She needed him. But he was afraid of returning to El Salvador with its penchant for gang violence and murder. His nightmares of El Salvador focused on a singular incident—the night he was almost beaten to death outside a bar, when a brawl turned ugly.

The same thugs who had beaten and threatened him years earlier were likely to be still living in town. There was no way to lie low in a village with a population of fewer than two thousand. His arrival would be public knowledge within twenty-four hours. If anyone still harbored a desire for vengeance, there wasn't any way to stop a lynching or revenge murder. Alvarenga understood the rules of street power. Murder victims were buried but never forgotten. There might be a bounty on his head even though he had nothing to do with that decade-old stabbing death. Alvarenga debated his options and settled on a strategy that was simple and aligned with his principles. If he survived at sea, he would return home to El Salvador with his head high. He would not run from the threat of violence. Fatherhood called.

CHAPTER 12

Another Slow Death

 December 1, 2013
Position: 5,500 miles off the coast
of Mexico
N 5° 35' 21.53" – W 176° 45' 33.52"
Day 379

S peeding west, far from the bountiful eddy that had supported him, Alvarenga was now consuming more than he was catching. His stock of dried fish was soon gone and his flock of birds began to thin. Even his water supply began to shrink as a week passed without a drop of rain. Having nearly died of thirst early in his journey, Alvarenga was extremely cautious. He slashed his water rations.

When his flock shrank to the final half-dozen birds, Alvarenga panicked. He spent entire nights awake, attentively awaiting the *whoosh* and *clack* of an incoming bird. His fish traps provided a meager catch and he could see all types of larger fish darting beneath his boat. He was tempted to dive in and swim after them but knew it was a futile mission.

When he cut his daily water ration to a minimum—two cups a

day—his body rebelled and he fought the urge to drink more. "As the fluid moves out of the cells you get a wrinkled look, sunken eyes, parched dried lips, tongue swollen, dry mouth," says Professor Michael Tipton, describing the symptoms of extreme dehydration. "Other organ systems have fluid requirements. The kidneys, for example, require fluid to maintain function. So renal function collapses. Mentally you're struggling."

Alvarenga shared his meager meals with his pet Pancho, who accompanied his master day after day. At night Pancho would slide his head under his wing and sleep next to the often awake fisherman. In the morning Pancho would sing, flap his wings and bring cheer to Alvarenga, who would ask his pet bird how he had slept as he optimistically announced, "Another day for the two of us!"

Day after day, as the drought of food and water worsened, Alvarenga cradled Pancho and watched the clouds in a silent plea for water. How could it not rain? He had become accustomed to nearly daily showers; now his drift felt like a grueling march through a liquid desert.

One by one Alvarenga ate the final birds until only Pancho remained. He warned Pancho that he was on the endangered species list. Though they had transcended deep into the realm of friendship, Pancho was filled with hundreds of calories of energy and valuable nutrients. "If another bird arrives, I don't eat you, Pancho," Alvarenga explained to his feathered friend. "And *pronto* a bird would land and I would eat it and tell him, 'Pancho! You're saved.'"

But finally there were no birds. Only Pancho was left. Alvarenga waited three days but still no turtle, fish or bird arrived. Looking at his companion Alvarenga solemnly declared his verdict. "Today it is your time, Pancho."

"I killed Pancho at night so I wouldn't have to look at him. I covered his head with a cloth and didn't want to use the knife so I snapped his neck." Alvarenga didn't have the stomach to prepare an elaborate meal or imagine cilantro and flavors. "I gulped him down, not like a bird that I would eat during the day where I would really enjoy the taste. I ate Pancho like a brute." For Alvarenga, eating his pet was cannibalism. "I ate him. But I didn't ask for him to forgive me."

———

The famished fisherman had nothing left to eat. His fingernails were gnawed nearly bloody. He chewed on a wooden plank until it turned into a pulp he could swallow. With his only knife, he cut off part of his beard, rolled it up and used drops of seawater to marinate the copper-colored hairball. He washed it down with freshwater siphoned from his dwindling stock.

Fish bones had nutritional value, he figured, so using the propeller he collected the stray bones from the deck and smashed them into a calcium-rich powder. It reminded him of being a small boy in El Salvador and watching his mother grind corn. The fish bone powder was chalky so he mixed it with water and ate a serving. It had the texture of cold, lumpy oatmeal.

The only remaining food was the barnacles that had colonized his hull since the second week of his journey and now studded the boat as if they were a thousand rudders. Each barnacle held a nugget of glistening flesh-colored meat. Succulent and slippery, they offered a luscious range of flavors and textures. It was the sharks' fault that Alvarenga hadn't already eaten them all.

Even for a fisherman with twelve years' experience in the open ocean there was no way to deal with the overwhelming terror of being at sea with so many predators. Oceanic whitetip sharks. Gray sharks. Copper sharks. Every time he stuck his head upside down into the water for an inverted survey of his thriving little ecosystem he imagined the damage from seven rows of teeth powered by a sleek body honed to hunt since sharks first appeared on earth 450 million years ago. Alvarenga played the odds. He'd done it dozens of times and harbored no concept of a cumulative risk with each dive.

But sport fishing guide Doug Lewis, who has spent years in the region, is all too aware of the risks. "You can see down deep into the water where it goes from blue to black, and if you've ever seen a big shark come up out of the black and materialize right near you it's literally like a ghost stepping through a veil. It's freaky."

Alvarenga followed a few simple rules for solo diving in the middle of the Pacific Ocean. The first rule was stay within a few yards of the boat. Without the boat he was doomed. No way could he live more than a week clinging to random pieces of floating garbage. The sun and sharks would combine forces.

"I always thought of my boat as a life-support machine," says Lewis. "That's your planet, that's the thing that's going to sustain you. Anytime you're away from that, or not firmly in it, there's a chance something could happen. Maybe you get a freak wave and it whacks you on the side of the head, unconscious. Game over. Whatever. It's when you're least expecting it that things go wrong."

Alvarenga's second rule was to keep swims brief, usually less than five minutes. There was often a lull between the arrival of sharks and their feeding frenzy; even if he was caught in the water with sharks, he likely would have time to exit. "Although sharks are around, they take their time," says Jody Bright, the sport fisherman who spends much of the year exploring the wilds of the Pacific. "A lot of times they come up and bump you, or rub on you. And then they swim away. . . . And if you can't see them, it doesn't mean they're not there."

For the first time, Alvarenga was forced to swim for food in the open ocean. On dozens of previous dives, he had eaten barnacles, but he had never gone overboard specifically to harvest food. Now he was sure the entire ocean ecosystem understood the risky nature of his new mission.

Opening his eyes underwater, Alvarenga glanced into the deep and saw two hundred feet of crystalline water, then a growing darkness forged of the same blacks and blues that colored the thunderstorms. But the clouds were naked in the sky and he could calculate their dimensions; the ocean depths seemed infinite.

Looking under his craft, Alvarenga took inventory of the habitual crowd, the regulars who migrated with him. His ecosystem had gone through a midnight changing of the guard. The mako sharks were now gone—marking the elimination of a particularly efficient hunter that has been clocked swimming at 54 mph. "The mako are completely unpredictable. They scare the piss out of me," says Bright. "I wouldn't get in the water with a mako for anything and when they come jumping around, I usually try to get down between the engines. They'll jump right into the boat."

The makos were replaced by primeval silhouettes as a swirling pack of fifty hammerhead sharks shadowed Alvarenga. They moved with languid calm, as if in slow motion. Alvarenga considered hammerheads more a curiosity than a threat. He had never heard of anyone being attacked by a hammerhead and routinely hauled them aboard. Alvarenga watched the shark pack migrate and evolve. Even when the sharks were not visible, he knew that could change in an instant.

Bright recalls one of his unexpected encounters: "I saw this little dot. And the thing zoomed up on me from a little dot to a seven-hundred-pound copper shark in a matter of seconds. It frightened the hell out of me. It stopped, like it had brakes. I still don't know how it did that. And it sat there for a second doing these telegraph movements, like saying 'Get the fuck out of my water,' and I listened."

No sharks approached Alvarenga. Instead he was surrounded by a cloud of triggerfish that flapped by, fins low on their back like wings on a bird. As they glided within arm's reach Alvarenga admired their psychedelic curves, dots and swirls—like seventies pop art with Caribbean colors. Known to attack scuba divers, triggerfish also devour baby turtles and small fish. Even Wikipedia describes them as "notoriously ill-tempered." The triggerfish had little fear of the hairy fisherman and came up close; he feared they were sizing him up. He imagined the bloodbath if dozens of these feisty "sea piranhas" attacked. Like being tortured with fingernail clippers, he thought.

Moving swiftly, Alvarenga took a deep breath and swam under his boat. Gliding his hands along the hull he harvested the clamlike crustaceans while his head swiveled, constantly on predator watch. As he perfected the difficult twisting motion needed to snap them off, collecting the shellfish in a scrap of T-shirt, he was repeatedly interrupted as his stiff beard floated up and got in the way. Fish guts, bird blood and months of gunk had solidified in his beard. In parts, the hair was as hard as wood. Frequently surfacing for air and floating near his boat, he could see no horizon, yet it was easy to imagine the vast world beneath his dangling shark-bait legs. Despite his fears and secret knowledge of the monsters of the deep, Alvarenga assumed that the ocean must be benevolent. How else could he still be alive?

Careful not to lose his catch, Alvarenga pulled himself aboard and collapsed. He was scared and tired—relief flooded his body— as if he had escaped an ambush. Dumping his booty on deck, he pried open dozens of the small creatures and extracted the pearls of meat. With his knife he diced until he had two cups of fresh barnacle ceviche. It was a gourmet meal and made excellent bait. When he tossed fragments of the meat into the ocean it instantly attracted triggerfish, which he grabbed. Alvarenga was again a full-time hunter-gatherer. Using meat from the barnacles, then from the triggerfish, he chummed his way up the food chain.

Small tuna—a delicacy he had not spotted in months—now appeared. "They would catch fish and then come next to my boat to rest or digest. That's when I would grab them. Inside their stomach was everything they had eaten, especially sardines and sea bass. I would slice open their intestines and find sea bass cooked in the gastric juices. I used to pretend it was grilled."

Alvarenga continued to watch his water stores shrink. He made a nervous countdown as one by one his stash of half-liter water bottles emptied. The daily rains were gone. Now he spent day after day stalled in the Doldrums, watching the towering storms explode around him.

Alvarenga's instincts then sensed a change. When the winds whipped across the ocean, he inhaled a deep, refreshing smell. The rains again began to pound down. He restocked his water containers and all around him signs of a new ecosystem appeared. For several days he drifted through a thick mass of branches and debris. The birds arrived again and began landing on his boat. They were more frequent and larger than ever. Alvarenga admired the thick chests and legs of these meat-heavy birds. His hunting skills, however, were hampered by exhaustion. It took him longer to catch birds, but finally he was once again able to catch more than enough for a day's meals. His rookery began to slowly fill up with a dozen birds.

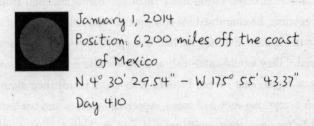

January 1, 2014
Position: 6,200 miles off the coast
   of Mexico
N 4° 30' 29.54" – W 175° 55' 43.37"
Day 410

Sailors navigating across the Doldrums—and few stick around a day longer than necessary—describe the weather as *disturbed, unsettled* and *confused*, which was also a fair description of Alvarenga's deteriorating mind-set. His trademark rationality, his prayers and his continuing ingenuity could not combat the sheer exhaustion of being trapped aboard a tiny boat full moon after full moon. "It felt like I was lacking in nutrition," said Alvarenga. "I just wanted to go to the corner of the boat and sit. I had less and less motivation to get up. Little by little I lost my strength. I realized this is how I was going to die."

Alvarenga didn't have the energy to complain, to worry or become angry. He retreated into a world of frustrated exhaustion. He was stuffed inside the icebox, where sweat dripped off him like he was running a marathon. He wondered, "Am I melting?" He could not go out in the sun for more than ten minutes without his skin burning. Veteran sailor Ivan Macfadyen, who has crossed the Doldrums in the Pacific numerous times, says, "The heat and sun would drive me batshit every day. I hid from the sun. It's sweelteringly hot and humid; it's just miserable when there's no wind. Even on a fully provisioned sailboat, it was still horrendous. And bear in mind that we try to cross the Doldrums area in a dead straight line to make it as short as possible. But to have drifted lengthwise along it? To be adrift? I can't think of anything worse. It's the equivalent of walking across a desert and poking your eyes out with hot sticks."

Inside his shelter Alvarenga banged his feet on the deck—the echo was a wake-up call reminding his mind that he was still in the here and now. But his feet felt wobbly and weak, as if his ankle were an untethered ball-and-socket joint. He had little strength, and no stability. Walking was now difficult. "I wasn't in physical pain but still I would scream," said Alvarenga. "I yelled to the four directions—'I want to get out of here. . . . Listen to me. . . . Someone, bring me food, bring me water. . . . I know you are listening.' I wondered, 'Am I going crazy?' Then I would collapse."

Venturing out on deck for ten-minute intervals during the day, Alvarenga developed a routine: he splashed water on his face, washed his body and delighted in the quick chills as the water drops ran down his body in rivulets. Scanning the horizon was a reflex, like looking both ways before crossing a street and taking stock of the neighborhood. When the seas were flat visibility was twenty miles, but it might as well have been two hundred or two thousand miles; there was nothing but nature with dimensions all her own.

Fresh garbage drifted by, overtaking Alvarenga in the current. He inspected the parade of industrial flotsam with a connoisseur's eye and was especially intrigued by floating plastic bottles with a mouthful of coffee-colored residue, like ground twigs mixed with water, sloshing in the bottom. The mixture smelled like ground pepper, but his curiosity was greater. Alvarenga sipped the dregs of what looked like macerated wood chips. His tongue and mouth went numb, his energy surged. He had no idea what he was drinking or where it came from but never hesitated to consume every last drop and chunk of the fibrous mystery drink. Later, when he discovered the source, he felt nauseous in knowing what he had so enthusiastically savored and swallowed.

Failure and frustration became more common. A sheet of plastic salvaged from the ocean was supposed to convert into a billowing spinnaker sail with rigging made from rescued fishing lines. After various prototypes, the dream of sailing ended in a pile of torn plastic. Alvarenga's lack of tools stymied his ability to build the designs that flowed up from his imagination. He needed nails. He would have given his left pinky for a size-seventeen wrench to unbolt and dump the 360-pound outboard motor. The motor weighed twice as much as Alvarenga and was a deadweight that slowed him considerably.

At the same time his spirits were flagging, a flotilla of boats kept the horizon abuzz. Alvarenga now spotted commercial shipping vessels every week, not only container ships but cargo ships of different sizes, headed in the same direction. Was he crossing through an international shipping lane? He hardly bothered to study the ships. "I barely imagined that they would save me. I would see one boat after another and would have lost my mind thinking about them."

Then a boat appeared on the horizon with a path leading directly toward him. As the multistory ship plowed the open sea, it looked like a knife blade aimed at him. Alvarenga was sure the two boats were on a collision course. The container vessel advanced until it was so close Alvarenga feared it might slice his boat in half. Would he have to jump off to avoid the crash? Fifty yards astern, the ship crossed his path as it slashed through the water. Alvarenga stared at the white hull. His eyes searched the captain's bridge, looking for a watchman. *"Ayuuuuuuda! Aquí! Aquí! Aquí!"* ("Help! Here! Here! Here!") Alvarenga screamed as he spotted three figures standing near the stern of the giant boat. Fishing rods in hand, the crew was high above him, trolling from their five-story-high perch. Alvarenga looked up in awe as the men waved. A shock of wonder filled his mind. Finally! He had been spotted. What kind of lifeboat would they use and how did one ascend that wall of steel? But no one ran for help. The men on the container ship didn't move. No sign they were radioing the captain, and not only was the giant ship not slowing but the casual waving continued even as they rapidly pulled away. The ship's wake bashed and slammed Alvarenga. Stunned, he screamed, then stopped waving and started wondering. Was it even real? Maybe it was a mad hallucination determined to break his mind. Alvarenga cursed the men, the ship and its captain. Yet again, he abandoned all hope of being rescued by a ship. That evening as he pondered the stars, Alvarenga relived the scene. He was now convinced it had really happened and his line of inquiry shifted. How could the container ship justify not stopping? Three crewmembers had waved. Alvarenga screamed his bewilderment aloud, "Do you think I am out here on a day trip?"

The near miss devastated Alvarenga. His mind weakened; his reflexes further slowed. His interest in living diminished. When salt water splashed into the bottom of his boat he spent several days floating, too distraught to bail. Alvarenga imagined the progressive stages of his own demise. He expected that, like Córdoba, he would slowly wither away. His desire to eat was succumbing to a more basic craving: to close his eyes. "I was tired of working. I lay down and stretched out. My blood had no strength left. The weakness was also in my mind, so much time thinking. I was always worried."

Alvarenga remembered Córdoba's bored stare, listless conversation and lack of interest in food. That same lethargy now contaminated his mind. Alvarenga's inventive determination and dark humor went flat. He didn't care. He stared at the roof of the icebox for hours, at times spending the entire day in his box, his mind frozen and stalled. Alvarenga felt he was watching his own death in slow motion. Hunger wasn't killing him; it was the far deeper pain of loneliness. He was desperate to escape this minuscule boat. He felt light-headed as if he might faint. He still recited prayers and tried to be positive but his will to live slipped away, one small decision at a time. There were new species of fish under his boat—sea bass and dolphins sped by—but he was too tired to care. "My body was gone. My strength was gone. I could barely turn over in the icebox. I was weak. I kept thinking about my death. It was too much for my mind."

Every death is unique and Alvarenga began by losing his toes. They felt dead. "I tried to warm them up, massage them," said Alvarenga. "My legs were asleep from the knees down. I couldn't walk. My body just didn't respond. I smacked my legs and felt nothing on my feet, my calves. They were hard and solid. Below the knee I couldn't feel anything. It was coming up my body."

Simple body movements were a challenge. Lunging for a bird was almost more effort than he could exert. Rolling off his sleeping bench was now an oft-botched routine. His hands remained strong, his eyesight keen, but the coordination between the two erratic. He missed birds. He grappled with sharks and felt them slip into the ocean. Then he began to smell an odor. "My body was like a cadaver. I was starting to rot and die. Was the salt preserving me?"

Despite his attempts to reinvigorate his muscles, it was too late. His body refused to follow orders. His legs "were starting to go stupid and didn't want to do anything." He had nightmares about death and a recurring fantasy that he was shopping for a pillow. "I was agonizing day after day. I had seen my friend die. First I fell down, and then I was going to start to dry out. My stomach was nearly gone. I could see my death was going to be very, very slow."

The rains were relentless. Alvarenga crawled and wailed. "I told God, 'I have enough water for the days that remain.'" And then it rained even harder. It started to fill up the bottom of the boat and Alvarenga succumbed. "I had always been a man of action, but now I just floated." As he laid on his back, staring at the stars, a foot of water sloshed and feathers floated by his face. At the bow, a dozen angry birds squawked and fought. He was oblivious. Floating changed everything. Why hadn't he thought of this earlier? He felt half dead, but at least he didn't have to deal with gravity anymore. "I was drying out. I felt that I was going to faint. Feverish. Depressed. No life left. I had lost my energy, I couldn't hold out any longer. I was dying of desperation. Of loneliness."

The ocean current was now so swift he could distinguish a clear wake behind his boat. But forward motion was difficult to judge without any landmarks. Calculating his direction was easy—all he had to do was fix on the morning sunrise or evening sunset. But eager for independent confirmation of his drift, Alvarenga started a new daily ritual. Every morning he tossed feathers into the wake of his drifting boat. He now took his course by comparing the line of feathers drifting out behind the boat and the first rays of the morning sun reaching over the horizon. The feathers no longer lined up with a southwesterly drift and confirmed his suspicion that he was now swerving back north.

Talking aloud, Alvarenga began to revive his phantasmal relationship with Córdoba. After fifteen lunar cycles, drifting through unknown territory and convinced his next destination was up to heaven, Alvarenga began to plumb his former mate for tips and insights about the upcoming journey. "My relationship with death was no longer one of fear. If I died, I died. That was God's will. I would not kill myself, but I was waiting, waiting for death."

CHAPTER 13

The Rooster

 January 15, 2014
Position: 6,400 miles off the coast
   of Mexico
N 3° 51' 21.61" – W 173° 10' 11.24"
Day 424

Alvarenga was collapsed on the deck of his boat when the sight of distant lights on the horizon jolted him awake. Large fishing operations use huge spotlights to help night crews avoid accidents and this looked like a million-dollar tuna hunt. But the lights grew and stretched so long it seemed like a coastal settlement. What else could it be but land? Staring at the glowing lights, Alvarenga fantasized he could join the people who lived in this unknown settlement. His understanding of Pacific cultures was limited to a few rumors featuring a preponderance of cannibals. Could this be their home? But fear of cannibals was overcome by a yearning to reach land regardless of the disposition of the welcoming party. He assumed that El Salvador was now so far away that he would have to get a job to earn enough money to buy a ticket back to his family. Alvarenga brainstormed and imagined the type of employment he could find ashore. He could always go back to baking bread. That he had been living illegally in Mexico for thirteen years, had no work papers, never held a passport and was now responsible for explaining the death of his only crewmember did not enter his thoughts. Alvarenga had little notion that he was now an international traveler in a hyper-digitalized world.

———

The more he looked at the lights, the larger he imagined the town. Or was it a city? He felt certain that hundreds of people lived there. Was he drifting by the island of Tukurere in the nation of Kiribati? Far from being cannibals, the Kiribati populace were devout Polynesians still speaking varied languages and faithful to the tradition that wayward souls who washed ashore deserved a generous welcome. Equal parts Darwinian and altruistic, this welcoming spirit is an essential characteristic of remote Pacific island life. Given the seasonal droughts that regularly ravish these islands, without a collective approach to water and food many of these populations would have long ago died of thirst and starvation. Rather than be cannibalized, as Alvarenga imagined, these indigenous communities were more likely to stuff him with free food and blanket him in love. The distance to shore was too far for a swim, even without sharks. As the lights faded and his hopes dimmed, Alvarenga was left to wonder if this sighting was another test by God. Or the latest torment by the Devil? He had passed close to land and feared he had just missed his last chance of salvation. Had he cheated death for all this time just to die so close to civilization?

Alvarenga felt as if he might drown in freshwater. The rain was relentless. Unlike the smaller thunderstorm cells farther east, these storms brought a full day of cascading downpour. So much water pounded down that Alvarenga was able to fill all seventy-three plastic half-liter bottles, and his five-gallon bucket and added fresh-water to his blue barrel. The water in the barrel had turned brown with silt collecting at the bottom. The fresh rains allowed him to dilute the mixture. "I looked at the water inside the boat and decided I didn't want to bail. Then I would bail. It would rain again. I would bail. My bones hurt. I wanted to rest, to recover my strength."

 January 29, 2014
Position: Tile Islet, Republic
   of the Marshall Islands
N 4° 37' 16.06" – W 168° 46' 33.77"
Day 438

A cold rain knocked visibility down as Alvarenga went whizzing along on a strong wind and a smooth current and progress was palpable. Coconuts bobbed in the water and the sky filled with shorebirds. Alvarenga stared. Then blinked. The muscles in his neck tightened. As his eyes crinkled in concentration, a tropical island emerged from the rainy mist. He wiped the raindrops from his eyes yet the mirage was still there. A green Pacific atoll, a small hill surrounded by a kaleidoscope of turquoise waters.

Slowly, the island came into focus. Alvarenga saw a palm tree jungle. There were so many birds it reminded him of his coastal home in El Salvador. These were not cross-Pacific migrators with the aerodynamic perfection of an albatross, but heavier shorebirds: eager to land, easy to trap. These coastal species lined up on his pole like targets in a carnival booth. Alvarenga couldn't help but continue to hunt and gather. His brain automatically prioritized such activities.

Alvarenga had forgotten the strength of these muscular shorebirds. As he grabbed one bird by the foot, a flashing strike of a beak drew a bloody welt on his forearm. Alvarenga yanked the bird upside down and fought against the madly flapping wings. Again, the bird snapped around and pecked Alvarenga. Enraged, he considered tossing the bird overboard but instead seized it and killed it instantly. The mangled bird lay at his feet. The commotion was over as quickly as it had begun and Alvarenga felt ashamed. Though he spent his life as a hunter both onshore and at sea, he had no taste for sport killing. The one time he had been brought along to watch a cockfight with colleagues back in Mexico he had huffed out, disgusted by the gratuitous violence.

As he looked at the island, Alvarenga's first urge was to dive overboard and swim to shore, but leery of sharks and unsure of his strength, he paused. He studied his destination. Hallucinations didn't last this long. Had his prayers finally been answered? Alvarenga's racing mind imagined multiple disaster scenarios. He could blow off course. He could drift backward—it had happened before. Or the island could dissolve into a nightmare taunting his weakened mind. He stared at land as he tried to pick out details from shore. It was a tiny island, no bigger than a football field, he calculated, though he could see just one side. He looked for huts, roads and boats—surely there would be fishermen. But it looked wild, without roads, cars or homes.

Alvarenga tossed a fresh trail of feathers behind his boat, then projected the route forward. It was a dead-center hit. He didn't see any surf break or white frothing—telltale signs of rocks or a coral reef. Alvarenga prayed to God and asked for waves to wash him ashore. "I kept reminding myself that it was farther than it looked, a good ways out, there might be animals, sharks or sharp rocks. So I held out. I kept telling myself to be calm, to take my time."

Alvarenga was so stressed and excited that he turned to food as a distraction from the unbelievable scene growing on the horizon. He retrieved the dead bird at his feet, ripped off the skin and began slicing away the connective tissue while guarding valuable nuggets of flesh. He stuffed his mouth in anxious bites and stared at the island. Dried triggerfish was a far more practical snack but Alvarenga needed to keep his hands busy. Plucking feathers was a monotonous, repetitive motion that allowed him to work away the stress and calm his mind. No sooner had he polished off one bird than Alvarenga killed, cleaned and ate a second bird. Then a third.

Another bottle with the strange wood shavings at the bottom floated by. Alvarenga chugged the dredges and drops of liquid despite the harsh, bitter taste. It was spicy, as if someone had poured ground pepper into the bottle, and perked him up, as if he had downed a coffee. Then he began to carve into a turtle he had captured a day earlier. He feasted anxiously as if he no longer needed to measure his food or water reserves. Two servings of turtle later, his belly bulging, he went into the icebox, seeking shelter from the rain.

It was a most inappropriate time for a nap. He was less than a half day's drift from land and headed for a collision course with salvation. What if the currents shifted? How would he swim to shore if he awoke miles farther away? But Alvarenga climbed into his icebox and lay faceup, his stomach bloated, and collapsed into a deep sleep. He dreamed of fresh crabs and imagined that he was ashore, speaking with people.

His siesta was less than an hour and when he rushed out of the icebox he was shocked. The island was right there, less than a mile away. With his knife, he cut away the ragged line of buoys. It was a drastic move. In the open ocean with no sea anchor he could readily flip during even a moderate tropical storm. But Alvarenga could see the shoreline clearly and he gambled that speed was of greater importance than stability.

In an hour he would be tossed ashore on a beach—though the tossing part looked rough. Alvarenga had negotiated surf breaks hundreds of times in his fully loaded fishing vessel; now he planned to abandon ship at the last moment. He would dive into the surf, away from the boat. No way was he going to fight this long only to get bashed on the head and killed like those unlucky fishermen who died in the tricky surf break back home in Mexico.

By early afternoon Alvarenga was gliding toward shore. He felt like a surfer, though he was probably traveling less than two miles an hour. Several football fields away from shore Alvarenga considered diving and swimming to land. But worried he might drown from exhaustion, he held out. The rain continued. Frigid drops pelted his body. Having been chilled miles above, in the attic of this roiling squall, the oversized raindrops felt like miniature ice cubes. Alvarenga began to shiver but dared not seek shelter from the storm.

After a half day of anticipation he waited until he was ten yards from shore, then perched on the rail, prepared to jump. The waves curled up ready to smash down. Protecting his head like a high-diver, he stretched out his arms and dove. His hands whacked the rocky bottom, but Alvarenga didn't lose the grip of his knife, which he cradled backward, the blade against his forearm. He stood up and laughed. The water reached his waist. Nearby, his boat slammed ashore and nearly flipped. The barrel went flying. A shriek arose from the trapped birds. Alvarenga ignored the instinct to chase his boat. He was headed to land. Wading didn't work; his feet were too tender and his leg muscles weak. Instead he floated on his belly and tried to swim the last few yards. The water was filled with jellyfish. He felt a burning sensation across his body. As the waves pulled him back he felt like he might be dragged out to sea. Treading to remain afloat, his head above water, he paddled "like a turtle" until a large wave picked him up and tossed him high on the beach, like driftwood. As the wave pulled away, Alvarenga was left facedown in the sand. "It took me a minute to touch the beach," he said. "I held a handful of sand in my hand like it was a treasure."

Crawling on all fours he moved higher up the beach, toward the dry sand. He didn't look back at the water. His pace was so slow that small slugs attached themselves to his legs and arms. Across his belly he felt them crawling and a sensation like blood-sucking leeches. "Dozens of them were all over my body." Using his last strength he pulled himself atop a log, twenty feet above the water line and shielded from rain by the palm canopy. His boat was sliding away, dragged down the coast by the waves. His lifesaving blue plastic barrel was missing. Alvarenga watched two of his captive birds escape. Broken wings akimbo, they waddled down the beach, crippled but free.

His body and mind overwhelmed by exertion and confusion, Alvarenga collapsed asleep. "When people have been in a situation where they have been willing themselves to survive, along comes a rescue boat, and they relax," explains Professor Michael Tipton. "They relax to the point where they collapse. Their blood pressure and their condition significantly deteriorates."

When he awoke Alvarenga found his body again covered with leeches or slugs. He angrily tore them off. His body was a wasted shell. Not only were his feet tender like those of a newborn infant, but his lower leg muscles were atrophied and so weak they could neither support his body weight nor pump the blood properly back to his heart. Long-term studies to prepare astronauts for the effect of weightlessness in space demonstrate that after four weeks in forced "bed rest" even highly trained athletes are unable to stand up. "The lack of being able to do thirty minutes' walking or general physical activity has fairly significant consequences for your cardio-vascular system, for bone mineralization, aerobic capacity, for blood pressure control," says Tipton. "All these things deteriorate when you've been restrained or confined for a long period of time. You might even expect him to pass out when he tried to stand up."

Crawling like a baby, Alvarenga headed toward a small rise, hoping to advance before dark—determined to get as far as possible from the ocean. As he crawled across the rocky land, Alvarenga stopped to pray. He had been saved from near death on so many occasions that he was sure there was a divine hand at work. He built a small altar out of sticks, stones and native flowers and asked for the strength to return to his flaccid legs and swollen feet. Then he ate the flowers.

Alvarenga could hear the crashing surf as he took stock of his new ecosystem, which was wall-to-wall palm trees sprouting from rich volcanic soil. He was astounded at the animal life. Calories were carousing in the branches. Birds nested high in the crown of the palm trees. Alvarenga began mapping their movements as he designed a hunting strategy—everything that was alive and moved was potential food. Alvarenga ambled up the slope like a grazing goat. As he crawled he stuffed plants and beach grasses into his mouth. Chewing with powerful bites, he didn't focus on taste. He was savoring the textures and smells of this exotic new world. Having survived on turtle blood, raw jellyfish and his own fingernails, the possibility that some plant species might be poisonous was not even an afterthought.

Nearly naked, crawling like an animal, he headed up the only incline he could find. Safety and a view would be his reward for a trip to the top. He wanted to sprint up and break free from the tyranny of slow motion. He had no such possibility. Even crawling was beyond his strength. He drifted off to sleep under the trees, a glorious new sound track easing his mind. Instead of the monotony of waves slapping at his boat's hull, now it was a symphony of sounds as the cold raindrops pounded into the rich foliage of the jungle island. Under the tropical canopy he felt shielded.

Alvarenga awoke in a panic. He was desperate to keep moving. He feared that if he stopped moving this fantasy would come to an end and he would awaken back on the boat in the open, endless ocean. He was determined to find a way home to El Salvador. He was determined to meet his teenage daughter, hug his parents and complete his promise to visit Córdoba's mother. But for now he was naked, cold and without food on a deserted island. "I went into the jungle totally naked like Tarzan," said Alvarenga. "I stalked the birds and planned to raid their nests for eggs. I thought that maybe during the day I should climb trees and then wait for them to come home to roost at night."

The island was littered with green coconuts, and had Alvarenga looked closer, he would have noticed fresh machete chops, tell-tale evidence of recent harvests. "I couldn't move very well, but I dragged myself the best I could, and started to collect the coconuts that were scattered around me. I smashed one open with a rock. That is how I started to eat coconuts. My stomach was so happy! My insides were overjoyed. They had not tasted anything like that for so long."

Dragging himself up, Alvarenga was curious if he might gain a view from the top of what he called "that small mountain" (actually a bump barely ten feet above sea level). From the "summit" Alvarenga eyed the colors, contours and inhabitants of this new ecosystem. He was relieved to be off the water but deeply regretted not chasing down his boat. Why hadn't he rescued the *panga*? What if he needed to get off this island? How would he travel? As he watched the sun go down, Alvarenga searched for clues that might help him decipher his new home. Where was he? Did people live here? The island was tiny but sat astride larger islands that chained together in a ring twenty-five miles across. The islands sheltered a smooth lagoon in the middle, which from the air looked like a huge wedding ring. Alvarenga saw not a single boat but the view was promising. Surely he could fish in the lagoon. But what would he use for hooks? Alvarenga promised that in the morning, he would scour the island for scrap metal and start building tools for his new life, but first he would try to rescue his boat.

Alvarenga fell asleep and when he awoke just before dawn,

around four a.m., he was soaked and cold. He pulled himself up and immediately spotted a cluster of lights on a nearby island. Civilization was near, but how to get there? Before he could follow that fantasy, he yet again fell asleep. But now it was a sleep haunted by the nightmare that he was still on the boat. His head ached when he awoke. For an hour he glanced around the island convinced that he was hallucinating.

The rain was so cold it made Alvarenga shiver although the air temperature was a comfortable 75 degrees. He longed for the security, familiarity and warmth of his home in the icebox. Why hadn't he thought of securing his boat onshore? Or kept his captive birds for food? His need to reach solid land had blinded him to common sense. No one allows a seaworthy boat to drift away without a fight, especially in the middle of God only knows where. What if he needed to abandon the island in a hurry? How would he escape? Swim. That's how he'd do it. He would swim to those distant lights spotted hours earlier. Was that a stupid idea? With legs barely strong enough to crawl, long-distance swimming was out of the question. Alvarenga gave himself advice, then shot down those very arguments. It felt like his brain had been hijacked by a dozen voices, each with a different disaster scenario.

The distinction between fantasy and reality remained blurry but Alvarenga saw a canal, a patch of sand, and figured the cove would be a good home so he crawled down the backside of "the hill." He would swim to the larger island. Suddenly, a flash of red caught his eye. It took him a few seconds to recognize that he was staring at a man's shirt. A red short-sleeve shirt hanging on a clothesline. His mind went wild. The island was inhabited. Then he heard a "a most glorious sound." A rooster crowed.

Alvarenga Washes Ashore

Pacific Ocean

Eninaitok Island

Ebon lagoon (protected)

Emi and Russel's home (Alvarenga found refuge here)

channel

Alvarenga spotted here

Tile Islet (pop. 0)

Alvarenga's path from the sea

Alvarenga washed ashore here

Highest point on Tile Islet (approx. 10 feet), Alvarenga spent first night here

0	200	400 feet
0	50	100 meters

N
W · E
S

CHAPTER 14

Who Is This Wild Man?

*A*yudaaaaaa! Ayudaaaaaa! Ayudenmeeeee!"* ("Help! Help! Help
meeeeee!") Alvarenga screamed. The famished fisherman was
crawling through a carpet of sodden palm fronds, sharp coconut
shells and tasty flowers. He descended from the rise and inched toward what looked like a wooden shack, a gaggle of chickens and a
lone pig. Who wore the red shirt on the clothesline? Was he armed
and dangerous? Do cannibals have roosters? Alvarenga's mind fired
in all directions. The tidal rhythm of life at sea had so accustomed
his brain to the sloshing and sliding of the Pacific that he was dizzy
standing on solid ground. He felt insecure on this crust of land.

The once-confident open-sea fisherman was unable to stand
for more than a few seconds. "I was totally destroyed and as skinny
as a board," he said. "The only thing left was my intestines and gut
plus skin and bones. My arms had no meat. My thighs were skinny
and ugly."

Under normal conditions, the stout Alvarenga might have
sprinted down the hillside. It would have taken seconds. Now it
took minutes for him to lurch from tree to tree, grabbing each
trunk like a man who'd had too much to drink. His feet moved
autonomously from his brain; despite clear orders they splayed in
seemingly random rebellion. His upper body was slightly stronger,

though there was no remnant of the explosive muscle power that had allowed him to win powerlifting contests among the tough fishermen on the docks of Mexico.

Alvarenga's heart was so weak it was unable to properly circulate blood up from his feet. He felt like he might faint. He sat on the sand at the edge of a blue lagoon so large it looked like a lake. Where was he? He had begged God to be washed ashore but now with his prayers answered, he received none of the imagined comforts. A deep anxiety chipped away at his confidence. Any animal larger than a dog was now classified as a predator. Especially humans.

During fifteen complete lunar cycles, Alvarenga had coached a fragile truce as despair and hope dueled for control of his mind. Standing on solid ground astride what looked and sounded like the outskirts of a small village, he had no way of anticipating the mental demons now poised to attack. His salvation from the sea, a miraculous escape, was now so imprinted on his brain that he never again would be free to imagine life without this trauma. He was literally and clinically "traumatized for life" and fully unprepared for contact with other humans.

Directly across the water, on the far side of a narrow canal, the red shirt was hanging on the clothesline. Alvarenga approached. Could he navigate the shallow waters? He stood up and, wobbling slightly, attempted to ford the fifty-foot channel separating the two islands. He howled in Spanish, "Does anyone hear me? Anyone!"

Across the canal, finishing up breakfast at her rustic beach hut, Emi Libokmeto heard the screams. "I got up and had a look. As I'm looking across to the other island, I see this white man there," said Emi, who works husking and drying coconuts on the island. "He is only in his briefs and he is yelling. He looks weak and hungry. My first thought was this person swam here, he must have fallen off a ship."

Alvarenga saw Emi and went into shock. "It terrified me. I was so scared. People don't exist, I told myself. How do people exist? How can there be people here if they don't exist? I tried hard to clear my head. Yes, yes, I am in the world. This is not a hallucination." Alvarenga's mind was going haywire. The same instincts that guided his solo survival at sea were short-circuited by his first encounter in nearly a year with a member of his own species.

Emi couldn't believe her eyes. The white man covered in wild hair was coming toward her. "My husband, Russel [Laikidrik], was very scared, he insisted we go back in our house and hide," said Emi. "But I wasn't scared. Just from looking at him I felt sorry for him so I urged my husband for us to go help."

From opposite sides of the canal the two parties approached. Alvarenga gingerly tested out the current, concerned he might be swept back to sea. Emi and Russel advanced with caution. "As we got closer we noticed the knife in his hand so we stopped," said Emi. "Russel was very worried and wanted us to turn back, but there was something about him. Something kept telling me this man needed our help and so I said to Russel that he needs our assistance. Plus, I was thinking to myself that he looks weak and there are two of us so if he tried anything we could control him."

Emi pointed at Alvarenga's hand, at the long knife, and yelled in English, "Put down! Put down!" and mimed doing so. Alvarenga balked. He needed the knife to dice coconuts and carve meat from the animals he was stalking and planning to hunt. His worn and trusty blade had saved his life dozens of times over the past year.

Why would he abandon a key element of his salvation? It was his only tool. The woman yelled again, with conviction. Her companion was a powerfully built man. Alvarenga recognized that the man could wrestle him down with ease and the small woman looked unlikely to back away. Russel, accustomed to the rugged manual work in the tropics collecting and chopping coconuts, repeated the motion indicating Alvarenga ought to drop the knife. Alvarenga understood their instructions and although he cherished his knife, he was too exhausted to argue or explain. He flipped his knife into the canal. It sank into the light-blue water and came to rest three feet deep. Without a weapon, barely able to stand and too exhausted to formulate a plan, Alvarenga dropped to his knees. He began to pray.

Emi was instantly moved to help the stranger. "For me this was a sign that he was also a person of faith and he had been through something traumatic and it moved me with an overwhelming feeling that we must help."

Fortunately for Alvarenga, the tide was slowly receding and the water in the canal was only waist high. Emi and Russel continued to wade toward him. Alvarenga was kneeling in the sand, swaying and obviously weak. He pointed frantically toward the far side of a nearby island and yelled in Spanish, "My boat, my boat. My boat is over there." But the couple didn't understand. As Russel and Emi approached, the wild man stopped making eye contact. Or maybe his eyes didn't focus anymore. He looked lost and as they got close he lowered his head as if he were trying to hide.

Russel stepped forward and reached down to stabilize the frightened man and discovered he was shivering uncontrollably. Russel peeled off his own shirt and pulled it over the man's head and then reached around to thread each bony arm through a sleeve. Doubting if the other man could even walk, Russel hoisted the stranger on his back and struggled to cross the canal with the bearded fellow clinging to him. "We took him back to our house. I got him a glass jar of water," said Emi. "He gulped it so fast. I poured him another glass of water and this time I motioned for him to slow down because I didn't want him to have a stomachache."

Safely onshore with his rescuers, Alvarenga broke down and began to sob. Emi and Russel also began crying. "I told my husband to hug him and comfort him with pats on the back," said Emi. "Like white people do."

Using Russel's spare clothes they clad their guest in a sweater, pants, shoes and socks. Even a belt. Although he felt physically warmed, Alvarenga was scared. "I was trying to not see people. I didn't want to see people. When they came close, I would cover my head. I wouldn't look at them. I wouldn't let them touch me. I thought maybe they were going to eat me."

Russel could tell the man was starving so he suggested his wife make a batch of pancakes while he went out to collect coconut husks to feed the fire. Emi tried to convince the fisherman to bathe. He declined, indicating he was too cold, and edged his chair closer to the fire. As Emi prepared pancake mix he sat with his feet practically touching the flames. It was the first time in a year he had seen fire. The flames danced and he looked at Emi. They both smiled.

Alvarenga bonded naturally with the lifestyle of the generous couple from this mystery tribe. These islanders lived on the edge of civilization. Their fragile hut was on par with his precarious *palapa* in Mexico. Stores of freshwater were stashed all around the house just like the seventy-three water bottles he had religiously guarded aboard *The Titanic*. When Emi lit the fire she took care not to use a second match. Alvarenga felt affection for such frugality. He understood the value of a single match.

"When the fire began to die down, I started cooking the pancakes. I can't remember how many I cooked but as they were coming off the pan, he began eating," Emi said. "In the end Russel and I only had one each. At one point he pointed at the plate of pancakes and motioned for us to eat. We motioned back to him, 'No, you eat.'"

Emi also provided plates of fresh coconut meat and glasses of coconut milk. Russel made another cooking fire and prepared a pot of rice. Alvarenga hinted they could eat the domestic animals, beginning with the rooster. "It was aggressive and big. I was thinking, 'What a good soup,' but the rooster gave me the eye and I couldn't catch it." Alvarenga then convinced Russel to slaughter one of the chickens and while he prepared the bird, Alvarenga "ate as many coconuts as she could peel. I ate so much she was scared."

After eating, Alvarenga felt invigorated not only by a full stomach but also by the fact that he had not been carved up. As his fear of Pacific island cannibals receded another deep fear arose: the fear of not moving. For Alvarenga, movement was synonymous with sanity. A migratory instinct pulled him to abandon the safety and shelter of this newfound refuge. "I was restless. After breakfast I wanted to walk," he said. "I went to the edge of the water but was afraid I might drown. It was terrifying. I couldn't even walk back to the house. They had to help me."

Alvarenga hadn't been under their roof more than three hours and already Emi and Russel were slaughtering animals, cooking up a second feast and handing him glass after glass of refreshing coconut water. Although he didn't know it, Alvarenga had washed ashore on Tile Islet, a small island that is part of the larger atoll. Ebon is the southern tip of the 1,156 islands that make up the Republic of the Marshall Islands and one of the most remote spots on earth. Airplane service is practically nonexistent and a boat leaving Ebon searching for land would have to churn either 4,000 miles northeast to hit Alaska or 2,450 miles southwest to Brisbane, Australia. Had Alvarenga missed Ebon, he would have drifted north of Australia, possibly running aground in Papua New Guinea, but more likely continuing another 3,000 miles until he hit the eastern coast of the Philippines.

"A long-standing tradition in the Marshall Islands is to share food," explains Jack Niedenthal, a documentary filmmaker who came to the Marshall Islands with the Peace Corps in 1981 and settled. "The cycle of long-lasting droughts and the remote nature of the island civilization have long prepared the islanders to be both flinty survivalists and generous hosts. A lot of the culture surrounds food; there are times when you run out of food. Everybody shares. It is a big thing. I ate some bizarre stuff on the outer islands because someone gave it to me. You learn to never refuse food from anybody. It is like saying 'I hate you.'"

After he finished eating, Alvarenga began signaling in an attempt to communicate with his hosts. He used hand signals to indicate that previously he had short hair and no beard. He also indicated that he used to be more robust. He motioned a bird sign and pointed at the fire and motioned no fire. He was trying to explain that he had eaten raw birds. Alvarenga drew a boat, a man and the shore. Then he gave up. How could he explain a six-thousand-mile drift at sea with stick figures? His impatience simmered. The frustrated fisherman began to shout in Spanish. God had guided him to this tropical oasis; why was basic conversation so difficult? For his entire life, Spanish had served to get him out of a jam, around corrupt policemen or into a tight skirt. But now he was incapable of even the most basic phrases. He asked for medicine. He asked for a doctor. "Painkillers. Bring me painkillers," Alvarenga pleaded. The native couple smiled and kindly shook their heads. "Even though we did not understand each other, I began to talk and talk," Alvarenga said. "The more I talked, the more we all roared with laughter. I am not sure why they were laughing. I was laughing at being saved."

Emi laid out a mat and a piece of foam the size of a single bed and covered it with a sheet. She placed the foam bed on the ground under the shelter of the roof. The rain had paused. It was low tide and the water had pulled back, exposing a white, sandy beach. Emi gave Alvarenga a pillow and told him to rest. "My mind filled with happiness. I was thinking how different is life when you are not lost." Alvarenga had a roof, a pillow and solid ground. "How tasty," he thought. "I closed my eyes. I was blocking out the world." He got up from his nap to pee on a tree. "I looked at my urine and remembered when I drank it."

Although it was day, Alvarenga asked that the light above his makeshift bed be switched on. "I slept and slept! What a luxury," he said. "Finally I didn't have the ocean slapping at my side. When I awoke I asked them to go get my boat over on the coast but they didn't understand."

Using pen and paper Alvarenga drew a boat. "Once we realized what he was trying to communicate, Russel left and headed in the direction of where he was pointing," says Emi.

Emi prepared a plate of rice and chicken and signaled to Alvarenga to pray and give thanks for the food. Alvarenga prayed then dumped a pile of salt on his food. Any spice the native cook offered, he eagerly added to his plate. "I didn't use any fork or spoon. It was ugly," he explained. "I shoved the food in my mouth with both hands. She served me lunch twice and I was still hungry."

After his third meal in roughly six hours, Alvarenga drank a cup of coffee. Emi was worried this wild man was going to eat until he was sick. She urged him to slow down. Alvarenga then spotted a bag of tobacco and asked for some leaves, rolled a huge cigar and puffed away for the first time since his last toke outside the Costa Azul lagoon. He almost fainted. Emi stared on in wonder.

Russel returned and told Emi the boat was "reefed" (washed ashore) on the next island down. He would wait for high tide to recover the boat. "After we ate, I got some paper and a marker and motioned for him to write," Emi says. "My intention was that we would deliver his writing to the Local Council as evidence that we discovered a person who washed ashore."

Russel and Emi could tell the foreigner was unsure of his own handwriting. The letters were large and crooked, like a child in first grade. They gave him a thick black marker to make the letters bigger and hopefully easier to decipher. Even had they been able to read Spanish they would have learned little from Alvarenga's haiku-like scribbles.

When Alvarenga finished his note, Russel climbed into a small sailboat and sailed off to deliver the unusual message. His journey was helped by a stiff wind and in less than an hour he arrived in Ebon, the main town and port on the island of the same name. When Russel arrived in Ebon, he saw a young boy riding past on his bike so Russel handed him the note with instructions to urgently deliver it to the chief of police or the mayor. "Let them know," Russel told the delivery boy, "that a man washed ashore."

The delivery boy found the mayor first and relayed the message. Mayor Ione DeBrum looked at the note and instantly recognized the Spanish word for "friend" but little else except for "Mom" and "Dad." DeBrum, a nutritionist by training, worried that the castaway might be dying from exposure. She packed a first-aid kit with IV solutions, coconut milk and ripe bananas to help stabilize what she figured would be a famished drifter. "I picked up the policeman that I have on the island and a health assistant because I thought I was going to see someone who was very weak." As DeBrum and the policeman headed to the dock, she also invited along Ola Fjeldstad, a Norwegian anthropologist conducting field research on Ebon Atoll. As they prepared a boat to cross the lagoon and scout out this report of a drifter, rumors of Alvarenga's arrival were already spreading across the island. A castaway raised all sorts of wild scenarios. Was he a drug trafficker? Or perhaps he fell off a sailboat?

———

Alvarenga was resting and ruing the stormy weather. It was gusty, cold, and the rain was pouring down again. "My bones, my body; everything felt totally collapsed. I was very malnourished after being adrift for so long."

Emi provided Alvarenga with a bucket of water, a bar of soap and a towel. "I smelled terrible," said Alvarenga. "There was an oil coming out of me, like fish oil." Alvarenga scrubbed his tender skin and looked at the bar of soap with curiosity. "I wanted to eat it. Then, since there was no shampoo, I tried to wash my hair with soap but it was impossible, it was all tangled. I managed to clean my face and my beard a bit."

After the wash, he sat and thought, "How do I get out of here?" Alvarenga began to brainstorm. He needed to consult his intuition and that meant talking aloud. Emi couldn't understand the man's animated conversation. But she sensed he was pleased with his musings so she started singing.

Emi's voice soothed Alvarenga. His desperation eased. Song allowed him to calmly take stock of this new world. Emi approached Alvarenga and looked at him with a tender curiosity. She tried to touch his hair. Alvarenga pulled back. "I said no but she kept wanting to touch my hair." The dance continued until Alvarenga convinced her. "I was not ready for that."

The only argument between Alvarenga and Emi erupted when he looked at himself in a handheld mirror. The image so shocked him that he violently threw the mirror. It smashed and led to an angry rebuke from Emi. Alvarenga for his part was glad to be rid of the only mirror in the house.

Alvarenga dreamed he was trapped in the open ocean. The boat crashed atop him and he fought to avoid drowning in the sea. He awoke screaming, "Where am I? I can't find my boat! I can't find my boat. Where is my icebox? My icebox!" Alvarenga was unnerved by his own behavior. "It took me an hour to understand. This is the world. This is the world." He repeated the phrase in the hope it was true.

As Alvarenga watched the birds in the trees, a commotion from the waterfront roused him. Emi began to jump and shout. He turned to see a motorized launch approaching. A uniformed man, like a police officer, was aboard as well as three passengers.

Alvarenga panicked. Was he being arrested? A policeman and three people in civilian clothes hustled off and began walking toward Alvarenga. He clenched his eyes shut. When he saw the official he assumed he was going to be arrested. It didn't matter that he had committed no crime. Having lived in Mexico for over a decade, Alvarenga was accustomed to injustice arriving in the form of uniformed officers. Foreigners in prison was an ugly tale that never ended well, he thought. He knew cases of El Salvadoran and Guatemalan immigrants who entered but never left the Mexican prison system.

But the first order of business was not to arrest him but for Alvarenga to submit to medical exams. The nurse's assistant took Alvarenga's blood pressure and did a cursory exam of his vital signs. He appeared weak but not critical. Russel's return interrupted the medical checkup. He called everyone's attention to a gruesome scene: the fisherman's boat, which he had recovered en route and towed to the beach. "Take a look," said Russel as he gestured inside the boat. The mayor, Ola the anthropologist, Emi and the police officer crowded around the boat. No one spoke. It looked like a movie prop. The deck was covered in a thin coat of green mold. The motor was stripped, like it had been pulled to pieces. Nothing shined anywhere on the boat; the surfaces were worn, the paint uneven. On deck, two plucked birds the size of chickens glistened, the pink meat a testament to their freshness. Seabird feathers caked the walls, stuck to the seats and floated in the water that sloshed across the filthy deck. A tangle of blue and white nylon cord was attached to the shards of Alvarenga's trusty sea anchor. Bird bones scattered the deck like whitened twigs. A dead turtle, partly eaten, lay next to an empty turtle shell. The entire boat was engulfed in the stench of death. "It looked messy, like it had been outdoors for quite some time," says Fjeldstad. "We kind of realized what happened when we saw that boat."

While the authorities took stock of the wreckage aboard his boat, Alvarenga made a quick decision: no way he was going back on the water. The policeman indicated for him to come. Alvarenga refused. Fjeldstad tried to explain in broken Spanish that they would go to a hospital and to a city where he could get help. Alvarenga's eyes didn't leave the water. Another boat ride? Impossible. He had been off the water for hardly twenty-four hours and they wanted him back in a boat?

Despite his resistance, the policeman and Fjeldstad hauled Alvarenga aboard a *panga* boat, practically an identical twin to his *Titanic*. He didn't writhe or seek to escape, but his mind fixated on this strange new reality. Who were these people? A chatter of unintelligible languages clacked around him. What country was this? Who were these dark-skinned natives who lived off coconuts in the middle of the ocean? Did they have contact with the world?

Alvarenga looked at his own boat with nostalgia. He stroked the rail as he said good-bye to his beloved craft. "I was giving thanks. I survived atop her. I wasn't sure when I would use her again. She saved my life."

Then the engine fired up, and the council boat turned around and motored across the lagoon. The bewildered Alvarenga was back at sea. "I couldn't believe that I was in a boat again. Give me a bike, a car to get out of there . . . anything but a boat."

"At first when we were on the boat going to the island he was looking around," recalls Mayor DeBrum. "The only thing I remember him commenting was 'Police. Police.' I tried to signal to him that the policeman wasn't in charge, and that we were taking him somewhere to help."

Fjeldstad handed Alvarenga a small notebook. "I was trying to ask him, Where do you come from? How long have you been out? What was your goal? We didn't get far. He was way too tired to make any effort to communicate. And since none of us spoke Spanish, we couldn't have a conversation with him. Our Spanish skills were pretty lousy, or nonexistent. So we made gestures. And he did nothing back. He was an empty shell of a human."

"I would draw boats, airplanes, it was impossible to communicate," Alvarenga said. "I wanted to cry."

As they motored across the lagoon, the policeman stared at the specimen before them. He had washed up and bathed but there was no hiding that he had been out at sea for a considerable time. His hair lay matted up like a shrub. His beard curled out in wild disarray. Fresh scars crisscrossed his browned hands. His ankles were swollen. His wrists were tiny and he could barely walk. Everything about him was mysterious. But it was his eyes that betrayed the depth of his trauma. He refused to look back and often hid his face. He had survived something terrible. His journey—whatever it was—had left a dark mark on the man. Even his hunger was otherworldly. The wild man consumed vast quantities of bananas, sandwiches, and pretty much anything put before him. His eating style was like that of a wild animal. He shoved food into his mouth. He ripped and shredded the meat, then crunched through the bones. Toward fellow humans, he showed no signs of violence or hostility. Alvarenga's mind had overwritten thirty-six years of socialization with a far more primitive mind-set. He didn't have the mental bandwidth for social niceties.

Alvarenga lay in the boat and observed as one of the crew trolled a fishing line. When the man snagged a two-foot fish from the lagoon, Alvarenga's face flashed with happiness. He gave a thumbs-up—a fisherman-to-fisherman congratulations. Then Alvarenga went to sleep. How long did he sleep? He never knew but estimated the entire trip took approximately twelve hours. The sun was going down as they neared the far side of the lagoon. Alvarenga was uneasy looking at the water for such long stretches. It wasn't good for his psyche. It would be months before he could comprehend that the entire trip lasted just fifteen minutes.

Alvarenga was now in a dense mental fog, his mind tortured by his inability to understand the language. Even the passage of time was unfathomable. During his drift he had watched the crescent moon grow slowly more bright, then attract monsters of the deep at full moon and finally go back to absolute darkness. The twenty-eight-day cycle felt natural. But hours and days were a mystery. And how could anyone possibly keep track of minutes? Alvarenga was certain that he had spent three full days with his glorious hosts Emi and Russel. He had slept entire nights, eaten multiple breakfasts and shared unforgettable dinners. In reality, he had been on their island less than twelve hours.

Alvarenga was also fighting bouts of agoraphobia, which is literally "fear of the marketplace." Vast, open spaces were associated with danger. His condition was deteriorating rapidly into the "opposite of claustrophobia," explains Peter Levine, author of *Waking the Tiger*, who has studied thousands of patients with PTSD and finds that many people, "when traumatized, don't have a cohesive memory. It is all shards of emotions, images and sensations but they don't fit together. Because of that the person isn't able to form a coherent time line. . . . I would guess that when Alvarenga was in somebody's home that is when he would have started to come apart."

Alvarenga's encounter with civilization was becoming increasingly tense. Nothing made sense. At sea he hadn't asked permission of anyone for anything. Every action had been free will. Adaptation to society was uncomfortable. Alvarenga preferred being alone. His personal space had been several thousand square miles of primeval ocean. Reduced quarters and being surrounded by people were enough to burst his fragile grip on sanity. Police uniforms in particular ratcheted up his fear. Why was he being taken prisoner—and by whom? His freedom was gone. But he could reverse that. Escape was possible. Alvarenga had beaten the sun, salt and waves—how difficult could it be to trick a few slow-moving humans? It wasn't time yet; first he needed to recover his strength. In his weakened condition he could do little but observe and plan an escape.

Alvarenga was unable to comprehend that he had just completed one of the most remarkable voyages in the storied history of seafaring. He didn't navigate, sail, row or paddle—he drifted. Unable to alter his course, he had been forced to build a world of survival starting with water and then branching into the depths of designing his own mental health program. He was extremely unlucky and terribly fortunate at the same time. "If you said someone left from the coast of Peru and drifted to Micronesia, that's completely unbelievable," says Shang-Ping Xie, the noted climatologist. "In the southern hemisphere, there's no rain to sustain life. People lost at sea off Peru have no chance of survival." But looking at the band of clouds just north of the equator, Xie has no doubts that Alvarenga's feat was possible: "Nature dictates our luck."

Who Is This Wild Man?

Drifting across the Pacific Ocean, watching the moon's light ebb and flow, Salvador Alvarenga battled loneliness, depression and bouts of suicidal thinking, yet he maintained his sanity by envisioning success. But surviving alone in a fantastic world of wild animals, vivid hallucinations and remote peacefulness did little to prepare him for the fact that he was about to be a pop celebrity, object of curiosity, target of derision and trending topic on Twitter.

CHAPTER 15

Found but Lost

Dusk stole away the light as Alvarenga arrived on the far side of the Ebon lagoon. He could see people gathered onshore. A crowd of bustling locals elbowed forward to glimpse this mysterious arrival. Four men carried the limp and sunbaked fisherman off the boat and upstairs to the second floor of what Alvarenga took to be a government office building. In the adjacent rooms he saw uniformed men and broadcasting equipment, including powerful walkie-talkie-style radios. "Looks like a police station," he thought.

A makeshift bed was arranged on the second floor of the building, between the room where Fjeldstad was living and the room where the police kept their gear. Alvarenga could make no sense of his new home. His energy was gone; at best he could walk the ten feet to the bathroom. Fjeldstad gripped his arm but Alvarenga shook loose. His independence and resolve were an intrinsic component of his survival. He could accept the generosity of strangers but survival depended on his own freedom to move.

As Alvarenga lay resting on the floor, islanders brought ramen noodles, coconuts and mosquito coils. Strangers popped into the room, snapped pictures with cell phones and vanished. The mayor's son was the unofficial interpreter. He had spent entire afternoons of his youth watching *Dora the Explorer* as she wandered the world, leaving millions of fledgling Spanish speakers in her wake. If Alvarenga had any possibility of bridging the cultural and language gap it was thanks to Dora.

The haphazard communication left Alvarenga baffled. He doubted if he would ever find someone who could fully understand Spanish. He needed urgent medical attention. "I was trying to get painkillers for my back. I wanted something for the pain," Alvarenga said. "I kept asking for pills, pills, pills! They didn't understand at all."

Alvarenga was now camped on the hard, ceramic floor of the Council House, the municipal offices on Ebon Atoll, which sits on the protected inner lagoon and is a sheltered environment, spared the rough waves and huge seas of the open ocean. A single main shipping channel exists for larger boats to enter or leave the port of Ebon, and between the spits of land, small channels form with the ebb and flow of the tides.

The government-owned Air Marshall Islands flies south to Ebon every week from Majuro, population fifty thousand, the Republic's capital two hundred and fifty miles north across the Pacific. But the runway at Ebon is short, the plane old and the service so irregular that locals jokingly call it Air Maybe. The only telephone on the island runs off a solar panel and a car battery, which means that by noon there's usually no juice left. A pair of radio operators can patch through government messages and official calls to the world, but the regular islanders of Ebon have little direct communication with the outside world.

The islands of Ebon tend to be tiny, often just a few hundred yards long and flat. The entire chain sits, on average, seven feet above high tide, meaning that since it was settled 3,500 years ago, the natives of Ebon have honed an intimate understanding and respect for the sea. They are accustomed to living aboard boats and with the constant possibility of being caught in a storm and dragged out to sea. Local navigators are some of the most talented on earth. Using a small outrigger sailing canoe known as a *walap*, the islanders are able to traverse large swaths of the Pacific, including the 2,500-mile journey to Hawaii. Long before the invention of the compass or sextant, navigators from these islands were able to calculate exact coordinates and complete monthlong journeys to reach distant isles. Even today the principal connection among the islands is via small boats. The Marshall Islands are one of the only refuges from Pacific storms in this part of the world. Many sailboats and commercial fishing boats stay moored for months during the raucous winter storm season. This international crowd of "yachties" tends to anchor down in "the Marshalls" as they wait out pounding rainstorms and avoid thirty-foot swells that make even the shortest island-to-island travel extremely hazardous.

"Over the many years I've lived in the Marshall Islands, dozens of islanders traveling between atolls in [the nation of] Kiribati have experienced engine problems, lost their way or been blown off course by storms, causing them to drift for weeks or months," writes Giff Johnson, editor of the local newspaper. "Many, of course, are never again heard from. But quite a few float into the Marshall Islands on small boats, some near death, others in relatively decent health. But they all have incredible stories to tell—which, in all likelihood, are largely true because castaways tend to tell similar survival tales of catching turtles, sharks and birds to stay alive."

Despite pristine diving, a rich marine life (interspersed with World War II relics) and beaches that look cut from the cover of a travel magazine, few international tourists visit Ebon. A visitor like Alvarenga from Mexico was a once-in-a-lifetime occurrence. Like a trophy fish hauled from the sea, Alvarenga was a curious specimen, an instant public attraction. As he rested on the ceramic floor the first night, surrounded by donated food and Fjeldstad's sketch pad, a parade of visitors came through. "Everyone was looking, staring, pointing, laughing, really interested," recalls Fjeldstad. "People on Ebon are naturally pretty curious. They were rushing toward him while he was in a position to not like that." Alvarenga noticed that the locals chewed a small (betel) nut, and when it was devoid of flavor, spit the remains onto the ground or into a bottle. He gagged when he realized that lost at sea, he had been gathering these same bottles, savoring this very spittle.

Alvarenga began to wonder if he was in jail. The policeman in the building seemed to be stationed not to keep out visitors, as Alvarenga had assumed, but to make sure he didn't leave. "People came and laughed at me," Alvarenga said. "They totally cracked up. Kids especially laughed at this hairy thing from the sea. I was skinny and weak and wanted to hide." Alvarenga was shocked. Why was everyone treating him like a freak show? He appreciated the gifts and there was not the slightest hostility, but what he most wanted was to be left alone, to go back home and return to life as usual.

"There's a lot of talk these days about a thing called resilience. That's the *in* term at the moment," says Dr. John Leach, a survival psychologist. "You've got built-in resilience, so you can bounce back when you get knocked [down] by a survival situation. My argument with that is that if you've gone through a survival situation, you've gone through a POW camp, or you've been taken hostage, or you've been through sea survival, you will not be bouncing back to *what* you were before. You will not be bouncing back to *who* you were before. Because you won't be the same person. If you think you are meant to be the same person, you can have problems. You've had an experience that has changed you. Coupled with that is that the society, the world you're coming back to, has certainly changed in their perception of you. They don't know how to handle you. Normally, most survivors want above all to be treated as normal. But the rest of the world can't treat them as normal."

Alvarenga was feeling increasingly stressed. His confused mind was searching for clues that would form into a coherent picture of his predicament. "How am I going to get out of this country? Will I adapt to this system, work for them and become part of the tribe?" Alvarenga dreamed he was trapped for years on Ebon Atoll. In his dream he was an old man. He envisioned his own death on Ebon. The nightmares increased his desire to escape. Alvarenga felt penned up, trapped and suffocating. He was addicted to freedom. Adrift at sea, he had lived without walls. His ceiling a blanket of blinking stars. The moon his calendar. "Without the stars it felt like someone had unplugged the world," said Alvarenga as he described his first nights indoors. "Even lost at sea, the stars reminded me that everything was okay. Looking at the roof made me uncomfortable."

"Somebody called on the radio to Majuro to report what had happened," said Fjeldstad. "That there's a guy arriving from we don't know where, but he's been out for quite some time. They explained that he needed health care."

The authorities in Majuro didn't believe the tale. And when the officials in Ebon insisted that the castaway was in poor health, Fjeldstad recounts, "They said, take his blood pressure. We did. It was pretty damn low. But they said, 'He'll be fine. We are *not* coming to get him.'" Although a government rescue was not forth-coming, rumors of a castaway began to circulate in Majuro.

Back in Ebon, Fjeldstad was increasingly frustrated by the lack of official help for Alvarenga. He decided to use the only tool available. He took his gripes to the only reporter he knew, Johnson at the *Marshall Islands Journal*. "I was thinking maybe he could push the government in some way, in the local newspaper," says Fjeldstad. "Let them know that something happened. But then all of a sudden it exploded worldwide."

Written by Johnson, the first story went out under the Agence France-Presse (AFP) banner on January 31, 2014, and outlined the remarkable contours of Alvarenga's story. The story was excitedly read in newsrooms around the world. Reporters in Hawaii, Los Angeles and Australia scrambled to reach the island to interview this alleged castaway. The single phone line on Ebon became a battle-ground as reporters from around the world tried to coax out tantalizing details from the Norwegian anthropologist. With Fjeldstad's firsthand reporting, Alvarenga's story was beginning to take shape. Two fishermen left Mexico. They drifted across the Pacific. Survived by eating raw birds. One man died from extreme hunger. The other survived fourteen months. There were many missing parts but that didn't stop the press. They filled in what they didn't know, added glorious details far from the truth and launched a mad rush to sort out a tale both so fantastic and so improbable that it was immediately compared to the fictional movie *Life of Pi*. But this story was possibly true and perhaps even included cannibalism. The glee evoked by that sinfully dark possibility moved media budgets around the globe.

Alvarenga's story had enough hard facts to make it plausi-

ble: the initial missing person report, the search-and-rescue operation, the correlation of his drift with known ocean current and
new details from Ebon suggesting he was extremely weak. A debate erupted in newsrooms and chat boards around the world. Was
this the most remarkable survivor since Ernest Shackleton or the
biggest fraud since the publication of the fictitious Hitler Diaries?
Adding to the confusion, Alvarenga was on a distant isle, shell-
shocked and unable to share more than fragmentary details of his
alleged expedition.

Ignorant of his growing fame, Alvarenga was going stir crazy
after two days cooped up in the Council House. He ached to see a
full display of stars. The walls made him anxious. "When are they
coming to get me?" he asked. "That was the first time I heard the
word *Marshalls*. I was told a boat from the *Marshalls* was coming
to get me."

Alvarenga could no longer wait passively; instead he devised a
secret plan. He would escape. "I wanted to go to the mountains to
be free. I felt like a prisoner," Alvarenga said. "I started hallucinating
that I was stuck in the icebox and really I was stuck in this room."

But with police and government officials constantly milling
around, there was little to do but spend hours with Fjeldstad on the
veranda, appreciating the small details of terrestrial life. Fjeldstad
recalls, "He was having joyous moments when he would just stare
into the atmosphere and sigh happily. We were sitting inside, and
children were playing outside, and he was saying, 'Listen, listen'—in
Spanish, of course—he was doing a kind of hand gesture. He was
like, 'Yeah, a child playing!'"

Fjeldstad improved the conversations a notch by flipping his
phone into Spanish and finding words that Alvarenga would rec-

ognize. On his second day ashore Alvarenga began to emerge from his stupor. "He was more mentally aware of his surroundings, and of himself. He was gradually realizing that he was safe. When we told him it was January 2014, he was repeating that to himself. He was shaking his head and saying, 'A year at sea.'"

Having used the moon as his clock, Alvarenga felt lost in the rigid world of solar time. Everything seemed rushed, stressful and arbitrary. He longed for the natural rhythm of sunrise, sunset and the quiet glow of the moon at night. When Fjeldstad left to buy fresh fish and the government officials went off to lunch, Alvarenga saw a chance to escape. "I went down the staircase, down a hall and was headed toward the door. I didn't look at anyone. I walked calmly. My eyes focused ahead." His plan was to live in the green hills he could see from his window. There would be food in the woods. And he would be on higher ground, providing at least psychological distance from the ocean. As he neared the main door to the outside world, a few steps from freedom, a policeman stepped forward and blocked Alvarenga's advance. The officer took him by the arm and escorted him back upstairs. "They were holding me like I was a terrorist or something," Alvarenga complained. "They gave me a pillow and a bed but also a guard."

The day after his escape attempt, a national police boat arrived in Ebon to evacuate the befuddled castaway. As Alvarenga was carried toward the patrol boat, nearly the entire 692-person population of Ebon was on hand to gawk and say good-bye. With typical Marshallese modesty, there were more handshakes than hugs. "I was the last one and he was really thanking me, with tears," says Mayor DeBrum. "I thought he was touched by the love of the people."

"Alvarenga thought we were there to arrest him. He put his hands together toward me like he was asking if we were going to handcuff him," says Captain Dennis Jibas, who was in charge of *Lomor*, the patrol boat. Captain Jibas felt sympathy for the lost fisherman. "The first place I took him was the freezer, asking him if he wanted to eat, and his sign language for yes was a thumbs-up."

Sleeping in the comfortable and cushioned officer's quarters, in a room devoid of portholes, Alvarenga was saved the trauma of ocean at eye level. During the rough ocean crossing, Alvarenga stayed belowdecks in a room conveniently located across the hall from the galley. Jibas says, "I personally checked on him and every time I went, he was busy eating: chicken, ribs, salad and rice, ramen, biscuits or anything the duty watch cooked up. This was very surprising to me. I really thought he was going to be seasick."

After twenty-three hours, Alvarenga noticed a bustle. He looked out the window on the deck and saw a handful of boats at anchor. "Wow! A real port," he thought. Alvarenga had arrived at Majuro. "Coming alongside our HQ wharf, he showed concerns about the number of people waiting there to see him," says Captain Jibas. "I don't think he liked being in crowds." Who were all these people? Alvarenga sensed that he was again the center of attention, exactly what a restless prisoner planning an escape didn't need.

Spanish speakers in Majuro were scarce, so when Norman Barth, deputy chief of mission at the United States Embassy, offered his fluent Spanish and volunteered to be translator, the Marshallese were pleased. Barth would be not only a translator but also an interrogator. The press had been speculating about the veracity of Alvarenga's tale for days; now it was time for officialdom to decide. Was Alvarenga's story true? What kind of hoax or criminal activity might be lurking behind this unbelievable tale? Was it even possible for a person to drift six thousand miles across the Pacific Ocean and survive to tell about it?

Had they been in Washington, Brussels or Geneva it is unlikely that the Marshall Island officials could have found anyone more qualified than Barth to get to the bottom of this mystery. Although his fluorescent green Hawaiian shirt, baseball hat and khaki pants painted him as a hapless tourist, behind those round-rimmed glasses was a mind honed to detect deception.

Over the course of his US State Department career, Barth conducted more than thirty thousand visa adjudication interviews in Mexico. His job was interviewing visa applicants and separating the scammers from legitimate refugees and legal immigrants. He was not a man easily duped and had spent years interviewing Mexicans. "If he says he's been drifting for a year, then I think, is this guy an impostor? Is this a hoax? Those are natural questions for a guy like me," says Barth. "I have seen all kinds of hoaxes and frauds and also all kinds of totally legitimate but incredible stories."

Barth, US Ambassador Tom Armbruster, a group of Foreign Ministry officials and Damien Jacklick, the director of immigration for the Marshall Islands, all crowded into the tight quarters of the police boat. Alvarenga was overwhelmed. It looked like the prosecutor, judge and jury had all shown up.

Barth, speaking Spanish, decided to go soft on the opening. "I said, 'Welcome to Majuro. Today is the first day of your rebirth.' As much as I was hoping that there would be some kind of reaction, there was nothing." After a few minutes of pleasantries, Barth drilled down on Alvarenga. "There was some confusion. He couldn't give me his date of birth. He said he was either thirty-six or thirty-seven." When Barth asked for his full name, Alvarenga was unable to provide exact spelling. He said, "You know, whatever."

"That was a data point for me," says Barth. "I thought, I don't know if this guy can even write. I don't think he knows how to spell." Alvarenga could barely keep his eyes focused on Barth, who was giving him the third degree about the spelling of his last name. This was the fourth time he had asked if it was A-L-B-A-R-E-N-G-A or A-L-V-A-R-E-N-G-A. "Fraudsters will often try to play on misspellings and so forth," says Barth. "That's one of the reasons I really wanted to get his name spelled properly."

Alvarenga told Barth he worked in southern Mexico as a shark fisherman for a man named Willy. Alvarenga was unable to give the last name of his boss, the name of the company or any other corroborating details. "I thought, this is your financial basis, whether you catch shark or not? And you're selling it to this guy Willy for a dollar fifty a kilo? That means you've got to get a hundred kilos of shark meat to get $150? More than being on the edge of poverty, he was right on the edge of subsistence. That was another data point."

"Physically I could tell he was hurting," says Jacklick, who watched Barth's interrogation. "It was hard for him to move around. He had problems with his joints; he wasn't bending his knees much, or his elbows much. I could see him go into this phase where he was reliving the whole situation. It took him a while to come out of it. I knew he was living it again, and picturing the whole thing, and trying to verbally describe it."

While Alvarenga fell into paranoia about prison and immigration law violations, the stunned officials gathered around the small table on the police boat in Majuro Harbor looked at him with growing awe and deep respect. Rather than arrest him they were more inclined to ask for his autograph or take a selfie with the grizzled survivor. Alvarenga's tale was so achingly honest that despite the contradictions in dates and details the overall arc was undeniably authentic. It felt like they were hearing history firsthand. It was as if they had been allowed to debrief Shackleton.

CHAPTER 16

Ambushed by Cockroaches

On February 3, 2014, as Salvador Alvarenga finished answering questions aboard the police boat in Majuro Harbor, a growing crowd gathered on the shore for a first look at the enigmatic visitor. The tiny knot of local journalists was now augmented by a crowd of curious onlookers, including a group of volunteer teachers from Boston, a pair of visiting anthropologists and the seasonal crowd of yachties waiting out storm season. For the past several days, the entire island had been abuzz with the news that a Mexican fisherman had washed ashore down by Ebon. The sketchy details pulled together for the first international article detailing Alvarenga's incredible journey had exploded into hundreds of breathless articles around the world. From every international flight that arrived in Majuro, a journalist or two deplaned and began to investigate the incredible tale.

Peering through a porthole, Alvarenga could see the restless crowd at the docks awaiting his appearance. Then he was told to move. It was time to get off the boat. He grabbed a can of Coca-Cola and shuffled toward the gangplank. A male nurse steadied him but the ramp was narrow so Alvarenga went alone. As he took his first steps, a chorus of questions, calls and shouts erupted. "Is that a Budweiser in your hand?" one bystander screamed.

Dressed in a baggy brown sweatshirt that disguised his reedy torso, he disembarked slowly but unaided. His round face and bushy beard made him look, in the words of one observer, "like a roly-poly, happy Santa Claus." Expecting a gaunt and bedridden victim, the crowd was engulfed by a wave of disbelief. Alvarenga cracked a quick smile and waved to the cameras. With his bushy beard and wild hair, several observers noted a similarity to the Tom Hanks character in the movie *Cast Away*. The photo of the bearded fisherman shuffling ashore went viral around the world. Briefly, Alvarenga became a household name.

As he was placed on a stretcher and loaded into an ambulance, a pack of photographers descended. "All those lights and spotlights in my face drove me crazy. It was like lightning so I pretended to sleep," said Alvarenga. "I survived the sea, but really thought I was going to die right there. I was not capable of answering questions. I could barely even walk."

Sean Cox, a volunteer English teacher living on the island, heard the rumor that the castaway was from Mexico. As a former Peace Corps volunteer in Panama, the six-foot-four-inch teacher spoke decent Spanish and figured he might be able to assist. He walked over to the hospital, weaved his way through a lax net of security and landed by the castaway's bedside. By nightfall he was Alvarenga's translator, trusted wingman, media shield and go-to man for junk food. "I don't really like the spotlight and I could tell that after what he went through at sea, he didn't really want a bunch of people swarming around, didn't want to soak up the fame," says Cox, who was working with World Teach, a nonprofit from Boston with long-standing ties to the Marshall Islands. "It was overwhelming."

With help from Barth's interview a first message went from the Marshall Islands to Mexico. The best clues to identifying Alvarenga were the name of his boat—*Camaroneros de la Costa #3*—and the registration number—0701343713-3. A call to the Fisheries Ministry in Mexico City was redirected to the division in the southern city of Tonalá. The official who answered immediately recognized *Camaroneros de la Costa* as Willy's outfit. Everybody in Tonalá and neighboring Paredón knew the garrulous and generous owner of a half-dozen fishing boats. The officials in Majuro were stunned when the Mexicans confirmed the boat had embarked from Costa Azul, a small Mexican fishing village.

Increasingly, the officials in Majuro received evidence that the fisherman's tale was possibly true, although several of the key details were off. Instead of "Salvador" the manifest had listed his name as "Cirilio," a nickname that Alvarenga had picked up as a child. But as the *Guardian* newspaper aptly noted, "Mexican official reports commonly contain mistakes." More evidence came in when the *Guardian*'s Mexico correspondent Jo Tuckman interviewed Chiapas search-and-rescue official Jaime Marroquin, who detailed a desperate search for Alvarenga and Córdoba. "The winds were high," Marroquin told the *Guardian* in the first confirmation of the search. "We carried out an intense search but we had to stop the search flights after two days because of poor visibility."

It was late evening when Mexican officials tracked down Alvarenga's supervisor. They dialed Mino's phone number in Costa Azul. It was his father, Jarocho, who answered the phone. "They asked for the registration number of boat number three," Jarocho recalls. "I gave them the number and they told me it was found, with a guy alive." Too old to sprint, Jarocho hurried down the dirt street to tell his son the unbelievable news. "*Mino! Mino! Mino!* Your boat showed up on the other side of the world *with a survivor!*"

Mino understood immediately. He was sure the survivor was his companion Chancha, who had never been far from his dreams. Mino went wild; he jumped into his pickup and made the thirty-five-mile journey—including police and military checkpoints attempting to slow the massive cocaine flow headed north—in a record thirty minutes. He charged into the Civil Protection offices in Tonalá, just off the coast. The official on duty confirmed the sketchy information. The boat *Camaroneros de la Costa #3* had been found in the Marshall Islands. No one had any idea where that was. They searched on Google and looked in awe at the breadth of the Pacific. Mino left the office and drove back to Costa Azul. He was crazy with joy. Who else could it be but Chancha?

Back in Majuro, doctors and nurses were running a series of tests on the frail fisherman. As a nurse withdrew blood, Alvarenga protested. "I told her she should be putting blood in rather than taking it out." Alvarenga appeared weak so doctors ordered intravenous hydration. "He was in psychosocial shock," says Franklin House, a doctor visiting the Marshall Islands from Texas who, thanks to his fluent Spanish, was drafted to diagnose the weakened castaway. "He acted like he didn't know how to respond to anything that was going on around him. I was impressed with how scarred up he was on his legs and arms."

When Dr. House returned to check on his patient later that day, he found him digging into a plateful of food, including a chicken breast and a large drumstick. "How's the chicken?" Dr. House asked.

"This chicken is really good," said Alvarenga. "Especially without feathers!"

"What do you mean by that?" Dr. House was confused.

"You don't know how many birds I ate during those thirteen months," Alvarenga said nonchalantly. "I ate them, feathers and all."

On February 4, Jack Niedenthal and Suzanne Chutaro—on assignment from CNN—awoke early and by 7:30 a.m. were inside the hospital setting up an interview with Alvarenga. "His legs were emaciated, like pencils, and he had cuts all over him. He was not in good shape," said Niedenthal. "He had all this hair, this beard. He looked like the wild man of Borneo."

Even before the interview began, Niedenthal found evidence that the frightened, bearded man was telling the truth. "He had no idea what a clip-on microphone was. He was freaked out by the microphones," says Niedenthal. "If this was a hoax he would be clipping that thing on. He was perplexed by the whole interview process." Alvarenga slowly opened up. He discussed his life at sea. He detailed eating raw fish, raw birds, fighting with sharks and nursing Córdoba until he died. His background story was that of a veteran shark fisherman who lost his motor and drifted from shore. In one segment, Alvarenga discussed suicide and drew an imaginary knife across his throat to illustrate how close he came to slicing his own throat. Forty-five minutes into the interview Alvarenga declared, "I can't do this," and popped the microphone off. He told the reporters he wanted to return to his hospital room. "They hung a NO VISITORS sign on his door," says Niedenthal. "And suddenly it was story over."

Niedenthal and Chutaro had snared a world exclusive, forty-five minutes of Alvarenga outlining his wild survival. Niedenthal sent the tape to Atlanta but didn't get the response he expected. CNN producers were livid. Nearly the entire tape was unsuitable for broadcast. The translator's voice could be heard throughout as he drowned out Alvarenga's answers. Only a few tidbits were broadcast. The short piece did little to enlighten the world about the veracity of Alvarenga's claims and left Niedenthal feeling guilty. A thoughtful filmmaker who produced pro-Marshallese documentaries, he was shocked at his own behavior chasing the story, at any cost. "Alvarenga broke down on camera. He wasn't ready for it. He never meant to be famous, or treated like a celebrity; he wanted to go back home. It was stressful for him to have that in his face. After not being around any humans, the last thing he wanted to do was talk to reporters."

Jacklick, the immigration chief, was fast becoming Alvarenga's confidant and worked overtime to protect him from the media. "José [Alvarenga] said from the get-go that he didn't want any interviews, or picture taking, none of that," says Jacklick. "I respected his wishes, and I protected him from the press the whole time. If anyone wanted to request an interview, they did it through me. And, of course, I denied all the requests."

On February 6, Alvarenga was released from the hospital in what proved to be a hasty and ill-advised diagnosis of good health. He was booked into a hotel under a fake name. "I wasn't in any condition to remember anything. My head was filled with bad thoughts. I was trying to get my mind back to normal," said Alvarenga. "And the reporters were asking me to do things that I shouldn't be doing. That is why I asked them to put themselves in my position. I was sick. I would tell my story but please give me time."

Jacklick arranged for a barber to visit Alvarenga's hotel. As the barber snipped and shaved, Alvarenga's face slowly emerged. Alvarenga smiled as the barber finished his work. Cleanliness was a part of his simple pride. When the barber passed Alvarenga a mirror to look at himself, he began touching his face in slow reverence. It was as if he was regaining his identity.

Though his hotel room had a view of the lagoon, Alvarenga felt trapped. "He opened up the blinds, saw the water and gave this look of disgust and said, 'How ugly,'" says Sean Cox. "He slammed the curtain shut and said, 'I'm tired of looking at that.'"

Alvarenga asked for and received chocolates, cigarettes and potato chips. "I'm sure his stomach was giving him problems," says Cox. "And I know it probably wasn't the best thing, but I was giving him whatever food he wanted."

As another flood of Alvarenga survival stories pulsed around the world, in El Salvador, a fourteen-year-old cruising the Internet recognized the name José Salvador Alvarenga. Same last name as her cousin Fatima, who was cooking across the hall with her grandmother at their home near the sea in Garita Palmera, El Salvador. "Fatima, look at this," she called out. "This guy has the same last name as you. They say it is your father."

Fatima was unconvinced until her mother studied the picture and "recognized his hands." Fatima began to cry. "God listened to my prayers! Finally I was going to know my dad. This is scary, I told myself. Then I cried and cried as I looked at my dad and thought about all that time in the ocean."

Several days later, Alvarenga was spirited out of his hotel room and taken to a government office to speak on a video call with his family, who had traveled to the Foreign Relations ministry in the capital of El Salvador. Alvarenga had last seen his parents during a brief visit seven years earlier. His daughter, Fatima, was then living with her mother in Guatemala. Alvarenga had not seen her since a year after her birth fourteen years earlier. Now Fatima was a teenager. The thought of a reunion with his grown daughter flooded him with fears. What if she refused to forgive him? What would be her first reaction to her estranged, yet world-famous, father? Would she see a dad or a deadbeat? "I couldn't really talk, it was too much," said Alvarenga once his family popped up on Skype. "My mom, my daughter, my dad was there. It was hard to believe it was true."

Fatima stared back, also in disbelief. This was her father? "He was shaven and he said hello and then he started crying," Fatima remembers. "I could not believe it, there he was. My dream comes true." But the connection was more of a group cry than conversation. Everyone felt awkward. Alvarenga was not ready for another shock to his already upended worldview. "Everything was scary. I was filled with terror. I cried a lot," said Alvarenga, who was now stalked by a crew of paparazzi. He nicknamed the press *cucarachas* (cockroaches). Before leaving his hotel room, he would ask his handlers to "check outside the door, I think cockroaches are near."

Steve Callahan, the author of *Adrift*, lived the same kind of madness when he returned to the United States after drifting across the Atlantic in a tiny, inflatable life raft. "The press pack is a bit like a shark feeding frenzy. They buzz around, all interested in you until they take a little bite, and then they swim off, never to be heard from again. And you're left an emotional rag, wrung out."

Alvarenga's medical condition steadily worsened. His feet and legs were constantly swollen. The doctors suspected the tissues had been deprived of water for so long that now they soaked up everything. The backs of Alvarenga's knees were so swollen he had trouble walking. A volunteer who was helping massage Alvarenga's legs and his feet says, "His skin was like a Barbie doll's; it felt plastic and fake. The poor man couldn't move; it was horrible."

After eleven days in the Marshall Islands, doctors determined that Alvarenga's health had stabilized enough for him to travel home to El Salvador. The US Embassy arranged for VIP treatment along the route, including tarmac boarding, an exemption from security checkpoints and doctors to examine Alvarenga at his stops in Hawaii and Los Angeles. Even for a seasoned traveler the trip would have been brutal—fifteen hours of flights and fifteen hours of layovers—and Alvarenga was flying for the first time. "It was my first time on an airplane. I didn't want to get on," Alvarenga said. "I had been saved from death at sea and now I was going to risk dying again."

As passengers filed aboard the plane, a pack of journalists pounced as they sought to pull out details of his story. No matter that Alvarenga could barely talk or that his brain was still fogged over by so much commotion, the reporters wanted a few exclusive words from the half-collapsed fisherman. The drought of fresh interviews over the past two weeks had made the reporters desperate; they leaned in, filmed, took pictures and ignored pleas to back off.

With headphones strapped on, his de facto bodyguard to his right and a posse of journalists looking for a chance to swoop in, Alvarenga nearly jumped out of his seat when he heard the roar of jet engines. Alvarenga began to shake; he was terrified. "He was very nervous," says Diego Dalton, the El Salvadoran diplomat who traveled with Alvarenga. "When the wheels left the ground, he was holding on really tight to his seat."

As the plane arched skyward, Alvarenga watched a few seconds of land whip by, then wide-open ocean. As he peered out the window Alvarenga feared he would be trapped at sea again. What if the plane fell into the water? Realizing that Alvarenga was becoming agitated, Dalton pulled the curtain shut and turned up the music. Alvarenga couldn't help peeking out the window. It was a mixture of fear and curiosity. "I thought about my entire trip," he said. "My mind started to spin and spin. I was hallucinating that I could see small boats down there."

Leaving Hawaii, Alvarenga flew to Los Angeles, where he spent the night in a hotel. Most of the press had lost his trail, but on the final leg of his trip two reporters booked seats across the aisle. As soon as Alvarenga was aboard they began to film. Dalton asked for privacy, insisting that Alvarenga was weak and needed peace and quiet. The reporters refused to turn off the cameras. Dalton turned to the pilot, Carlos Dárdano, for help. "Listen, you're flying business class, so first of all, behave like you're in business class," Dárdano scolded the stunned reporters. "If I want, I can kick you out of the plane. I don't care if you've paid business class out of your own pocket. So behave, and let the passenger have a relaxing flight."

Alvarenga was exhausted by the constant press harassment. When would they leave him alone? When would he get his life back? Without his cloak of anonymity to protect him, Alvarenga was floundering. He was an instant celebrity catapulted into the grind of the news cycle at just the moment he was trying to find both his own self and his place in society. He was in an awkward place, one inhabited by many war veterans and survivors of deep trauma.

As his final flight descended toward El Salvador, Alvarenga began to tremble. "He was very nervous," said Dalton. The thirty-hour trip across the Pacific Ocean was nearly over and Alvarenga prepared to face not only a mad crowd of paparazzi but also blunt questions from his daughter, Fatima. He had abandoned her when she was one year old. She was a mystery daughter and he was the dad who had deserted her. Throughout the worst moments adrift, Alvarenga's spirits feasted from a bountiful vision. He had promised to trade in his party-boy lifestyle for the joy of life as a doting dad. But that role had been an invention of his imagination, a response to a deep psychological need in a moment of maximum stress. Now he had to adapt that fantasy to the embarrassing reality that he couldn't even pick out his fourteen-year-old daughter's face from the crowd at the airport.

CHAPTER 17

Call of the Sea

R ather than meet his family as scheduled, after he landed in El Salvador Alvarenga was immediately hospitalized and given a new battery of tests. After a week of being locked up on Ebon and a second week hiding and running from the press in the Marshall Islands, Alvarenga was no longer the obliging patient. His feisty independence roared back. He was on his home turf, where everyone understood Spanish. Now he was free to think, travel and speak out as he pleased. "They wanted to put all these monitors on me but I said no. I would never let them do that to me," Alvarenga recounted. He refused to be tethered down by tubes. "In the Marshall Islands they told me I didn't need them [the tubes]. If I had let them hook up all those instruments I was fucked."

Alvarenga was not interested in being interviewed by doctors. He was sick of journalists. He understood what ailed him: he needed to get back home, to escape these smocked specialists who questioned him by day, gave him pills at night and served boring meals hardly worth eating. Hospitals were for sick people. He was tired of being treated like an invalid. Mom's food would rekindle his strength. His daughter's presence would boost his morale.

Alvarenga believed he didn't need a doctor to diagnose what was wrong. He was suffering from a yearlong tortilla drought.

Nearly every day of his journey at sea he had imagined toasted tortillas. During his two weeks in the Marshall Islands he begged for corn tortillas but was told to wait, that no one ate tortillas in the middle of the Pacific. But here in El Salvador, he was sure tortillas were nearby. Within hours of being checked into the hospital in Santa Tecla, Alvarenga placed an order—as if he were in a take-out restaurant—for a heaping plate of hot tortillas. The nurses refused his petition. Alvarenga insisted. A doctor was called in to explain dietary restrictions to the insistent patient. "They denied me tortillas," said an indignant Alvarenga. It was an affront to his national pride—how could a Salvadoran be denied his birthright? Alvarenga began to scream, "Tortillas! Bring me tortillas!" The nurses broke out in laughter and cheerfully brought him a tiny plate of white rice.

Alvarenga's doctors were not tricked by the fisherman's bravado and demands for tortillas. They suspected that he was descending into a psychological pit, not unlike post-traumatic stress disorder, in which flashbacks, nightmares and feelings of guilt wreak havoc on an already confused mind.

Finally, after hours of waiting, Alvarenga's mother, Maria, was allowed to see her son. She prayed as she entered the room, giving thanks to God for the miracle of having her son back from the brink. She was certain that only God's generosity explained his extraordinary survival. Maria hugged her son, Salvador, for the first time in years as they both sobbed. "I was mute, I couldn't talk," Alvarenga said. His mind also focused on giving thanks. While he did not pray aloud or verbalize his vigorous belief in a God above, Alvarenga felt protected. He now shared his mother's unshakable faith. During his ordeal, Alvarenga's religious convictions were sparked by his more religious crewmate, Ezequiel, and then internalized. After the death of his companion, Alvarenga felt accompanied by a faith he couldn't define but rarely questioned.

For nearly an hour, mother and son quietly shared silence. She prayed; he gave thanks. Then it was time to meet his daughter. When Fatima entered, Alvarenga was still mute. Fatima massaged her father's hands as she silently gawked at his rough skin, assorted tattoos and deep scars. "She did not pressure me about anything. I just managed a couple of words," said Alvarenga. "I liked it when she touched my head, my feet. I felt her presence."

Fatima was shy as she first held his hand and then hugged her father. "He had a big smile but he was not present, he was kind of sinking," she said. She was scared by the look of her father's "swollen and shiny" legs. But she was quietly ecstatic. "All my prayers had been answered, now I had a father." Fatima wanted to ask her father dozens of questions. She was curious about his time at sea. What kind of food did he eat? How did he sleep? Was it scary? Had he seen mermaids?

The doctors in El Salvador were well aware that Alvarenga's mental health was fragile so they strictly restricted visits. A policeman was posted outside Alvarenga's room. The bedridden survivor wrote a note to the press asking to be left alone, yet cameras still flashed inside his semi-private room and a reporter dressed as a doctor made a crude effort to steal a few words from the prone but now feisty fisherman. Alvarenga was no longer surprised by the paparazzi attacks. "I remember this really tall guy, he told me he was a psychologist. But really he was trying to steal my story," Alvarenga said. "He offered me a telephone if I told him my story. I said no; then he said he would give me a refrigerator."

For nine days, Alvarenga was hospitalized. He was diagnosed with anemia and doctors suspected his diet of raw turtles and raw birds had infected his liver with parasites. Alvarenga believed the parasites might rise up to his head and attack his brain. Deep sleep was impossible.

When he managed to fall asleep his mind erupted in nightmares, flashbacks to his fear of returning to his small village in El Salvador, where he had been badly beaten years earlier. "I dreamed I was being chased by people who wanted to kill me. I'm not sure who or why, just that they wanted to kill me." His dreams were also filled with images of birds. "I would imagine that I was talking to the birds, then eating them and then getting sick."

The vision of eating raw birds and falling ill was a flashback to Córdoba's tragic death. Alvarenga thought often about the young man. It was the part of his story that everyone wanted to hear and the most painful to dredge up. Their relationship was born of mutual suffering. It was forged by smashing waves, freezing rain and slow starvation. Alvarenga felt no guilt for the young man's death, yet he longed to have Córdoba by his side. If only the young man had learned to eat seabird ceviche. Alvarenga imagined their joint celebration. It was not the same to celebrate alone. Alvarenga acknowledged Córdoba's key role in his own survival. He had learned to pray from Córdoba and the storytelling tools he employed to keep his own sanity while adrift and alone for ten full cycles of the full moon were fruits of his earlier efforts to motivate his dying shipmate. He was anxious to complete the promise to deliver a message to Córdoba's mother, Ana Rosa. Alvarenga had vowed to visit her in El Fortin, the small village just north of Alvarenga's former home in Costa Azul, Mexico. As soon as he was strong enough, he would travel to Mexico and deliver those final words directly to Córdoba's mother.

———

On February 19, Salvador Alvarenga finally arrived home as reporters snapped photos, party music blared and relatives lined the entrance to his family's five-room cinder block home. Arely Barrera, his former girlfriend and Fatima's mother, appeared nervous and unsure of her role in his new life as folk hero. They shared a timid hug. When he saw Fatima, Alvarenga grabbed his daughter and announced, "I love you, and I am not going to let you go!" Fatima hugged him even harder.

But Alvarenga did not adjust well to life at home. "I turned on the shower and ran away from the water. I was so traumatized that I preferred to use a bucket," Alvarenga said as he described the difficulty of assimilating to simple routines. When his bathing bucket mixed with a handful of red dirt, Alvarenga screamed and went running from the sight. His brain confused the murky red water with a bucket of fresh turtle blood.

During the first days, he spoke barely a word to Fatima. She would sit on his bed and look into his eyes, wondering how he survived more than a year adrift at sea. He smiled at her but for weeks delayed his first talk. Finally he gathered the energy and clarity to open his heart to his daughter. "I know I didn't raise you and that all those years are lost," he said. "But Dad is here to give you advice, to help you learn right from wrong."

Fatima was dubious. "Why didn't you ever come back for me? You forgot me!"

Alvarenga explained that she was the reason he survived at sea, how he fought to stay alive in order to see her, to help raise her. "I asked God to be with you, that he let us be together."

Fatima countered that before his ordeal, he had been safe on land for years and made no effort to find her or reach out. "Why did you leave me?"

"I was a party guy, I was drinking and using drugs. I had big problems." Alvarenga gave her the straight truth, though he did not detail the near-fatal beating that had also influenced his decision to leave town.

The new father and teenage daughter hugged. It was not the magical moment of bonding that either had imagined, but at least it was no longer a fantasy. Despite the difficult questions and painful answers, they each felt a deep relief at being united. "I called him 'Dad,'" said Fatima, who could see that her parents' breakup was imminent. She would soon have to choose between living with her mother, who was moving to Guatemala, or remain with her father in El Salvador. She had already decided. She was staying with her dad.

Alvarenga was in a stupor for weeks, barely able to communicate. "He was very strange," Fatima said. "His legs were swollen and he could hardly walk. He was always tired. He would just sit in bed with the fan running in his face. Even talking made him tired. You had to speak really slowly and some words he didn't understand. I never saw him cry. I think he did that at night." Fatima's initial elation at having her father home was complicated by her fears that "he might stay like that and then I was going to be alone again. But bit by bit, he got better."

Asked what it was like to have a father after so many years without, Fatima paused. "At first he felt like Daddy number two. My grandfather Ricardo was like my first father and he [Salvador] was like my second father." Week by week, her father migrated out of the zombie phase and was able to focus on day-to-day life as the two began to share more time. "Then we laughed a lot," Fatima said, describing long sessions hunched over a cell phone watching YouTube videos together. "My favorite game is to ambush him. I hide behind the dresser or in the corner and make sounds. Then I jump out and he starts shaking." Fatima never understood the absolute panic she caused her father with her innocent pranks.

"I have a lot of questions but I'm not sure if he will answer them," Fatima admitted. "When I ask him about his trip, he looks like he is tranquil, but I can tell that on the inside he is suffering. He looks down, he turns tense and his face changes color."

Fallout from his trauma at sea was constant. Alvarenga remained hyper-vigilant to the most basic environmental changes. When he heard objects bump together, he thought of turtles. "I still imagined that I smelled like fish," he admitted. But he no longer feared the sea and was contemplating the challenge of heading back out. "I could be a shrimper, they only go out twelve miles," Alvarenga confessed. "Even if my motor died I could still make it back in."

Fatima rejected the idea. "I told him no. What if he got lost again and did not make it back?"

Walking along the beach with Fatima, he beamed with pride when a photographer snapped pictures of them together. "I love it and she can't believe it," said Alvarenga as he hugged Fatima.

Having a famous father made life at school easier for Fatima. Classmates constantly asked her to explain how her dad ate raw birds, caught sharks with his hands and fought off the shadow of suicide. "I have more friends now," said Fatima. "I am kind of shy but people thought I was stuck up so they didn't talk to me. Now they talk to me more even though I am the same as always." Her classmates called her Naufraga ("Castaway") in honor of her dad.

As Fatima described life with her father, a workman at the family home in El Salvador poured cement from a bucket, while a second worker used a wooden 2x4 to smooth out the surface. Alvarenga watched with care: this was not just any floor. This was the dance floor. Soon the house would be filled with partygoers, flowers, catered food and music. Fatima was turning fifteen, which in Central America can require an event as extravagant as a wedding. She had the dress, was practicing the waltz and best of all counted on a prized guest: her dad.

———

Of all his worldly possessions there is probably nothing more cherished by Alvarenga than his first car, a 2005 Chevrolet Aveo sedan. He washed it frequently. Made plans to paint it and enthusiastically described slick racing stripes or gaudy color combinations. Although he had no license, he drove hours every day. He didn't drive fast or far, often slumbering along at 5 mph, the window down, radio blaring as he chatted with childhood friends or flirted with admirers. His pace was slower than a bicycle. It was not speed he sought but movement. As if he'd become addicted to drifting, Alvarenga had a need to move. The drive around town was four miles and then he looped back outside his parents' flour mill. It was his therapy. Fatima sometimes accompanied him, proudly riding shotgun and laughing at her dad's repeated circles and repeated jokes.

In many ways Salvador Alvarenga was overly protective of Fatima. He didn't like her talking or texting with boys her age. When these teenage boys came by to visit, Alvarenga gruffly ran them off, despite Fatima's assertions that they were only friends. But he also endowed her with some of his vaunted survival skills. Her favorite food is "turtle heads with salt" and her main after-school activity driving lessons with her dad. In macho El Salvador, where the roles available to women are limited, many women still don't know how to drive. Alvarenga broke tradition and taught Fatima the value of independence. On the rocky roads around town, he invited Fatima to take the wheel.

As Fatima started up the automatic transmission, her father smiled. The engine was running but Fatima still cranked over the key, eliciting a grinding howl of protest from the ignition. She shifted into drive and jammed the accelerator. Gravel whipped out like buckshot and a cloud of dust briefly eclipsed the cornfields across the street. Fatima smiled as she corrected a wide left arc to avoid whacking a fence post. "I feel confident. Really confident," she announced. "I like to drive fast but Dad is worried that if a cow crosses I won't be able to stop." Her father turned to admire his daughter's plucky confidence. She stalled on a rocky patch of unpaved road, and then shredded the ignition again. Salvador, who babies his car, seemed unfazed by the violent shriek. What did it matter if his daughter couldn't drive on land? His world was at sea, battling the wind, steering a course through the waves and savoring the distance from the furies of life on land.

———

As soon as his health permitted, Alvarenga made plans to return to Mexico. His trip was a fusion of two missions. First, he needed to complete his promise to his dying mate, Córdoba. Lost at sea he had sworn to bear witness and explain the circumstances of young Ezequiel Córdoba's death to his family. Second, he needed to visit his former colleagues at the fishing community. Although Alvarenga could barely walk, he felt obliged to fulfill his commitments.

In March 2014, six weeks after he washed ashore, Alvarenga was back on an airplane, this time a short flight to Tapachula, Mexico. His fisherman friends turned out en masse, but after initial greetings Alvarenga wanted to move on. He was in an urgent rush to meet Córdoba's mom and deliver the young man's dying words. Alvarenga had no transportation, so he crowded into a van filled with reporters. The journalists drove him to the meeting with Ana Rosa, Córdoba's mourning mom.

The ramshackle village of El Fortin sits just north of Costa Azul. It is a dusty hamlet where electricity and freshwater are still luxuries. Few residents own cars and except for a twice-a-day van, there are few opportunities to drive out of town. But like many villages in this coastal section of Chiapas, life and work are centered around the sea.

Protected by thick walls of mangrove forests, El Fortin is home to several hundred brave fishermen who either throw nets in the lagoon or risk the commute into the wild open ocean. Córdoba's brothers were fishermen, pulling manta rays from the calm waters of the lagoon or heading over the horizon on full-day deep-sea ventures to catch sharks.

As Alvarenga awaited his audience with Ana Rosa, the other Córdoba brothers puffed their chests in a clear provocation toward the last man to have seen their brother alive. Alvarenga was in no mood to fight. Even smiling was difficult. He was there as the bearer of bad news, a messenger of death. He needed to complete his vow to his deceased companion. He needed to speak alone with Córdoba's grieving mom.

For two hours, Alvarenga sat with Ana Rosa, answered her questions and explained Ezequiel's slow death. Doña Rosa asked for more details. Did her son suffer? Alvarenga explained that her son Ezequiel had died in peace. "Then she couldn't listen anymore. She cried so much and asked me what I did with the body. I told her."

Córdoba's brothers were not convinced. They had doubts and continued to question Alvarenga. He invited them to ride along on the hour drive to the fishermen's headquarters in Paredón. If they wanted to know the details of their brother's death they were invited, but no one took up the offer. Alvarenga was eager to leave the tense scene. He had answered all their questions, delivered the message to Ana Rosa and, most important, received her blessing. "She listened and said she did not blame me, that my conscience should be free," said Alvarenga. "She said she would never think that I had killed her son."

Having completed his obligation to Córdoba, Alvarenga now focused on his personal objective: to investigate why his buddies had not found him on the first day of the fateful storm. He doubted they had really looked. His last radio call came when he was just twenty miles offshore. Why hadn't they rescued him during those first hours?

As he traveled to Paredón, a deep anger rose up. If they had mounted a proper search-and-rescue operation he would never have gone adrift. When Alvarenga arrived in the fishing village of Paredón, Willy and Mino, his boss and his supervisor, were smiling and ecstatic to see their lost colleague. Alvarenga was angry. He met his former bosses not with a smile or a hug, but a direct accusation.

"You think I am worthless?" Alvarenga targeted his hostile questioning at Mino, his former supervisor.

"Hey, Chancha," said Mino. "Don't be saying that. I know what you are thinking."

"Okay, explain it to me," said Alvarenga. "I'm listening."

"We went out for three days looking for you," said Mino as he described how a total of four boats had patrolled the sea and found not a single piece of wreckage or gear. Mino detailed the entire rescue. The boats. The airplane. Alvarenga was skeptical so Mino went to his home and returned with a file of the search report, complete with official papers and even the name of the pilot who had come down from the city of Tuxtla Gutiérrez to fly the search plane.

Alvarenga now felt guilty and made a confession to Mino and Willy. "I gave your boat away," Alvarenga told Mino. He explained how he had gifted the boat to Emi and Russel on the other side of the world. "Don't talk to me about boats," said Mino, who even in hard times was known as a generous supervisor. "You're alive. That's all that matters. Boats we have."

The fishermen organized a small get-together at Mino's house. They had music, friends and a steady stream of rum, grain alcohol and beer. Alvarenga skipped the booze—he was dizzy enough being on land. He didn't down a single drink, smoke a cigarette or joint. He was looking for ways to slow down, not agitate his already rattled mind.

As his colleagues drank, Alvarenga raised another sensitive topic. Was it true they had all attended his funeral? Alvarenga felt betrayed. How could they hold a funeral for him if he was alive? Why hadn't they maintained faith?

"They told me how they threw flowers at sea and drank coffee [a tradition at fishermen's funerals]," said Alvarenga. "I was waiting for them to say they had kept hope that I was alive but they *coffeed* me. I started to shake. I went into a trance thinking about that. 'They *coffeed* me.'"

Alvarenga was incredulous. "I was suffering," he told his colleagues, "and you guys were enjoying a coffee here? I was begging for food and you smoked pot!"

"Yeah, we *coffeed* you, Chancha," admitted Trumpillo.

"You should have sent me food," responded Alvarenga.

"We smoked, we drank," admitted Trumpillo. "We were thinking about you."

"Instead of thinking, you should have saved me," said Alvarenga.

Alvarenga's unruly accusations masked his deep relief at rejoining his colleagues. Here in the fishing shacks, the slapping of the ocean sounded not like a tortured reminder of his nightmare at sea but an invitation to return home. Although they cultivated the image of outlaws, these fishermen were governed by a strict set of rules, but not the kind of guidelines that would ever be written or published. Alvarenga's funeral ceremony had followed that same logic. Los Tiburoneros (The Sharkers) failed to understand Alvarenga's anger over the fact that they had honored his life with flowers, candles and coffee. That was tradition. It was greater than any one man.

Eating plate after plate of mahimahi ceviche, Alvarenga's trademark bravado surged. Physically he was shuffling like a disabled war veteran, but he had been onshore for six weeks; his mind was now better able to sort friend from foe. Here with his buddies, he began to share the details of his lessons from survival at sea. "I don't waste food now," he told his colleagues. "I used to throw a kilo of tortillas in the sea, for the fish. When I was lost I thought a lot about that. Now I find someone who is hungry and give it to them. I know what it means to be suffering from hunger or thirst."

Several Sharkers insisted that they too could have survived what Alvarenga endured. His response was laden with warning: "I hope for your sake you never have to try. You will cry; you will suffer. You don't want to suffer as I did."

While his friends smoked marijuana, sipped tequila and piled up empty beer cans, Alvarenga held forth. He had always been able to keep his audience's rapt attention. Now he was a storyteller with a world-class adventure. Here there were no taboos. And no land-lubbers. If any crowd could appreciate his epic struggle at sea it was The Sharkers. And if anyone was likely to be lost at sea as a cast-away it was the men in this room. Alvarenga knew this was a tough crew who could handle the exhausting physical challenges of being lost at sea, so he explained a less obvious facet of survival: his mental health. "Don't give up hope, remain calm," he urged. "What could be worse than what happened to me? I always thought that every-thing would work out. What further suffering could there be than what I lived through? I didn't give up." His friends cried, toasted and hugged their beloved Chancha. It was as if a ghost had stepped from their past and brought them stories from the afterlife. As they celebrated and drank, Alvarenga listened again and again to the de-tails of his own funeral as his overjoyed friends opened bottles of tequila in his honor and shouted their joy.

Chancha was alive!

Call of the Sea

The Sharkers cultivated a bad-boy rebel image that was only partly fiction. They were accustomed to living on the cusp of sudden death. As they killed sharks and tuna, butchered bait and measured the weather, their world was a mix of death, danger and beauty. They were the last of a centuries-old tradition of men and the sea. A final generation condemned to fish ever more distant from shore, in an ocean that had been nearly fished out. Many of them realized that within ten years they too would be hanging up their hooks and finding jobs on land. There simply weren't many fish left in the sea. Few of the men wished this life upon their sons. But for now they were *Sharkers*, a wayward tribe of men who spent more time at sea than on land, savored the rough beauty of life at sea and reveled in a deep tribal loyalty.

Willy and Mino and a close friend known as Pulga pulled Alvarenga aside and assured him the loss of the boat was insignificant. They showered him with compliments and stuffed his pockets with orange 500-peso (US$35) notes. "Come back," they urged. "You always caught more than anyone else." Alvarenga considered the offer. A boat. A job. His old life back. In his pocket 15,000 pesos (US$1,200) tempted him to jump back into his Wild West life. Mino, Pulga and Willy wanted him back. The call of the sea was magnetic. It would kill his mother if he did. It might kill him if he didn't. He was a man of the sea. But he was also a father; for now he'd try his luck on land.

Author's Afterword

During the year I interviewed Salvador Alvarenga, I literally saw the transformation of a man before my eyes. Salvador migrated from the arid land of zombies to the green pastures of fatherhood. Initially he had a deep fear of not only the ocean, but even the sound of water. He slept with the lights on and needed to have constant company nearby. Now he enjoys short boat trips, the rock and roll of a small voyage out to sea.

He spends more time with Fatima now, cracking jokes and providing driving lessons to a daughter he dotes upon. This is not to say that he is not forever marked by his trauma. Heavy rain and the crack of lightning are still enough to send him shivering. But after weeks together during my most recent visit to El Salvador, I can say it is his smile that most dominates his face—a broad smile, a hearty laugh and loving family. His dream of renewal, of being a dedicated father, appreciative son and loyal friend has now been fulfilled.

Over the course of the past year, I had much turf to cover. First, I had to discover if his tale was even true. To be honest, I initially doubted the story. Who survives fourteen months at sea? Only a Hollywood screenwriter could write a tale where such a journey ends happily. But as I started to dig, the evidence immediately began to favor Alvarenga's version of events. His background story was never in doubt. He was a well-known and beloved coastal fisherman with a history of surviving against the odds. From the small village of Costa Azul, there were dozens of witnesses who saw him leave shore for what was supposed to be an overnight fishing gig. When, in mid-November 2012, he was trapped by a ferocious storm he radioed a desperate SOS to shore. I interviewed witnesses up and down the coast. When he did not make it home, a search-and-rescue operation lasted for days; even airplanes were sent for him.

Nowhere did I see evidence of a fake or fraud. Furthermore, when Alvarenga landed (with the same boat) thousands of miles away in the Marshall Islands, he was steadfast in his rejection of interviews and press attention—even posting a note on his hospital door begging the press to disappear. This was hardly the attitude of a publicity-seeking scammer. What I repeatedly discovered during my journalistic investigation was a humble man with an endless list of friends and colleagues who detailed his amazing survival skills, buoyant humor and implacable will to live.

Spending time with Salvador was an adventure and an education that I will never forget. One afternoon after his rescue, as we were driving along the Pacific coast of El Salvador, we came around a bend opening up to a lush valley. He spotted yeasty clouds piled high and dark. He began to cry. I was baffled and asked what was wrong. "Those clouds, those clouds, they were the ones that would bring me water. When I saw them I knew I wasn't going to die."

In the smallest details I saw both the scars and the lessons of a survival so brutal yet so achingly human that it has forever marked this remarkable man. "I now appreciate small pleasures," Salvador told me. "Think about it, I didn't see another person for over a year! Or a tree. Or a fruit. Or a tortilla and that is the most blessed of all for me. Not one tortilla."

Author's Afterword

How many of us appreciate the joys of a simple tortilla?

But of all the conversations we shared this past year, I most remember when I asked why he wanted to collaborate on a book. Of course, we both hoped a book would be financially beneficial, but what else motivated him to spend hour after hour with me, telling all the details of his story? I quote at length his answer.

"I suffered so much and for so long. Maybe if people read this they will realize that if I can make it, they can make it. Many people suffer only because of what happens in their head; I was also physically being tortured. I had no food. No water. If I can make it so can you. If one depressed person avoids committing suicide then the book is a success.

"Be strong. Think positive. If you start to think to the contrary, you are headed to failure. Your mind has to be relaxed as you think about survival. Don't think about death. If you think you are going to die, you will die. You have to survive and think about the future of your life, that life is beautiful! How can you imagine taking your own life? There are challenges and punishment in life but you have to fight!"

Note on Time and Mapping

Salvador Alvarenga kept track of time using the cycles of the moon. He was always clear as to how many months he had been adrift. The chronology in this book is a combination of his memory, studies of ocean currents and documents provided by search-and-rescue officials. Special thanks to Nikolai Maximenko and Jan Hafner at the University of Hawaii and Art Allen of the US Coast Guard for their generous work to re-create Alvarenga's voyage.

Note on Translations and Profanities

The Sharkers of Costa Azul use a rich combination of slang and profanity, and in bringing their story to life the translations have been made to convey the essence—not the literal words—of what they said. Although I have lived in South America for seventeen years and am fluent in Spanish, the vernacular of Mexican fishermen was not always easy to translate into English. My apologies for not being able to fully convey their rich humor and cheerful vulgarity.

Acknowledgments

During the course of the year that I researched and wrote this book not only did I travel to practically every major airport in Central America but I was also privileged to enter the world of coastal fishermen in Mexico. It is a land of brutality and poverty but also a noble world filled with trust, generosity and honest living.

I am just the author. Salvador Alvarenga is "The Miracle Man" as the *Marshall Islands Journal* so rightfully christened him. I raise my favorite beer mug in a toast to a great survivor.

As a young reader, I always dreamed of meeting Papillon, the French convict who stirred the world with his 1969 autobiography outlining dashing escapes and stoic resistance while imprisoned in French penal colonies in South America. It was years later that I understood Papillon to be a fiction, as legendary French publisher Robert Laffont admitted before his death. Now I have been blessed to share a year with a real-life Papillon, a modest fisherman who crossed the Pacific Ocean, surviving on brainpower, faith and an endless surplus of optimism.

I want to thank my seven daughters, who put up with Dad being away for weeks on end, always supporting me and brainstorming about what makes a great book. Before too long, I will be editing your manuscripts. I missed you dearly, Francisca, Susan, Maciel, Kim, Amy, Zoe and last but not least my little Akira. Finally to my loving partner, Toty, who never tired of dropping me off

Acknowledgments

at the airport, suffering through impossibly bad Skype connections and keeping our family emotionally united.

Special kudos to my head of research, Bud Theisen, without whom this book would never have been so complete. From tracking down turtle experts to finding world-class meteorologists, Bud was always one step ahead. His role in crafting this story was fundamental and much appreciated.

Also thanks to readers Larry Chollet, Charles Graeber, James Bandler, Samuel Logan, Steven Bodzin and everyone else who read chapters and provided feedback. Lawyers Jeff Masonek and Matt Sugarman took care of the legal details, and at Simon & Schuster's Atria Books imprint I was privy to a dedicated team starting with my editor Peter Borland, who was intensely enthusiastic and encouraging about this project. Along with publisher Judith Carr, Suzanne Donahue, Lisa Keim, Paul Olsewski, David Brown and Daniella Wexler each helped make this book come to life. In El Salvador, photographer Oscar Machón was a generous and solid partner.

George Lucas at Inkwell Management was a star as he negotiated the US contract and answered my million e-mails about the project. My agent, Annabel Merullo, and her colleagues Tim Binding, Rachel Mills, Laura Williams and the team at Peters, Fraser & Dunlop were the instigation for this entire project. Thanks yet again to the keen eye of Annabel!

Finally I would like to thank all the fishermen and their families in Mexico who provided interviews for this book, including Jarocho, Parka, Mino, Willy, Nacho, La Vaca, La Parka, Pulga, Caracha, Pitoya, Nacho, Doña Mina, Doña Reina, Eddy, Laura, Indra, Lionel, Joe in Puerto Escondido, Pedro Vasquez, Omar as well as

Acknowledgments

Rey and The Wolfman, who sat for interviews from inside jail. José Antonio Arreola saved the entire project by returning one very full notebook left in his taxi in Paredón, Mexico. Thanks again, José!

Fatima, Ricardo and Maria Alvarenga shared their home in El Salvador with me during weeks of interviews with their son and father. Carlos Guzmán was forever patient as he organized the logistics of setting up interviews with Salvador.

Finally, another thanks to Salvador Alvarenga. May we all show such grace, humor and humanity when life drives us to the edge of sanity. He is a wonderful teacher and a man who drives better at sea than on land.

Jonathan Franklin
Santiago, Chile

July 2015

Acknowledgments

It was these scientists, diplomats and individuals who, through their generous time, helped me understand the wilds of the Pacific Ocean, the science of survival, the depths of extreme trauma and the firsthand experiences of Salvador Alvarenga. Thanks to all the folks mentioned below (and those not mentioned).

Art Allen	US Coast Guard
Joseph J. Flythe Jr.	Senior Associate, HRS Consulting Inc.
	Former US Coast Guard rescue swimmer trainer
Robert Monroe	Communications Officer, Scripps Institution of Oceanography, UC San Diego
Daniel Deutermann	US Coast Guard (Ret.)
	Managing Director, The Squadron
Blair Witherington	Archie Carr Center for Sea Turtle Research, PhD University of Florida
John Leach	Author, *Survival Psychology*
	Department of Sport and Exercise Science University of Portsmouth, UK
Mario Aguilera	Assistant Director of Communications, Scripps Institution of Oceanography, UC San Diego
Damien Jacklick	Chief of Immigration, Marshall Islands

Acknowledgments

Norman Barth	Deputy Chief of Mission, US Embassy, Marshall Islands
Emi Libokmeto	Islander in Ebon who rescued Alvarenga
Russel Laikidrik	Islander in Ebon who rescued Alvarenga
Jan Hafner	Scientific Computer Programmer, International Pacific Research Center, University of Hawaii
María Elena Figueroa	Community leader, Chocohuital, Mexico
Tom Armbruster	Ambassador, US Embassy, Marshall Islands
Dr. Franklin House	Visiting physician, Marshall Islands
Shang-Ping Xie	Climatologist, Scripps Institution of Oceanography
Sean Dylan Cox	Translator/confidant of Alvarenga in Marshall Islands
Steve Callahan	Author, *Adrift*, consultant on film *Life of Pi*
Suzanne Chutaro	Reporter, *Marshall Islands Journal*
Laurence Gonzales	Author, *Deep Survival: Who Lives, Who Dies, and Why*
Todd Mulroy	Director of World Teach, Marshall Islands
Ola Fjeldstad	Anthropologist working on Ebon
	Roommate with Alvarenga during first days

Acknowledgments

Luca Centurioni	Physical oceanographer
	Director of the Global Drifter Program, Scripps Institution of Oceanography, UC San Diego
Daniel Cartamil	Marine Biologist, Scripps Institution of Oceanography, UC San Diego
Jack Niedenthal	Filmmaker in the Marshall Islands
Diego Dalton	El Salvadoran diplomat
	Deputy Head of Mission, Salvadoran embassy, Japan
Nikolai Maximenko	Senior Researcher, International Pacific Research Center, School of Ocean and Earth Science, University of Hawaii
Michael Tipton	Professor of Human and Applied Physiology
	Coauthor, *Essentials of Sea Survival*
Michael Terlep	Cultural anthropologist, Marshall Islands
Matt Riding	Cultural anthropologist, Marshall Islands
	Alvarenga translator first days in Majuro
Jason Lewis	Global explorer, writer
Jacob Eurich	Marine biologist, underwater photographer, James Cook University
Ivan Macfadyen	Veteran sailor, racer, writer

Acknowledgments

Ione DeBrum	Mayor of Ebon Atoll, Marshall Islands
Jody Bright	Pacific fishing expert, boat captain
	Tuna tournament director
Doug Lewis	Sport fisherman crew, musician, writer
Giff Johnson	Editor, *Marshall Islands Journal*
Peter A. Levine	Trauma specialist
	Author, *Waking the Tiger: Healing Trauma*
Jaime Marroquin	Civil Protection Secretary, Chiapas, Mexico
Dennis Jibas	Captain of the RMI patrol boat *Lomor*, Marshall Islands
Rafael Gutierrez	Local rescue coordinator in Puerto Escondido, Mexico

extracts reading groups
competitions books new
discounts extracts extracts
competitions discounts
books new events reading groups
competitions new extracts reading groups
events books
reading groups new extracts discounts
books new titles reading groups
interviews
events extracts events
discounts new
new books events interviews new books extracts
events new
discounts extracts discounts
www.panmacmillan.com
extracts events reading groups books
competitions books extracts new